BANKRUPT BRITAIN

An atlas of social change

Daniel Dorling and Bethan Thomas

First published in Great Britain in 2011 by The Policy Press

The Policy Press
University of Bristol
Fourth Floor, Beacon House
Queen's Road
Bristol BS8 1QU
UK

t: +44 (0)117 331 4054
f: +44 (0)117 331 4093
tpp-info@bristol.ac.uk
www.policypress.co.uk

North American office:
The Policy Press
c/o International Specialized Books Services
920 NE 58th Avenue, Suite 300
Portland, OR 97213-3786, USA
t: +1 503 287 3093, f: +1 503 280 8832
info@isbs.com

© The Policy Press 2011

ISBN 978 1 84742 747 2 paperback
ISBN 978 1 84742 748 9 hardback

British Library Cataloguing in Publication Data
A catalogue record for this report is available from the British Library.

Library of Congress Cataloging-in-Publication Data
A catalog record for this report has been requested.

Cover image courtesy of Stockphoto Pro
Cover design by Qube Design Associates, Bristol
Printed in Great Britain by Henry Ling, Dorchester
The Policy Press uses environmentally responsible print partners

MIX
Paper
FSC FSC® C013985

Dedicated

to David Cameron and Nick Clegg

Other related titles published by The Policy Press

  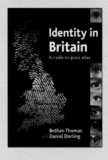 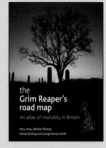 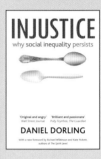

Gordon, D., Davey Smith, G., Dorling, D. and Shaw, M. (eds) (1999) *Inequalities in health: The evidence*, edited collection of 20 chapters.

Shaw, M., Dorling, D., Gordon, D. and Davey Smith, G. (1999, 2000) *The widening gap: Health inequalities and policy in Britain*.

Mitchell, R., Dorling, D. and Shaw, M. (2000) *Inequalities in life and death: What if Britain were more equal?*

Davey Smith, G., Dorling, D. and Shaw, M. (eds) (2001) *Poverty, inequality and health: 1800–2000 – a reader*.

Dorling, D. and Thomas, B. (2004) *People and places: A census atlas of the UK*.

Wheeler, B., Shaw, M., Mitchell, R. and Dorling, D. (2005) *Life in Britain, using millennial census data to understand poverty, inequality and place: Ten summary reports and a technical report*.

Dorling, D., Rigby, J., Wheeler, B., Ballas, D., Thomas, B., Fahmy, E., Gordon, D. and Lupton, R. (2007) *Poverty, wealth and place in Britain, 1968 to 2005*.

Thomas, B. and Dorling, D. (2007) *Identity in Britain: A cradle-to-grave atlas*.

Shaw, M., Davey Smith, G., Thomas, B. and Dorling, D. (2008) *The Grim Reaper's road map: An atlas of mortality in Britain*.

Dorling, D. (2010) *Injustice: Why social inequality persists*.

Contents

Acknowledgements

We are extremely grateful to David Dorling for reading through an entire early draft of this work; to Julia Mortimer at The Policy Press for commissioning it; to Jo Morton for superb copy-editing; to Dave Worth for the design and layout; and to the rest of the team at The Policy Press for their unstinting patience and support; to the people who decided in the final year of the New Labour government to open the floodgates and let the data out; but not to those who replaced them and have already begun in earnest to cancel so many of the surveys and data collection projects that allow what is shown here to be known in the first place, often for the first time.

We need to know who is living where in Britain and how people's lives are changing, for better or worse. That is, unless you believe that there is no need to plan, perhaps because you believe that the free market will result in the optimum outcome and that anyone who suffers under it deserves to suffer for the greater good. In the coming years it will be far harder to produce the kind of evidence we show here. Many government statisticians and analysts are being made redundant as we write. Others are having their time diverted away from providing the continuous stream of information that they have so carefully amassed, and are being channelled instead towards destructive tasks such as introducing competition where it will be harmful rather than monitoring progress or the lack of it. We would like to acknowledge the huge amount of work done by others to collate the numbers that we have turned into maps here. And we would like especially to acknowledge all those who are working now to ensure that in future we will still be able to plan, once the current madness has passed.

Patrick Wright began his 1991 masterpiece *Journey through the ruins: The last days of London* (London: Radius) by dedicating it to Margaret Thatcher. It was not meant as a compliment. For the avoidance of doubt, our dedication is similarly intended.

Data was obtained from Big Brother Watch; Data Unit Wales; the Department for Children, Schools and Families; the Department for Environment, Food and Rural Affairs; the Department for Transport; the Department of Communities and Local Government; the Department of Communities and Local Government Floor Targets Interactive; the Department of Energy and Climate Change; the General Register Office for Scotland; Google docs; the Government Equalities Office; Health Solutions Wales; Her Majesty's Revenue & Customs; the Home Office; Information Services Division (ISD) Scotland; the Insolvency Service; Local Government Chronicle Elections Centre, University of Plymouth; the Ministry of Justice; the National Atmospheric Emissions Inventory; the NHS Information Centre; Nomis; the Office for National Statistics; Office for National Statistics Neighbourhood Statistics; the Organisation for Economic Co-operation and Development (OECD); the Scottish Government; Scottish Neighbourhood Statistics; the Social and Spatial Inequalities Group at the University of Sheffield; the Statistical Directorate of the Welsh Assembly; StatsWales; UK Local Government on the Web; the Welsh Assembly Government; and Worldmapper.

Maps are based on boundary data provided through EDINA UKBORDERS with the support of the ESRC and JISC and use boundary material which is copyright of the Crown.

Introduction

Bankruptcy is being unable to discharge your debts, being unable to pay those to whom you owe money. It also has a further, figurative meaning of lacking in some quality, such as *moral bankruptcy*. The British state is far from bankrupt in the traditional financial definition of bankruptcy. It is still well able to pay its creditors. The British state is currently bankrupt in how it treats those who are more vulnerable, especially the poor, the young and the sick.

Attitudes to the extent to which Britain is bankrupt, morally, economically or in any other way, vary geographically:

> In England, for instance, Londoners are three times more inclined than the residents of the industrial Midlands to believe that 'the economy is on the mend' and that over the next year it will improve. That gap is hardly surprising, considering that it took time for the recession to overflow from London's City banks to the factory floors of the Midlands, and that it will take a similar length of time, if not even longer, to chase it away from the households of jobless factory workers than from the homes of the beneficiaries of lavishly state-subsidized bank dividends and the profits of outfits servicing the rich.[1]

Everything has a geography, including, perhaps especially, belief.

Whether you believe that what we are about to show constitutes evidence of various forms of bankrupt or broken Britain, or whether you can see signs of bullishness or optimism in the maps that follow, will depend as much on what you bring to this book as on what is in it. However, to understand what follows you need to know some things about the geography of UK statistics. We use this introduction to explain that geography and, in particular, how we have chosen to map the country. Looking at these maps, you may well appreciate for the first time the many different ways in which Britain is divided up for administrative purposes.

Often we don't map all of the country. In this atlas we have not included Northern Ireland at any point. We have in the past drawn an atlas of the UK including that country on almost every page.[2] What that atlas and much other work reveals is that Northern Ireland really is, demographically and in terms of economic and other trends, essentially different. The patterns that are found and the ways in which they have been changing bear little resemblance to the other constituent countries of the UK. Given that, and the political separations, and above all the fact that some of the data we show here simply aren't publicly available for small areas within Northern Ireland, we concentrate in this work on England, Wales and Scotland, or what we refer to in shorthand as Britain.

Often in the pages that follow, Scotland and/or Wales have had to be excluded because the data for a particular topic were not available in a comparable form to that for England. Occasionally we have data for one or both of Scotland and Wales, but not for England. The maps shown here give access to the widest and most comprehensive sets of British data ever released. This is thanks to the former Prime Minister, Gordon Brown, who, in his last year in office, decided to make as much government information as possible widely and freely available. The data used here are the most recently available at the time of writing and, although much of these data rely on extrapolations from the 2001 Census to produce the 2008 and 2009 mid-year estimates of population that are so often our denominators, no actual census data are plotted here. Data from the 2011 Census will not be available until 2012 at the earliest. If cuts are made to official statistical services and the research centres which have in the past distributed census data then the results of the most recent census may well be delayed. We hope this volume gives an indication of trends in the meantime.

As this atlas went to press towards the end of March 2011 there was little sign of any serious recovery. We started researching and writing this atlas in the winter of 2009; the 'Politically bankrupt' chapter was first drafted immediately after the general election in May 2010, while the 'Financially bankrupt' chapter was first written in the early autumn of that year. By the spring of 2011 we began to wonder whether we might have started to write this atlas prematurely. We had been able to include cuts from the Emergency Budget of June 2010 but submitted the manuscript to the publisher shortly before the Comprehensive Spending Review of October 2010. On the other hand, much of the material which we map in the pages that follow is no longer being collected and many of the relevant websites have been removed, apparently without being archived at the National Archives. If we had not begun this atlas when we did, it could not have been written.

This is a unique atlas: it will not be possible to produce an update of all the topics included here in the future, due to the effects of government cuts on data collection and dissemination. Many of the surveys we have relied on to plot out the current status of Britain have recently been cancelled. With the abolishment of the Audit Commission and the removal of local authority performance targets, much of the data will probably not be collected in the immediate future. Even if individual councils continue to collect this data and publish it on their own websites, there will be no central repository recording how all councils are performing; and much of the utility in such data is to see how councils are performing compared not only to their neighbours but also to other councils with similar demographic and social characteristics.

The accompanying website to this atlas (www.policypress.co.uk) contains updates to some of the key data we have collected, as far as possible, together with updated maps where relevant. Thus, at its point of publication, this printed atlas, and the accompanying website, is, we believe, the most authoritative record to date of the changing social geography of Britain. Future projects will almost certainly have to be a little more limited in scope.

The cuts implemented by the Emergency Budget of June 2010 were capped at 2% and were a precursor of far deeper cuts of £81bn in total imposed by the Comprehensive Spending Review in October 2010. These cuts will impact on many of the topics we have mapped in this atlas. The subsequent Budget of March 2011[3] downgraded the national projection for economic growth in the coming year to just 1.7% (the previous estimate had been 2.1%). As these estimates are almost always optimistic, we may well be entering a decade of growth hovering around 1% per annum, a historic low.

The perilous state of the country's finances means that public borrowing is forecast to be £146bn in the 2011/12 financial year. However, this is £2.5bn lower than the Chancellor of the Exchequer George Osborne's forecast in the Emergency Budget. He has been cutting even more than he predicted then.

We will not know for some time whether he kept within that initial 2% cap. Academics have calculated that, given George Osborne's published plans, he aims, by 2015, to reduce the share of the UK's GDP that is spent on public services to a proportion that is lower for the first time ever than that spent in the United States.[4] The UK is set to become the most neo-conservative of all the world's richest countries in terms of how small the state will be.

In Chapter 1 we estimate what might in future be the increased unemployment rate from the reduction in public sector employment. Over the next few months we will see how close our projection comes to reality. Tax, tax credit and benefit changes will impact on the numbers of people living in poverty, as well as reducing the amount of money that the more affluent have to spend. The Institute for Fiscal Studies estimated in March 2011 that real household incomes across all of Britain fell by 1.6% from 2008 to 2011.[5] Austerity had already begun even before the first significant impact of the public sector cuts was felt in April 2011.

There are likely to be dramatic changes to the patterns of residential bankruptcy (Chapter 2). As interest rates have remained low, benefiting mortgagees, repossession rates have decreased; if interest rates were to rise (which is increasingly likely given rising inflation) we could see a dramatic reversal of the picture in the very near future. Changes to housing benefits and council rents will impact adversely on tenants and may well lead to an increase in homelessness (although there are suggestions that in order to ameliorate the figure the official definition of homelessness may be changed by the Coalition government).

Chapter 3 considers the political bankruptcy of Britain. With a referendum on the voting system due on 5 May 2011, and the proposed gerrymandering of parliamentary constituencies, we will see significant changes to the political landscape in the future, and the system possibly being brought into even greater disrepute. The council elections due in May 2011 will provide an indication of how the population of the country is reacting to the cuts and ideological changes that the Coalition government is imposing on the people. Almost all of the worst of what is being imposed was not in either of the two Coalition parties' election manifestos. In a sense we have been robbed of our freedom to choose.

Recessions tend to be accompanied by increases in burglary and theft. There are already indications that burglary is rising; changes to anti-social behaviour legislation and cuts to services may well impact on teenage pregnancy rates and reduce effective child protection as there will be fewer adults paid to protect, including those providing assistance in school classrooms, as well as traditional social workers. As Chapter 4 makes clear, money impacts on morals.

With so many people being adversely affected by the cuts – in terms of their employment, reductions in the support available when out of work, and the subsidised legal and advisory support that they will soon not be able to access – it is probable that more people are going to become emotionally affected by the hard times to come (Chapter 5). However, as the relevant surveys we used to monitor the emotional state of the nation have been discontinued for many of these topics, it will be difficult to ascertain the effect of these changes. ONS has been tasked by the Prime Minister to instigate a new index of happiness, and it is to be hoped they will point out how many existing useful data time series which already measured aspects of well-being are being discontinued.

Just as we will find it harder in future to measure the impact of current adverse conditions on people's well-being, we may also not be able to tell (as well as we currently can) how areas are performing on

environmental matters, as described in Chapter 6. Much of the data, for example on recycling rates, may well no longer be centrally collated. In his March 2011 Budget the Chancellor scrapped the fuel escalator, which would have increased petrol prices. We should expect there to be more pollution as a result than there would have been if drivers had been further discouraged from driving.

For people who drive large gas-guzzling cars and who keep their job, especially for those who are very well paid in the private sector and may even enjoy bonuses, the immediate future may appear, superficially, to look rosier. Personal direct taxation for these people will not be increased during 2011/12 despite the country's dire predicament. In England, no matter where they live, they will not be paying more council tax, as that has been reduced or frozen everywhere. If they claim 'non-dom' (non-domicile) status they will only pay the £50,000 levy and no further tax on their overseas income, no matter how much they award themselves in pay. And some bosses will even make a profit out of recent changes. Corporation tax is to be cut by 2% from April 2011.

The bankers who were closest to the economic crisis were again, by 2011, awarding themselves multi-million pound bonuses. Government had talked tough but did not act to prevent them from doing this, even in regard to those banks in which we all had become a majority shareholder. In the run-up to the spring of 2011, the more unfair the outcome of the measures the government took, the more they talked of fairness. This atlas shows how their actions are beginning to increase division in British society. All of this leads to a dispiriting outlook. It is probable that in the immediate future we are likely to see an increase in the general bankruptcy of British society.

How to use this atlas

To understand this volume first you need to understand the maps, which may look a little strange. As it is difficult to discern the patterns in the centre of cities (that encompass a small area but have large populations), we have used cartograms, where the size of each area is represented as proportional to its population. In previous atlases we used hexagons, which are easy to create but lose topology: as a hexagon can only have six immediate neighbouring hexagons, any place that in reality has more or fewer neighbours is not accurately represented. Here we use a new approach, using cartograms that maintain as far as possible the original shapes, and accurately depict an area's neighbours. A further advantage of these cartograms is that every place has its own individual shape, and it is therefore easier to locate places on the cartograms rather than having to locate one hexagon among many.

These cartograms were created using the algorithm developed by Michael Gastner and Mark Newman.[1] In these cartograms every area has been scaled to be proportionate to the whole population that live there, while maintaining topology and minimising distortion to local compass directions. The cartogram transformation was undertaken using the utility developed by ScapeToad.[2]

We have used a variety of different geographies in this atlas, because of the availability of differing datasets. General election data is, of course, available for parliamentary constituencies. Much health data is reported for (soon to be abolished) Primary Care Trusts in England, NHS Boards in Scotland and Local Health Boards in Wales.

Much of the data on children is reported by local education authority, while fire and rescue data come at the level of the Fire and Rescue Services. Most of the data we map are reported for local authorities, but this has been complicated by the reorganisation of some authorities in 2009. As there has been so much administrative reorganisation over the years, for long-time series maps of data going back over many decades, we present our findings by ancient counties.

Depending on the data source, a 'year' may be a calendar year, a financial year or an academic year. The data sources for the maps, figures and tables are collected at the very end of the atlas.

The key maps that follow show these differing geographies, and identify where changes to boundaries over time have occurred.

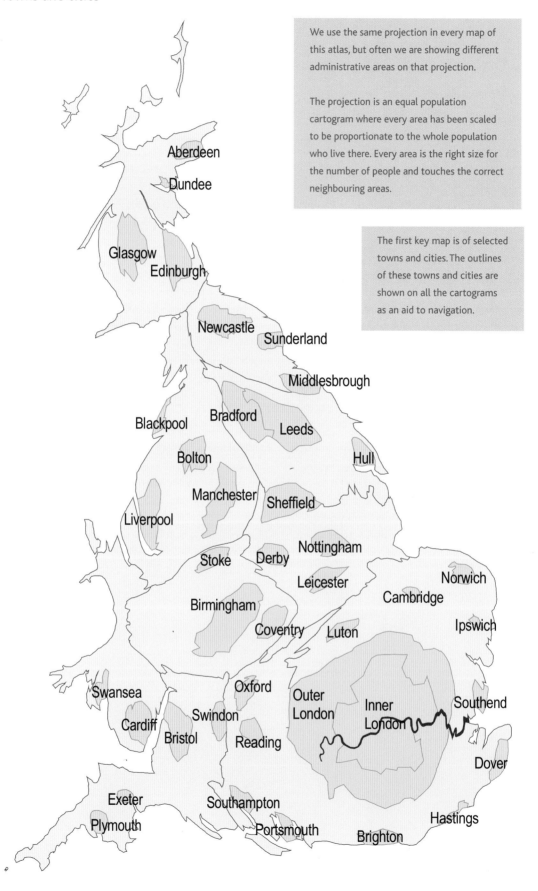

We use the same projection in every map of this atlas, but often we are showing different administrative areas on that projection.

The projection is an equal population cartogram where every area has been scaled to be proportionate to the whole population who live there. Every area is the right size for the number of people and touches the correct neighbouring areas.

The first key map is of selected towns and cities. The outlines of these towns and cities are shown on all the cartograms as an aid to navigation.

Aberdeen

Dundee

Glasgow
Edinburgh

Newcastle
Sunderland

Middlesbrough

Blackpool
Bradford
Leeds

Bolton
Hull

Manchester
Sheffield

Liverpool

Nottingham
Stoke
Derby
Leicester

Norwich
Cambridge

Birmingham
Ipswich

Coventry
Luton

Swansea
Oxford
Outer London
Inner London
Southend

Cardiff
Swindon
Bristol
Reading

Dover

Exeter
Southampton

Plymouth
Portsmouth
Brighton
Hastings

Government Office Regions

This second key map shows just the regional and national boundaries of Britain. Note how all the regions were designed to be of roughly similar population size.

Scotland

North East

Yorkshire and
The Humber

North West

East Midlands

West Midlands

East of England

Wales

London

South
West

South East

Local authorities 2001: The North (and East Midlands)

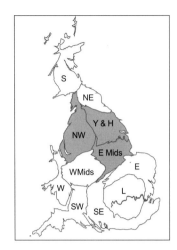

This third key map shows the boundaries of local authorities as they were defined in 2001 within just three of the regions.

In 2009 there was some local authority reorganisation; where this happened it is indicated on these locator maps.

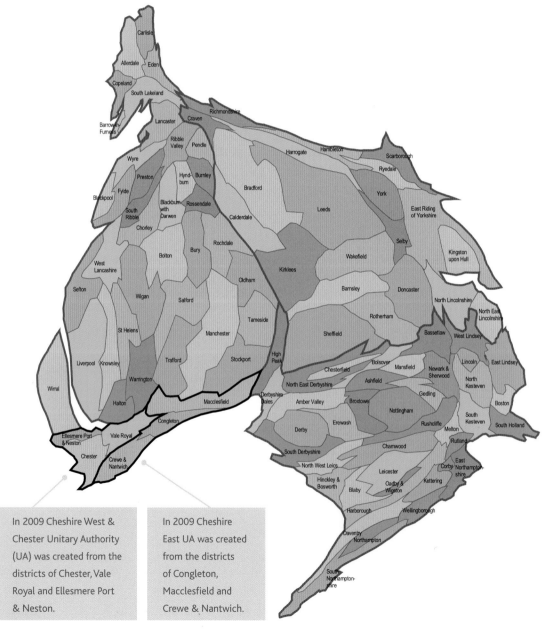

In 2009 Cheshire West & Chester Unitary Authority (UA) was created from the districts of Chester, Vale Royal and Ellesmere Port & Neston.

In 2009 Cheshire East UA was created from the districts of Congleton, Macclesfield and Crewe & Nantwich.

Local authorities 2001: The South East

In 2009 Bedford district became a unitary authority.

In 2009 Central Bedfordshire UA was created from the districts of Mid Bedfordshire and South Bedfordshire.

Local authorities 2001: Scotland and the North East of England

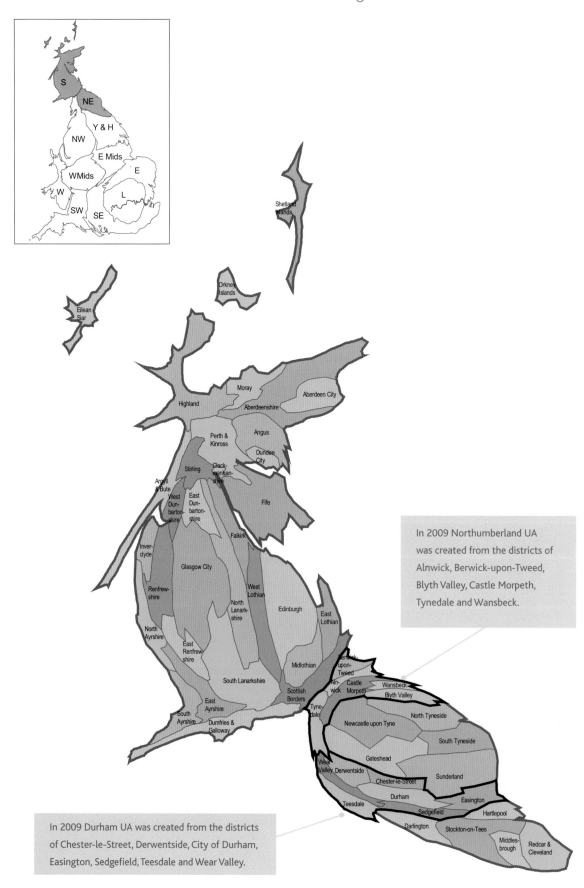

In 2009 Northumberland UA was created from the districts of Alnwick, Berwick-upon-Tweed, Blyth Valley, Castle Morpeth, Tynedale and Wansbeck.

In 2009 Durham UA was created from the districts of Chester-le-Street, Derwentside, City of Durham, Easington, Sedgefield, Teesdale and Wear Valley.

Local authorities 2001: Wales and Western England

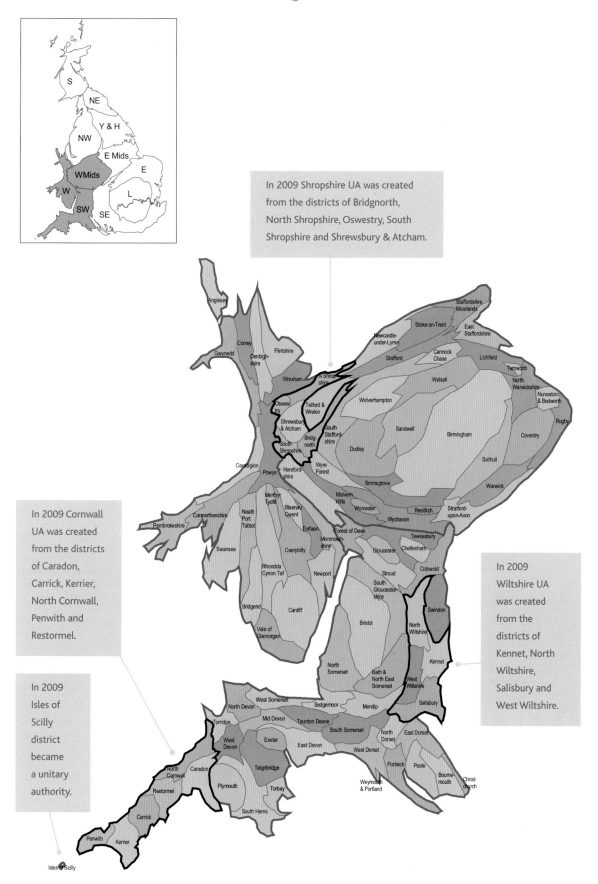

In 2009 Shropshire UA was created from the districts of Bridgnorth, North Shropshire, Oswestry, South Shropshire and Shrewsbury & Atcham.

In 2009 Cornwall UA was created from the districts of Caradon, Carrick, Kerrier, North Cornwall, Penwith and Restormel.

In 2009 Isles of Scilly district became a unitary authority.

In 2009 Wiltshire UA was created from the districts of Kennet, North Wiltshire, Salisbury and West Wiltshire.

Local education authorities 2009: The North (and East Midlands)

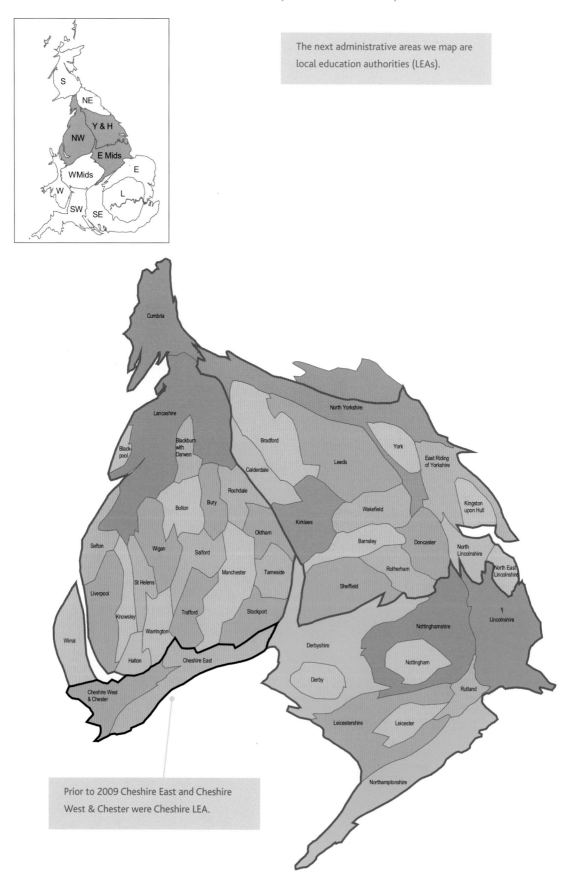

The next administrative areas we map are local education authorities (LEAs).

Prior to 2009 Cheshire East and Cheshire West & Chester were Cheshire LEA.

Local education authorities 2009: South East England

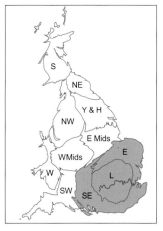

Prior to 2009 Bedford and Central Bedfordshire were Bedfordshire LEA.

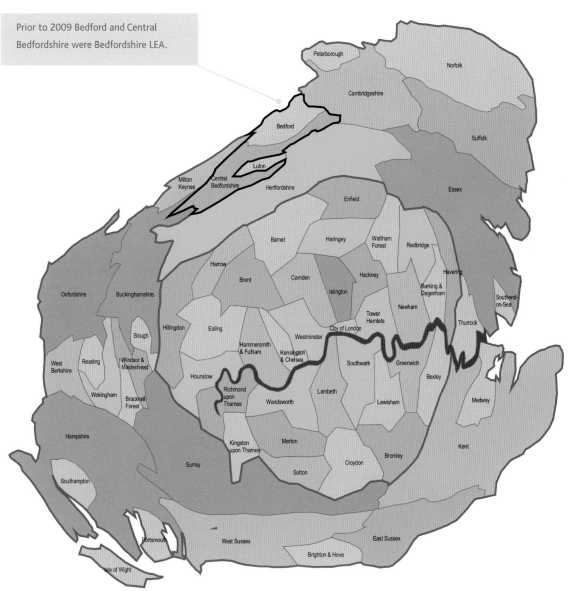

Local education authorities 2009: Scotland and North East England

Local education authorities 2009: Wales and Western England

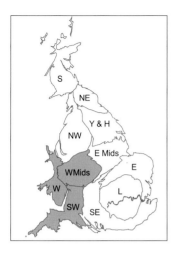

Ancient counties: England and Wales

Ancient counties, or Lieutenancies, are the areas represented on behalf of Her Majesty the Queen by a Lord Lieutenant. These are almost always old counties, sometimes called ceremonial counties.

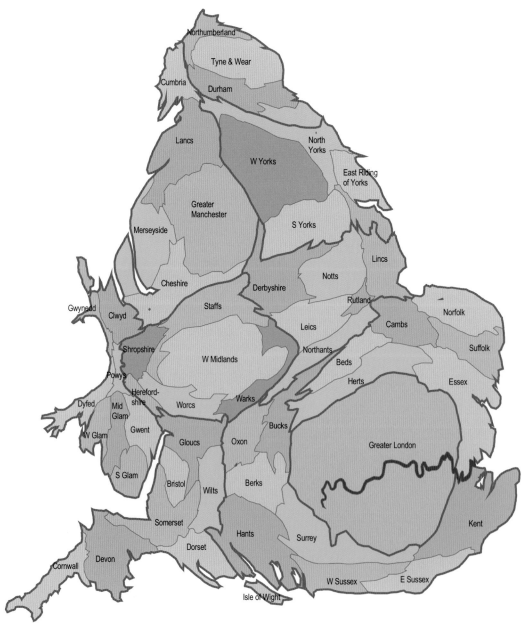

Ancient counties: Scotland

When we have data for different points of time for incompatible boundaries we aggregate the numbers up to these counties which almost always neatly encompass smaller areas of different eras. Thus, these counties are often used in constructing historical data series.

Parliamentary constituencies 2010: The North

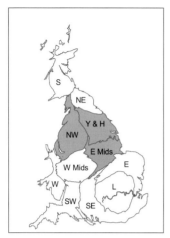

Westminster parliamentary constituencies are the smallest geographical areas we plot in this atlas. They have the benefit of all being of very similar population sizes and so all being roughly equally visible on a map shaped by population.

Parliamentary constituencies 2010: The South East

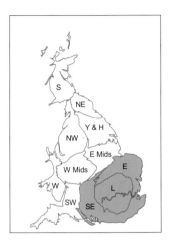

Parliamentary constituencies 2010: Wales and Western England

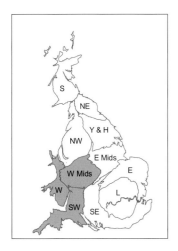

Primary Care Trust areas and NHS Board areas 2007: Scotland and North East England

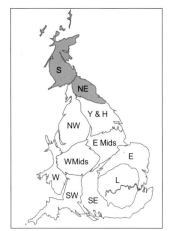

Primary Care Trust areas have been defined to organise primary care services, that is the care provided to people when they first have a health problem, by doctors, dentists, pharmacy services and so on. They are often quite different in size and shape from many of the other administrative areas for which key maps have been included so far.

In Scotland the equivalents are known as NHS Board areas.

Prior to 2007 the Argyll & Clyde NHS Board had responsibility for the area outlined in black. It was then split, most going to Greater Glasgow & Clyde and part to Highland.

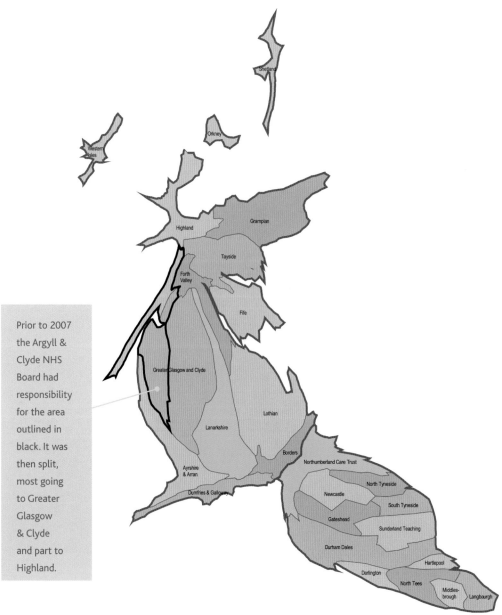

Primary Care Trust areas 2007: The North

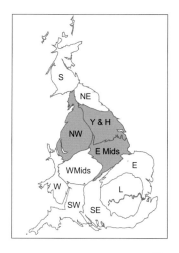

Primary Care Trust areas 2007: South East England

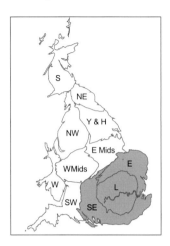

Primary Care Trust areas and Local Health Board areas 2007: Wales and Western England

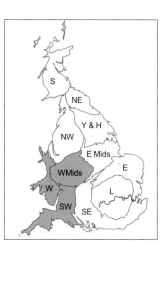

In Wales the equivalent bodies to Primary Care Trusts are known as Local Health Boards.

Fire and rescue service areas: Britain

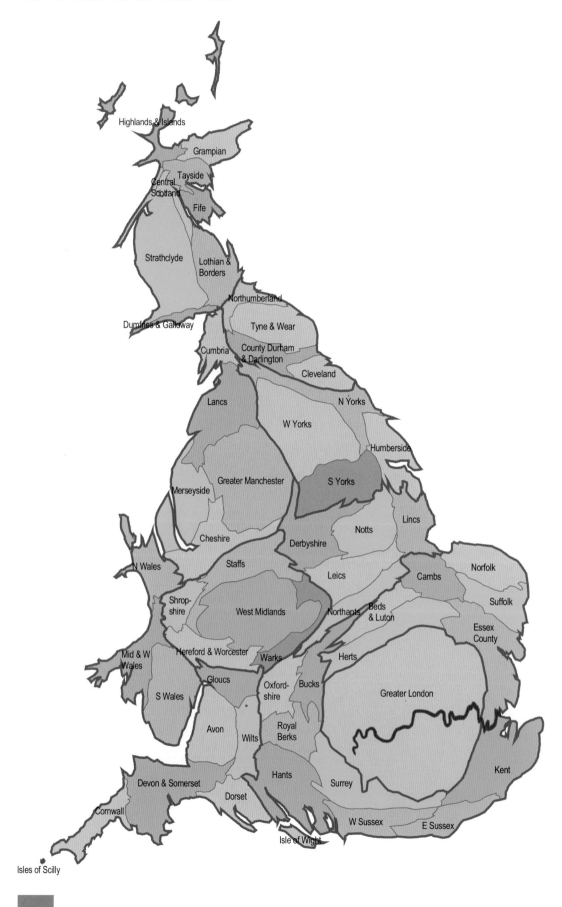

Accompanying the whole page maps are tables showing the areas with the 5 highest and 5 lowest rates, together with, if applicable, the greatest and smallest changes.

We have written this book assuming that you will not necessarily want to begin at the beginning and slowly work your way through to the end. Now that you understand the boundaries that we have used, you can read it in any order that you wish. We would recommend you read a complete chapter to get the complete picture, but you can dip in and out of chapters.

If you are in a hurry to see the conclusions we reached, having drawn all these pictures of this small island and its most recent travails, then turn now to the final chapter, but it is perhaps better to have a look at some of the detail first and make up your own mind about what it suggests, rather than just relying on our final summary. For now, a last word from Zygmunt Bauman, on what it is that matters, why the lines which divide us matter, and how the norms of life can be negotiated for the better:

> Nothing in history is predetermined; history is a trace left on time by multiple, dispersed and disparate human choices, seldom if ever coordinated. It is much too early to foresee which of the two interrelated functions of borders will eventually prevail. Of one thing we can be pretty sure, though: we (and our children) will lie on the beds that we, collectively, are making for ourselves (and for them). And through drawing borders and negotiating the norms of life on the frontierland, those beds *are* made. Knowingly or not, by design or by default, purposefully or inadvertently … Whether we want it, or not.[3]

Chapter 1 Financially bankrupt

A nation in hock to pawnbrokers
(*Metro* newspaper headline, 6 September 2010)

Introduction

People in the UK know times are hard. This can be seen from the levels of short-term debt (credit card, payday loans and so on), and from the difficulties many are having repaying long-term debt (mortgages, student loans and so on). Even back in 2008 personal short-term debts were higher as a proportion of assets in the UK than in most European countries (see Figure 1.0.1). Too many of us had 'maxed-out' on credit cards and other short-term loans. The small group who benefited from lending all this short-term debt were profiting to the detriment of the many. In 2008 – the most recent year for which we have data – in Europe, only Greece, Poland and the Slovak Republic had personal borrowing levels higher than those in the UK, and UK levels were only slightly lower than those in the United States. Personal debts in the UK in 2008 formed 6% of all households' financial assets. Many households have no or very small debts. Many other households have what for them are huge debts in proportion to their income. Short-term debts tend to be highest among those who have least. The interest paid on those debts is redistributed indirectly to savers. Savers are disproportionately found among those who have most.

On top of those short-term debts are long-term debts, often seen as a sensible way to borrow, as rates of interest are much lower on mortgages than on credit cards or payday loans. However, long-term debt is similarly a mechanism that transfers wealth from those who borrow to those who lend. As house prices in Britain soared in the years up to 2008, saddling yourself with a huge mortgage became less and less attractive but less and less avoidable for people who were tired of the insecurity of renting and sick of high home rental prices. According to the charity Credit Action, as of September 2010, total UK personal debt (both short- and long-term)

stood at about £1.5 trillion and was predicted by the government's Office for Budget Responsibility to rise to £1.8 trillion by 2015, growing by £159 million a day – every day – for the next five years. When it came to precise figures, here is how Credit Action presented the implications of some of these huge numbers:

> This would take the average household debt to £72,341 per household. UK banks and building societies wrote off £10.9bn of loans to individuals in the last 12 months to end Q2 [second quarter] 2010. In Q2 2010 they wrote off £3.47bn (£2.14bn of that was credit card debt). This amounts to a write-off of £38.06m a day. Total UK personal debt at the end of July 2010 stood at £1,456bn. The twelve-month growth remained at 0.8%. Individuals owe more than what the whole country produces in a year. Total lending in July 2010 rose by £0.3bn; secured lending increased by £0.1bn in the month; consumer credit lending rose by £0.2bn (total lending in Jan 2008 grew by £8.4bn). Total secured lending on dwellings at the end of July 2010 stood at £1,239bn. The twelve-month growth rate rose slightly to 1.0%. Total consumer credit lending to individuals at the end of July 2010 was £217bn. The annual growth rate of consumer credit rose by 0.2% to 0.2%. Average household debt in the UK is ~ £8,628 (excluding mortgage).[1]

It is at the point when they and their creditors begin to see their debts as unsustainable that people are forced to consider bankruptcy.

It was the much smaller proportions of national debt rising which highlighted the borrowing and lending crisis most acutely in Britain. Private lenders do not much fear individual borrowers. Borrowers have no unions, they cannot act collectively. Private debt can be racked up to very high levels and the interest squeezed out of people's earnings and welfare benefits (even though £38 million a day is still being written off). It is when governments borrow that lenders are far more wary of lending more and more. Governments are seen as least likely to default on their debts, but when they do default, lenders are – for once – unable to secure a profit.

How much debt do we hold? Start with average personal household debt in the UK, at around £8,600 excluding mortgages. Next add on to this the national debt. Exactly how national debt should be measured is much disputed. Annual

national debt is the short-term difference between the net borrowing and lending of what is called the 'consolidated general government sector'. By EU accounting rules this is made up of central government, state government (devolved administrations in the case of the UK), local government and social security funds. The debt is how much greater the running costs of these bodies are than is their annual income from taxes and other sources. At 11.9% of GDP, national debt adds a further £6,550 per household to that average short-term personal household debt.[2] If we take the amounts quoted by Eurostat in 2008 and 2009 (Figure 1.0.2), then, as a proportion of GDP, national net debt in the UK is the third highest in Europe (after Ireland and Greece) and the largest by far in absolute terms. Greece and Ireland are, of course,

Figure 1.0.1: 2008 Personal short-term debt of households as proportion of financial assets

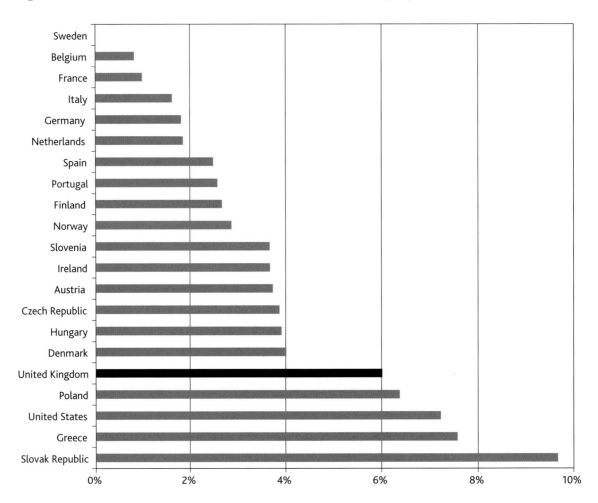

Notes: Financial balance sheets – non consolidated; includes non-profit institutions serving households (Swedish reported figure is 0.0048%). Denominator: Financial assets; Numerator: Short-term loans

sheltered from the threat of currency speculation by being in the Eurozone.

Thus, in *absolute* terms the UK has both the highest personal and the highest national debt in Europe (see Figure 1.0.1 and Figure 1.0.2), and in relative terms the highest debt per capita apart from Greece, which, it is vital to remember, has been sheltered within the Eurozone and for which an international bail-out package has been arranged. In the UK there might instead be a run on the pound. Expressed per household, combined short-term personal and national debt in the UK, by 2010, stood at around £15,150 for every average household group (2.37 people) in the country. Some 57% of that was private short-term debt, and 43% was national short-term debt.

When these figures are compared with average household earnings they appear shocking. Almost half of all households live on an annual income equal to or lower than this after housing costs have been

taken into account.[3] However, in comparison with average household wealth, which for England stood at £371,000 by 2008,[4] the annual debt is a paltry 4% of that figure.

One household's bankruptcy is another's unearned income; one country's deficit is another's surplus. Without massive private lending there would be no borrowing, without the Bretton Woods international finance system, national debts could not be this great. All this was only very recently created, and all of it is sure to change as it has already changed so much, just through our lives and our parents' lives. But knowing this is little consolation when you are told personally that the money has run out, both the money in your own bank account, and what you share with others through government. In this first chapter we map out, as succinctly as we can, the state of play as we see it now – when it comes to who is most likely to become personally insolvent, to live in poverty, to lose their job, and to see their local council services and national services cut. We often

Figure 1.0.2: 2008 (blue) and 2009 (black) National net debt as a proportion of GDP

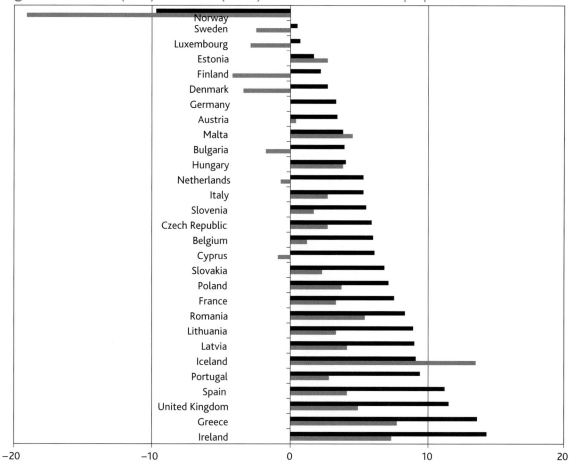

refer to median values: 50% of the population are above this value, and 50% below. It is important to realise that these figures are often much lower than the mean or average values, because in finance there is little restraint on how much some people can have. We end the chapter on who still benefits from others being in so much debt, where the wealth is concentrated and who is not being taxed, leaving the cuts to fall on others who have less to begin with.

1.1 Bankruptcy, insolvency, individual voluntary arrangements and debt relief orders

As debt rises, and defaulting on that debt rises, there is also an increase in the possible ways in which that defaulting can be managed. The language and rules are complex, and constantly changing, but the patterns revealed by the statistics of debt are far simpler.

Map 1.1.1 shows the distribution of adults declared insolvent in 2009 in England and Wales. We have had to exclude figures for Scotland from this map: because they are not disaggregated there by local authority; because the law and hence statistics there are very different; and because major changes were introduced in April 2008 making comparison over time within that country (and with the rest of Britain) very difficult. If Scottish data could be included on this map then it would be in Scotland that the darkest shades would be seen. In April/May/June 2010 some 5,378 personal insolvencies were declared in Scotland, a rise of 4% on the quarter before.[5] If this were to continue then in the 2010/11 financial year some 22,800 people would be declared insolvent in Scotland. This is a much higher figure (when considered in proportion to population) than that in England and Wales where, between 2008 and 2009, annual total insolvencies rose from 104,110 to 131,583.

The area where personal insolvency is least common in all of England and Wales is the City of London. Very few people live there but it is still interesting that only eight residents were declared insolvent there in 2009 (7.6 insolvencies for every 10,000 adults living there). Rates of insolvency are lowest within London mainly because business is doing well, and consequently employment rates remain high and wages buoyant in London and much of the South East of England. One of the key businesses of the City is lending money and then chasing it up when it is not paid, especially from people who become insolvent. Rises in insolvency in one part of the country maintain and create profit for others elsewhere, not least in London. Profit is made from lending to those who can meet their repayments, and the penalties for being in arrears ensure that profit is also made from those who default. Another reason why insolvency rates are lower in London is that adults there tend to be younger. Rates of insolvency are highest in those parts of the country which are most economically distressed and/or which have a more elderly population who have had more time to accrue debt.

The highest rate of insolvencies in 2009, at 56.4 per 10,000 adults, was recorded in Mansfield in Derbyshire, where the rate increased by 23 adults per 10,000 in the year to that high point. Map 1.1.2 shows the geographical patterning of where insolvency rates rose the most, and the clustering/scattering of the few areas in which insolvency cases actually fell. The greatest fall was in the City of London; there were 17 cases of insolvency among residents of the City in 2008. Thus the absolute number of cases there more than halved in the year to 2009, while the rate of insolvency fell by 8.8 adults per 10,000 adult residents. The maps show that the few decreases tend to be in London and the South East, while the greatest rises in insolvency have been in the North.

There are many ways in which a person can become insolvent, although as most of the maps of the particular administrative routes show very similar patterns, we don't show each map here. Bankruptcy is the traditional route. The highest rate of bankruptcy in 2009 was recorded in Torbay in Devon (34.9 bankrupts that year per 10,000 adults). To file for bankruptcy people have to have fairly substantial assets, so bankruptcy rates tend to be a little higher in more affluent areas. The next most common form of insolvency is to come to an individual voluntary arrangement (IVA) with your lenders. This saves them and you money and reduces legal bills when there clearly are few assets to fight over. In 2009 IVAs were most commonly drawn up in Easington in County Durham (23.3 drafted per 10,000 adults). The lowest rates of IVAs were

Map 1.1.1: 2009 Adults declared insolvent (per 10,000 adults), local authorities, England & Wales

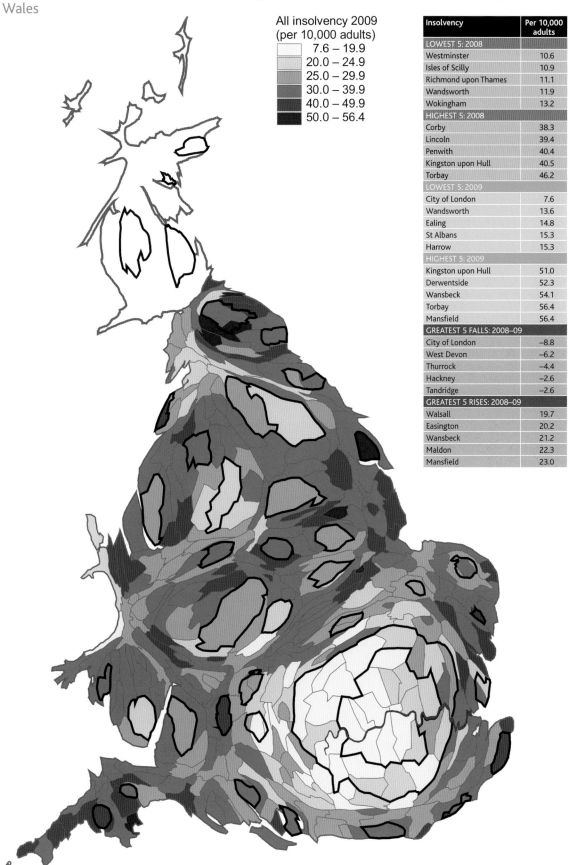

All insolvency 2009
(per 10,000 adults)

	7.6 – 19.9
	20.0 – 24.9
	25.0 – 29.9
	30.0 – 39.9
	40.0 – 49.9
	50.0 – 56.4

Insolvency	Per 10,000 adults
LOWEST 5: 2008	
Westminster	10.6
Isles of Scilly	10.9
Richmond upon Thames	11.1
Wandsworth	11.9
Wokingham	13.2
HIGHEST 5: 2008	
Corby	38.3
Lincoln	39.4
Penwith	40.4
Kingston upon Hull	40.5
Torbay	46.2
LOWEST 5: 2009	
City of London	7.6
Wandsworth	13.6
Ealing	14.8
St Albans	15.3
Harrow	15.3
HIGHEST 5: 2009	
Kingston upon Hull	51.0
Derwentside	52.3
Wansbeck	54.1
Torbay	56.4
Mansfield	56.4
GREATEST 5 FALLS: 2008–09	
City of London	−8.8
West Devon	−6.2
Thurrock	−4.4
Hackney	−2.6
Tandridge	−2.6
GREATEST 5 RISES: 2008–09	
Walsall	19.7
Easington	20.2
Wansbeck	21.2
Maldon	22.3
Mansfield	23.0

recorded in the City of London (1.9 per 10,000), then Westminster (3.0 per 10,000) and Kensington & Chelsea (3.1 per 10,000).

Finally, there are some people whose assets are too meagre even for IVAs to be appropriate. Debt relief orders (DRO) have been available since April 2009 to people who do not own their home, who have no assets other than (at most) a car worth less than £1,000 (and if so all other assets must be worth less than £300), who owe less than £15,000 and who have an income, after all necessary expenditures, of less than £50 a month. These 'insolvents' are

following something similar to the Scottish 'Low Income, Low Asset' (LILA) route into bankruptcy, which '… allows people who meet the relevant criteria to apply for their own bankruptcy without proving apparent insolvency or having creditor concurrence'.[6] Map 1.1.3 shows the national distribution of DROs issued per adult during the first three quarters of the operation of the scheme. Uptake has been greatest in Berwick, on the Scottish border (14.1 cases per year per 10,000 adults). No cases of a debt relief order being granted were recorded in the City of London.

Map 1.1.2: 2008–09 Change in insolvency, local authorities, England and Wales

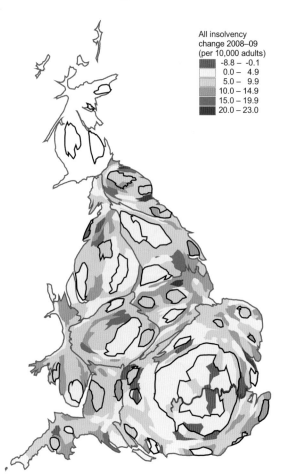

All insolvency
change 2008–09
(per 10,000 adults)
- -8.8 – -0.1
- 0.0 – 4.9
- 5.0 – 9.9
- 10.0 – 14.9
- 15.0 – 19.9
- 20.0 – 23.0

Map 1.1.3: 2009 (Q2 to Q4) debt relief orders issued, local authorities, England and Wales

DROs Apr–Dec 2009
(per 10,000 adults)
- 0.0 – 1.9
- 2.0 – 2.9
- 3.0 – 4.9
- 5.0 – 9.9
- 10.0 – 14.1

1.2 Children living in poverty due to financial deprivation

There are many different ways of suggesting that financial bankruptcy (widely defined) is high and rising in Britain. It is well known that of all the countries of Western Europe, the UK has among the highest rates of child poverty and by far the highest rate given the wealth of the country.[7] The only countries in Europe that have similar rates of child poverty tend to be those which are very poor overall. For many years the UK has had enough money to be able to ensure that almost none of its children grow up in poverty, but has chosen not to do so. In more recent years the UK has aligned its measures of child poverty with those of the European Union so that now, when we talk about national poverty statistics, we are using widely agreed measures. The exact definition of child poverty now used in the UK is 'The proportion of children living in families in receipt of out-of-work benefits or in receipt of

tax credits where their reported income is less than 60% of median income'.[8] That income cut-off in 2008/09 was £244 per week before housing costs are taken into account (BHC): or £12,688 annual household income. However, after the average household has paid for housing this amounts to only £10,712 to live on.[9] A household receiving an annual income of that level or above is deemed not to be poor.

The latest national child poverty statistics disaggregated by area are those for the boom year 2007 and were released by Her Majesty's Revenue & Customs for local authorities in England and as part of the Scottish Neighbourhood statistics data in Scotland. No comparable data have yet been released for areas within Wales. In England in 2007 more than one in five (some 21.6%) of all children were deemed to be living in poverty, a rise of roughly one extra child in every hundred on the figures released a year before (20.8%). Map 1.2.3 shows the national

Map 1.2.1: 2006 Children living in poverty (%), local authorities, England & Scotland

Children in poverty 2006 (%)
- 4.1 – 9.9
- 10.0 – 19.9
- 20.0 – 29.9
- 30.0 – 39.9
- 40.0 – 49.9
- 50.0 – 60.3

Map 1.2.2: 2006–07 Change in children in living in poverty (% point), local authorities, England & Scotland

Children in poverty change 2006–07 (%)
- -1.4 – -0.1
- 0.0 – 0.9
- 1.0 – 1.9
- 2.0 – 2.9
- 3.0 – 3.3

Map 1.2.3: 2007 Children living in poverty (%), local authorities, England & Scotland

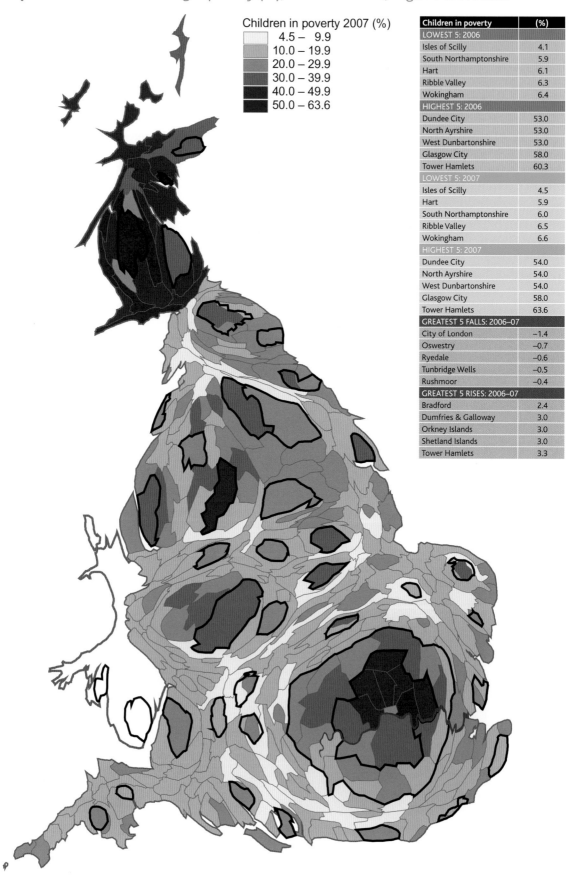

Children in poverty 2007 (%)

	4.5 – 9.9
	10.0 – 19.9
	20.0 – 29.9
	30.0 – 39.9
	40.0 – 49.9
	50.0 – 63.6

Children in poverty	(%)
LOWEST 5: 2006	
Isles of Scilly	4.1
South Northamptonshire	5.9
Hart	6.1
Ribble Valley	6.3
Wokingham	6.4
HIGHEST 5: 2006	
Dundee City	53.0
North Ayrshire	53.0
West Dunbartonshire	53.0
Glasgow City	58.0
Tower Hamlets	60.3
LOWEST 5: 2007	
Isles of Scilly	4.5
Hart	5.9
South Northamptonshire	6.0
Ribble Valley	6.5
Wokingham	6.6
HIGHEST 5: 2007	
Dundee City	54.0
North Ayrshire	54.0
West Dunbartonshire	54.0
Glasgow City	58.0
Tower Hamlets	63.6
GREATEST 5 FALLS: 2006–07	
City of London	−1.4
Oswestry	−0.7
Ryedale	−0.6
Tunbridge Wells	−0.5
Rushmoor	−0.4
GREATEST 5 RISES: 2006–07	
Bradford	2.4
Dumfries & Galloway	3.0
Orkney Islands	3.0
Shetland Islands	3.0
Tower Hamlets	3.3

proportion of dependent children up to age 19 who meet all the government's poverty criteria living in households earning less than the official threshold of 60% of median income. This is income measured before housing costs are taken into account, which further reduces the number of children who can be counted as poor. The measure is equivalised to allow for the fact that households with more members have higher living costs overall (although less per member).

The highest rates of childhood poverty in 2007 were found in Tower Hamlets, where more than 60% of children were deemed to be living in poverty by this measure. The next highest rates were found in Scotland, where a majority of children in the following areas lived in poverty: Glasgow City, Dundee City, North Ayrshire, West Dunbartonshire, Inverclyde, East Ayrshire, Dumfries & Galloway and North Lanarkshire. Far more children in London would be deemed to be living in poverty had the government included the cost of housing in its definitions. Fewer than one child in 13, and as few as one in 22, live in poverty in West Oxfordshire, Mole Valley, Uttlesford, Harborough, Wokingham, Ribble Valley, South Northamptonshire, Hart and the Isles of Scilly.

In Glasgow the proportion of children living in poverty did not rise between 2006 and 2007. However, in all the other poor areas mentioned above it rose by at least one extra child in 100. In contrast, in none of the areas of least poverty has there been such a rise, and in a few areas of low poverty those rates are even continuing to fall. Map 1.2.1 shows the child poverty map for 2006 and Map 1.2.2 shows the map of change between 2006 and 2007. The greatest increase in child poverty, of 3.3%, was recorded in Tower Hamlets. Within England rates then rose most within Hackney (by 2.4%), Oldham (by 2.4%), Bradford (by 2.4%), Birmingham (by 2.1%) and Burnley (by 2.1%).

Child poverty fell in only 29 of the 386 areas shown here in Map 1.2.2. Everywhere else it rose slightly, and with the recession it is likely that it has risen greatly almost everywhere since, but it will have risen most where it was highest to begin with. This is because of the distribution of new economic distress which we show below. Whatever their intentions, the outcome of the policies of successive

British governments has been to reduce poverty levels most in areas which were already wealthiest. Between 2006 and 2007, after the falls in the City of London, the greatest decreases in child poverty were recorded in North Devon (-0.4%), Rushmoor (-0.4%), Tunbridge Wells (-0.5%), Ryedale (-0.6%) and Oswestry (-0.7%). The next highest reductions were in the Chiltern district, where in 2006 only one child in 11.9 was poor; by 2007 it was only one in every 12.3. It is from the Chiltern district that top bankers often commute into the city to work during the day. It is from Tower Hamlets that those who clean their offices overnight typically travel.

And, of all children, it is the youngest who are most likely to be living in poverty.

1.3 Pensioner poverty and inequality due to financial deprivation

Of all pensioners, it is the oldest who are most likely to be living in poverty – that is, living on less than 60% of median household incomes, equivalised for household size. Of pensioners living in poverty, 43% live alone, and 59% own their home outright.[10] Before the cost of housing was taken into account, 20% of pensioners were found to be living in poverty in Britain in 2009 by this definition. However, this proportion falls to 16% once housing costs are included, mainly because so many pensioners do own their homes outright.

That almost three out of every five pensioners living in poverty are actually home owners is not as surprising as it first sounds. Pensioners are more likely than any other group to own their home as, simply due to their age, they are most likely to have completed mortgage payments on a property, usually while still earning a wage. Owning a home is not without cost, though, and the cost of maintaining their home can drive pensioners on low income into poverty. These poorer pensioners usually own property that is worth relatively little compared to the overall housing market, often situated in more run-down areas. Pensioners of all ethnic minorities are more likely to be living in poverty than are white pensioners, and some 49% of Pakistani and Bangladeshi pensioners live in poverty even after housing costs are taken into account and despite an even higher proportion among this group being

Map 1.3.1: 2007/08 Median annual pension income (£), local authorities, Britain

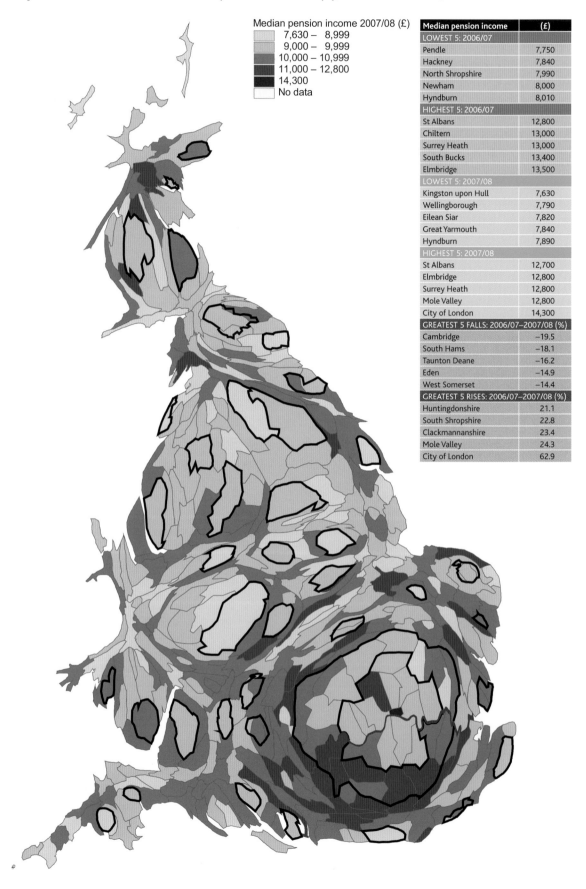

Median pension income 2007/08 (£)

- 7,630 – 8,999
- 9,000 – 9,999
- 10,000 – 10,999
- 11,000 – 12,800
- 14,300
- No data

Median pension income	(£)
LOWEST 5: 2006/07	
Pendle	7,750
Hackney	7,840
North Shropshire	7,990
Newham	8,000
Hyndburn	8,010
HIGHEST 5: 2006/07	
St Albans	12,800
Chiltern	13,000
Surrey Heath	13,000
South Bucks	13,400
Elmbridge	13,500
LOWEST 5: 2007/08	
Kingston upon Hull	7,630
Wellingborough	7,790
Eilean Siar	7,820
Great Yarmouth	7,840
Hyndburn	7,890
HIGHEST 5: 2007/08	
St Albans	12,700
Elmbridge	12,800
Surrey Heath	12,800
Mole Valley	12,800
City of London	14,300
GREATEST 5 FALLS: 2006/07–2007/08 (%)	
Cambridge	−19.5
South Hams	−18.1
Taunton Deane	−16.2
Eden	−14.9
West Somerset	−14.4
GREATEST 5 RISES: 2006/07–2007/08 (%)	
Huntingdonshire	21.1
South Shropshire	22.8
Clackmannanshire	23.4
Mole Valley	24.3
City of London	62.9

home owners.[11] Recently Her Majesty's Revenue & Customs (HMRC) released data on taxable incomes disaggregated by area and status (including pensioner status) which now allows us, for the first time, to compare how pensioners fare financially across the country and how that geographical pattern is changing. In the most recent year for which data are available, HMRC takes a sample survey of 600,000 individuals from information held by their tax offices on persons who pay UK tax. This includes all but the least and the most affluent pensioners. The least affluent have insufficient income to pay tax; the most affluent find ways of avoiding tax, often acting as if they are just visiting the UK and are normally domiciled abroad, but they are a tiny group, so their exclusion does not skew the figures shown here too much.[12]

The highest median pension income, from all sources combined, recorded for any area in the most

recent tax year for which HMRC has released data (2007/08) is £14,300 for those individuals resident in the City of London. This is a small group of people but increasingly the City and a couple of neighbouring areas are revealing extreme statistics which help to illustrate just how skewed British society has become. At the other extreme, in the city of Hull, pensioners have a median annual income which is barely half of that: £7,630 a year (£21 a day).

In the poorest 100 of the 407 areas for which HMRC has released median pensioner total incomes (before tax), all median annual pensioner incomes fall short of £9,230; in the next 100 areas all are less than £9,820; in the next, all are less than £10,400; and in the next they are all less than £12,200. It is only in seven areas of the country that the average pensioner will have an income in excess of £12,200. As well as the City of London these seven include Elmbridge, Mole Valley, Surrey Heath, St Albans, Winchester and Waverley.

Map 1.3.2: 2007/08 Mean annual pension income (£), local authorities, Britain

Mean pension income 2007/08 (£)
8,420 – 9,999
10,000 – 12,499
12,500 – 14,999
15,000 – 19,999
20,000 – 23,500
No data

Map 1.3.3: 2006/07–2007/08 Median annual pension income change (£), local authorities, Britain

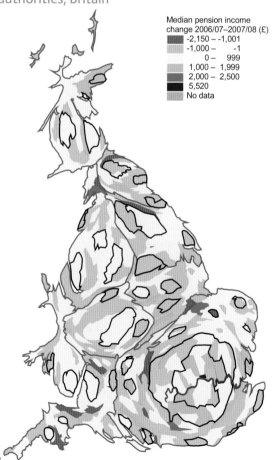

Median pension income change 2006/07–2007/08 (£)
-2,150 – -1,001
-1,000 – -1
0 – 999
1,000 – 1,999
2,000 – 2,500
5,520
No data

Map 1.3.1 shows the national distribution of median pensioner income for all areas.

The reason why many more pensioners than the 20% quoted above are not deemed to be living in poverty is that the incomes just quoted are for individual pensioners. Many pensioners live as couples and their combined household income means that many of these couples live just (or not far) above the poverty line. Furthermore, that poverty line is reduced for single pensioners living alone as their living costs are deemed to be lower than those of a couple. However, while this might be true of food costs it is unlikely to be true of heating costs, or the costs of age-related disability, such as travelling by taxi (which is no dearer for two than for one), home help and paying for other jobs which in their younger days many older people did themselves.

A significant minority of pensioners remain very well-off. Map 1.3.2 shows mean pension income in each district of Britain, a figure which is heavily skewed by the high incomes in retirement of a very few individuals. By 2007/08 the highest mean individual incomes for all pensioners in any local authority area were found in the City of London, then in Kensington & Chelsea, and then Westminster. These mean averages were £23,500, £23,100 and £20,700, respectively. The lowest mean pensioner incomes were found in Hull, Sandwell and Stoke-on-Trent, at £8,570, £8,500 and £8,420, respectively.

Map 1.3.3 shows how median annual pensioner income, in pounds, in each area, has changed between the most recent years for which data are available. Here are some percentage figures for change in median income to compare with those mapped absolute figures. In the three districts with the poorest pensioners, the incomes of pensioners between 2006/07 and 2007/08 fell: by 6.6% in Stoke, 7.6% in Sandwell and 12.7% in Hull. In all these cases these falls will be due to reductions in sources of income outside of the basic state pension affecting people in these areas more badly than elsewhere in the country.

In stark contrast, over exactly the same period, pensioners' incomes in the City of London rose by 13.0%, in Kensington & Chelsea by 3.6% and in Westminster by 8.9%. Incomes in Kensington

& Chelsea may have lagged as investment income began to fall during the start of the economic slump. By the median income measure, the highest rise recorded was an extra £5,520 a year in income for the average pensioner living in the City of London between 2006/07 and 2007/08. The biggest fall was an average of £2,150 in South Hams. In Stoke the fall in median incomes per annum was of 'only' £590. It was low because many pensioners there did not have much above the minimal income guarantees that they could lose. And, of course, losing more than £10 a week in income is not a small decrease when you are living hand to mouth, just as gaining many thousands of pounds is not much of a windfall to a pensioner who already has millions.

1.4 Working-age poverty due to unemployment

When the full extent of the economic crash of 2008 became clear, the great fear was a return to widespread mass unemployment. Between July 2008 and July 2009 the proportion of working-age adults claiming unemployment benefit rose in every single parliamentary constituency. This was possibly the first time such a uniform increase in numbers of unemployment benefit claims had occurred across all of Britain. The situation appeared dire. Talk was of a return to the 1930s. The rise was slowest, less than a percentage point, in the most remote areas: Skye, Westmoreland, Dwyfor Meirionnydd and Orkney & Shetland. Claims rose most quickly in areas where particular manufacturing plants were immediately affected, often through loss of financial support as credit dried up. Rates rose by at least three percentage points in Walsall North, West Bromwich West, Rotherham, Wolverhampton South East, Birmingham Erdington, South Swindon, Walsall South, Merthyr Tydfil & Rhymney and West Bromwich East. By July 2009 over one in ten of the working-age population of Birmingham Ladywood, the most affected constituency, were claiming jobseeking (unemployment) benefits.

Government intervened. The largest increase in employment created in the subsequent year was an extra 60,000 jobs in the National Health Service. Unemployment rates actually fell in some months up to the end of the last New Labour parliament. Although Birmingham Ladywood's claimant rate

Map 1.4.1: 2009–10 Unemployment benefit claims (% change), parlamentary constituencies, Britain

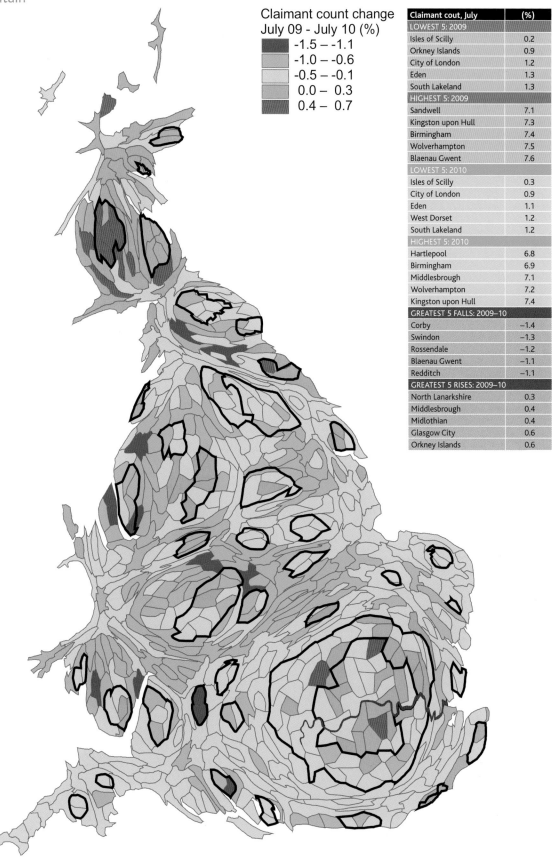

Claimant count change
July 09 - July 10 (%)

- -1.5 – -1.1
- -1.0 – -0.6
- -0.5 – -0.1
- 0.0 – 0.3
- 0.4 – 0.7

Claimant cout, July	(%)
LOWEST 5: 2009	
Isles of Scilly	0.2
Orkney Islands	0.9
City of London	1.2
Eden	1.3
South Lakeland	1.3
HIGHEST 5: 2009	
Sandwell	7.1
Kingston upon Hull	7.3
Birmingham	7.4
Wolverhampton	7.5
Blaenau Gwent	7.6
LOWEST 5: 2010	
Isles of Scilly	0.3
City of London	0.9
Eden	1.1
West Dorset	1.2
South Lakeland	1.2
HIGHEST 5: 2010	
Hartlepool	6.8
Birmingham	6.9
Middlesbrough	7.1
Wolverhampton	7.2
Kingston upon Hull	7.4
GREATEST 5 FALLS: 2009–10	
Corby	−1.4
Swindon	−1.3
Rossendale	−1.2
Blaenau Gwent	−1.1
Redditch	−1.1
GREATEST 5 RISES: 2009–10	
North Lanarkshire	0.3
Middlesbrough	0.4
Midlothian	0.4
Glasgow City	0.6
Orkney Islands	0.6

remained unchanged and the highest in the country, with 10.7% of the working-age population still claiming by July 2010, in many places claimant rates fell, while in Scotland, Inner London and the North East, claims still rose.

Some areas were especially badly affected despite central (Westminster) government action. The six constituencies, out of 632 mainland seats, which experienced the greatest increases in unemployment between July 2009 and July 2010 were Glasgow South West, Glasgow North West, Glasgow Central, Glasgow South, Glasgow North East and Glasgow East. Map 1.4.1 shows these percentage point changes in unemployment rates for all areas. Map 1.4.2 shows how unemployment claimants were distributed in 2005 (when the New Labour government came into office for its last term). Map 1.4.3 shows the most recent picture, which reflects rising joblessness over that final New Labour five-

year period, but also the falls in many places within that last year.

It is important to point out that what is being mapped here is the Jobseeker's Allowance (JSA) claimant count, which records the number of people claiming JSA and also National Insurance credits at Jobcentre Plus local offices. Government websites do state that this is not an official measure of unemployment, but it is the only indicative statistic available for areas smaller than local authorities. Over the years increasing numbers of people have been moved (or have moved themselves) from claiming unemployment benefits when they could not find work, to claiming various sickness benefits. In some cases, if an appropriate job were available then these people could take it, despite their illness. Having an illness and especially having a disability does not necessarily mean you cannot work. In other cases, prolonged exposure to repeated unemployment may

Map 1.4.2: 2005 Unemployment benefit claims (%), parliamentary constituencies, Britain

Claimant count July 2005 (%)
0.5 – 1.9
2.0 – 3.9
4.0 – 5.9
6.0 – 7.9
8.0 – 9.3

Map 1.4.3: 2010 Unemployment benefit claims (%), parliamentary constituencies, Britain

Claimant count July 2010 (%)
0.9 – 1.9
2.0 – 3.9
4.0 – 5.9
6.0 – 7.9
8.0 – 10.7

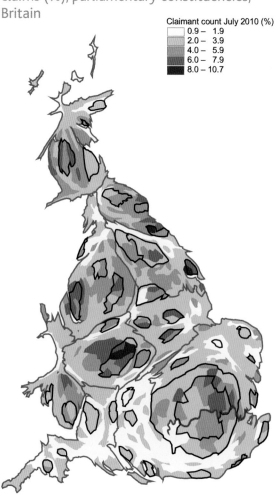

make you incapable of the kind of work you once could do, through loss of confidence and self-esteem.

To put the changes shown here into context, Map 1.4.4 takes the annual series back to 1983, when there was widespread mass unemployment. However, note how little the South East of England was affected then. Note also how in 1989 and 1990 almost all areas other than Glasgow, Liverpool and Hackney turn much lighter as unemployment rates fell and then rose again in the short recession of the early 1990s. However, in this series it is the period 1999 to 2010 that is most remarkable, when claimant rates became low almost everywhere. A key reason for this was that by then the vast majority of working-age adults out of work were in receipt of different forms of benefit (other than Jobseeker's Allowance), or were studying or had retired early. Nevertheless it was a remarkable period, which is only now ending. Table 1.4.1 lists where unemployment rates were highest and lowest each year, giving a simpler summary of how the geography of unemployment is changing.

Table 1.4.1: 1983–2010, Areas with most and least unemployment benefit claimants in July, local authorities, Britain

Year	Worst-off Area	Rate (%)	Best-off Area	Rate (%)
1983	Knowsley	18.6	Mid Sussex	2.9
1984	Knowsley	18.7	City of London	2.1
1985	Knowsley	18.9	City of London	2.6
1986	Knowsley	18.9	City of London	2.4
1987	Liverpool	16.9	Hart	2.1
1988	Liverpool	15.1	Horsham	1.2
1989	Liverpool	12.8	Mid Sussex	0.8
1990	Liverpool	11.6	Surrey Heath	0.9
1991	Hackney	14.7	Aberdeenshire	2.1
1992	Hackney	16.5	Shetland Islands	2.6
1993	Hackney	17.5	Shetland Islands	2.9
1994	Hackney	16.8	Ribble Valley	2.4
1995	Hackney	15.9	Hart	2.2
1996	Hackney	15.2	Hart	1.6
1997	Hackney	12.1	Wokingham	0.9
1998	Hackney	10.5	Hart	0.6
1999	Hackney	8.6	Hart	0.6
2000	Hackney	6.9	Hart	0.5
2001	Tower Hamlets	5.8	Rutland	0.4
2002	Tower Hamlets	5.7	Rutland	0.4
2003	Hackney	5.8	Rutland	0.6
2004	Hackney	5.5	Rutland	0.4
2005	Hackney	5.5	Purbeck	0.4
2006	Tower Hamlets	5.7	Rutland	0.6
2007	Birmingham	5.2	East Dorset	0.5
2008	Birmingham	5.2	Rutland	0.6
2009	Blaenau Gwent	7.6	Orkney Islands	0.9
2010	Kingston upon Hull	7.4	City of London	0.9

Map 1.4.4: 1983–2010 Unemployment benefit claims (%), local authorities, Britain

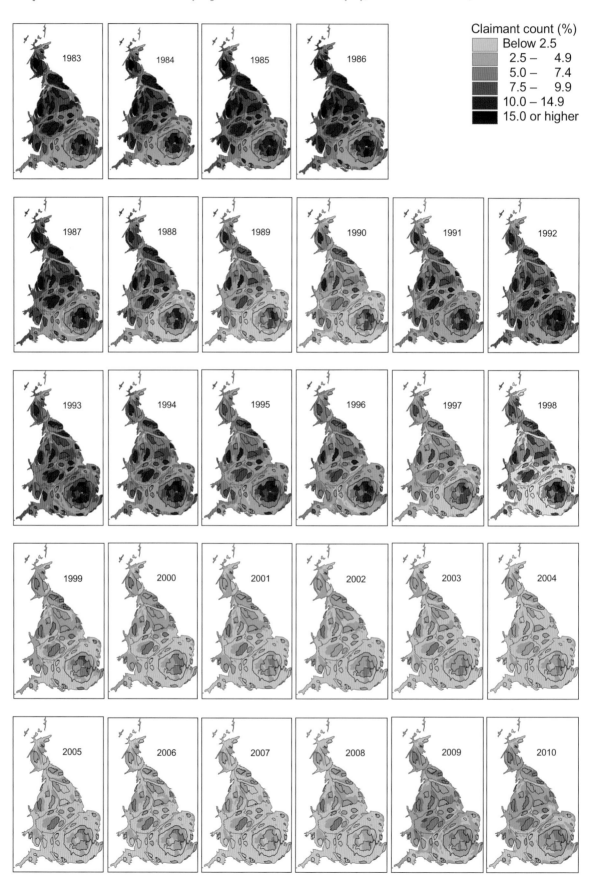

Claimant count (%)
- Below 2.5
- 2.5 – 4.9
- 5.0 – 7.4
- 7.5 – 9.9
- 10.0 – 14.9
- 15.0 or higher

1.5 In work poverty due to low or falling earnings

Just as most people who are out of work would like to work, and most who are in receipt of benefits are usually not in receipt of unemployment benefits, most people in poverty live in a family where someone is in work but where that work is too lowly paid for them to escape poverty. Income inequalities in Britain are among the widest in the affluent world. The largest group of poor households living in Western Europe live in Britain.[13] As official unemployment rates fell during the late 1990s, and for almost all of the decade that followed, and as many mainly-out-of-work groups, such as students, took temporary part-time work to supplement their income, it was increasingly low wages that created new cases of poverty, despite the guarantee of a minimum wage.

It is very hard between census years to determine how many people live in households with only one low-earner in each part of the country, or to know in each place how badly part-time employees and/ or female workers are paid as compared with full-time workers (and/or men). What we can measure is how earnings of people in full-time work vary across the country and how they have been changing most recently. We do this using results disaggregated by area and published in the government's Annual Survey of Hours and Earnings (ASHE).

Methodological changes took place in the ASHE during the collection and processing of the 2007 round of that survey, so we concentrate here only on levels and changes since then.[14] In 2007 the (mean) average man in full-time employment in Britain received £525 a week and the average women in full-time work £320, according to the full 2007 sample. The mean average for all people was £423 a week. The vast majority of the population in work earned below these averages because the arithmetic means are skewed by high earnings. Most full-time workers were not paid this much and, furthermore, because so many people now work less than full-time, for the first time in many decades, average wages in many places are beginning to fall.

Map 1.5.1 shows the changes in mean rates of gross weekly pay in each district of the country. In 118 districts mean average pay of full-time employees

fell between 2008 and 2009. It fell the most in absolute terms in the district of Eden in Cumbria, followed by West Berkshire, Thanet in Essex, Windsor & Maidenhead, South Oxfordshire, Tandridge, Spelthorne, South Bucks, South Lakeland, Chester-le-Street, Tunbridge Wells, Elmbridge, Herefordshire, and the Forest of Dean. The falls were hitting affluent as well as poor areas, although a fall of the same number of pounds a week in a poor area is a much higher proportionate fall in household income, and these are households where a higher proportion of income has to be spent on necessities.

In other parts of the country annual mean full-time incomes rose in the year 2008/09 despite the economic crisis. As we pointed out above, there are some businesses which profit from hard times and it would appear, give or take some random variation, that these are most concentrated where weekly earnings increased most: in West Oxfordshire (by £71 a week), Vale of Glamorgan (£76), Chester (£76), Winchester (£78), Blaby (£78), Guildford (£79), Wychavon (£83), Kerrier (£90), Ryedale (£116) and Rutland (£118). However, it must be remembered that these figures come from surveys of employers. When we consider the tax returns of individual employees we find a far greater range of outcomes (see Section 1.7).

Map 1.5.2 shows the outcome of these changes. By 2009 mean weekly earnings exceeded £1,000 in Kensington & Chelsea, the City of London, Westminster and Elmbridge. They were lowest, between £426 and £392, in Boston, Restormel, Blackpool and Blaenau Gwent. In 2003 people employed in the best-off district in Britain (Kensington & Chelsea) earned on average £837 more per week than did people in the worst-paying area (Blackpool, where average wages were then £354 a week). In 2004 that gap between the highest and lowest paid rose to £882; in 2008 to £912 and in 2009 to £1,046. By 2009 it was again Blackpool and Kensington & Chelsea appearing at either end of the league tables; people in Kensington & Chelsea were, on *average*, earning 3.3 times more than those in Blackpool.

Finally, Map 1.5.3 shows the median full-time take-home pay in each district in 2009. Most people earn much less than mean earnings, which are skewed by the few highest earners. For example, in Blackpool in

Map 1.5.1: 2008–09 Change in mean full-time weekly earnings (£), local authorities, Britain

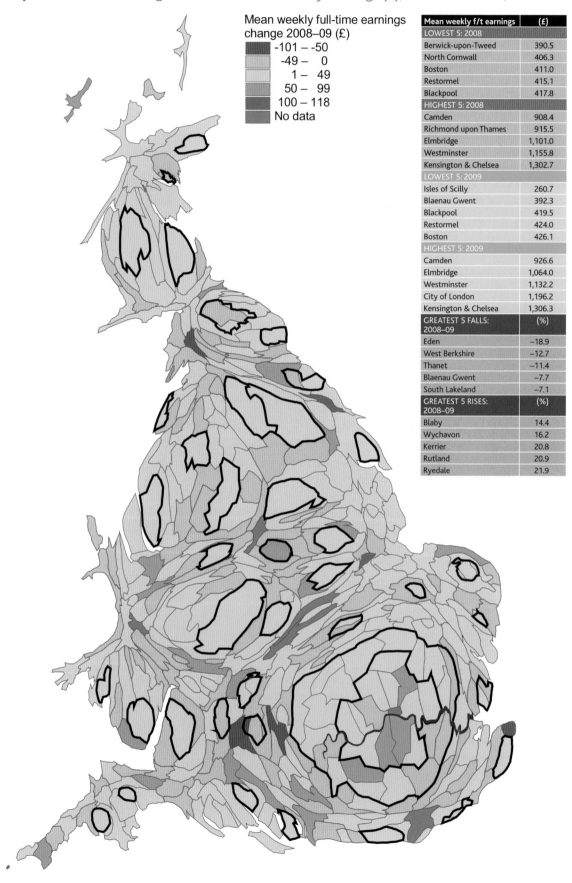

Mean weekly full-time earnings change 2008–09 (£)

- -101 – -50
- -49 – 0
- 1 – 49
- 50 – 99
- 100 – 118
- No data

Mean weekly f/t earnings	(£)
LOWEST 5: 2008	
Berwick-upon-Tweed	390.5
North Cornwall	406.3
Boston	411.0
Restormel	415.1
Blackpool	417.8
HIGHEST 5: 2008	
Camden	908.4
Richmond upon Thames	915.5
Elmbridge	1,101.0
Westminster	1,155.8
Kensington & Chelsea	1,302.7
LOWEST 5: 2009	
Isles of Scilly	260.7
Blaenau Gwent	392.3
Blackpool	419.5
Restormel	424.0
Boston	426.1
HIGHEST 5: 2009	
Camden	926.6
Elmbridge	1,064.0
Westminster	1,132.2
City of London	1,196.2
Kensington & Chelsea	1,306.3
GREATEST 5 FALLS: 2008–09	(%)
Eden	−18.9
West Berkshire	−12.7
Thanet	−11.4
Blaenau Gwent	−7.7
South Lakeland	−7.1
GREATEST 5 RISES: 2008–09	(%)
Blaby	14.4
Wychavon	16.2
Kerrier	20.8
Rutland	20.9
Ryedale	21.9

2009 mean earnings were £420 and median earnings were £372 a week, whereas in Kensington these figures were £1,306 and £933, respectively. The inequality ratio between these two extreme districts falls, by this way of counting, to the median full-time employee in Kensington & Chelsea earning 2.5 times more than the median in Blackpool. This is still a huge difference, but it is muted by taking out the highest-earning employees of Kensington & Chelsea. And even higher earners can be identified when we consider tax records in Section 1.7 below, especially among the self-employed who, by definition, cannot be included in an employment survey of employees.

These maps show that there are far fewer very high earners in Blackpool; and that the overall effect of the direct London weighting and the indirect way in which basic average wages in London tend to rise faster than elsewhere, is clear and simple: rising inequality.

Map 1.5.2: 2009 Mean full-time weekly earnings (£), local authorities, Britain

Mean weekly full-time earnings 2009 (£)
261 – 399
400 – 499
500 – 599
600 – 799
800 – 999
1,000 – 1,306

Map 1.5.3: 2009 Median full-time weekly earnings (£), local authorities, Britain

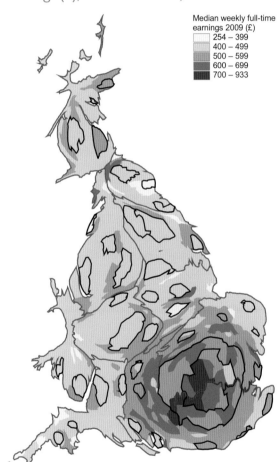

Median weekly full-time earnings 2009 (£)
254 – 399
400 – 499
500 – 599
600 – 699
700 – 933

1.6 Public sector cuts: local and national implications

In June 2010 the Department for Communities and Local Government published what is likely to become one of the most infamous documents of the economic depression/recession, titled *Local government contribution to efficiencies in 2010/11*.[15] This document set out some of the most unfairly distributed cuts ever to be imposed on local government in England. The poor and the poorest areas of the country were targeted to receive the deepest and most sustained cuts. This mirrored the effects of the national budget of that month which was also found, on examination by the Institute for Fiscal Studies,[16] to be highly regressive. It is not a coincidence that almost all of the areas to suffer the greatest service cuts contained a large majority of people who had voted against the two parties that had come to form the new Coalition government.

What matters in government reports are the figures. For instance, the cuts this document specified will result in more people, and especially young children, being killed, because road safety funding is to be cut by £37 million:

> Road safety funding – £37.797m. £20.592m is proposed to be removed from road safety revenue grant (paid out via area based grant) in the last four months of 2010/11 and £17.205m road safety capital grant originally due to be paid in May. This represents a reduction of 27 per cent in the revenue grant and all of the capital grant. (page 10 of the report)

Road safety funding is higher in areas where there are more children who need to be taught about the danger of roads, and so these cuts have different effects across the country. There are, of course, many other cuts specified than those to road safety.

The key figures in the document are presented in very small type in its Appendix D. Map 1.6.1 shows these figures. It shows where the main cuts would hit most, least, and not at all. These are the first, relatively modest, local government cuts, of 'just' £6 billion. However, not a penny of that £6 billion is to be saved by the citizens of generally well-heeled districts such as Chiltern, South Bucks, most of

Devon, Christchurch, most of Dorset, Cheltenham, the Cotswolds, Winchester, Broxbourne, most of Hertfordshire, Tunbridge Wells, Harrogate, most of Oxfordshire (but not Oxford), all of Surrey, the Malvern Hills and another hundred or so generally 'leafy' and mostly 'Tory' or 'Liberal Democrat' areas. Some of the counties these districts lie in will see cuts, but all of less than 0.9% and some as small as 0.6% of their budgets. The smallest reported cut of all, of just 0.1%, will be to the budget of the Corporation of the City of London.

It is mostly in the North and in northern cities where the local cuts will be greatest, initially reducing budgets by 1% and 2%, in places like: Sheffield, Barnsley, Bradford, Bolton, Corby, Kingston upon Hull, Gateshead, Stoke-on-Trent, Sunderland, Salford, Nottingham, Stockton-on-Tees, Hartlepool, Doncaster, Redcar & Cleveland, Liverpool, Knowsley, Middlesbrough, St Helens, Blackpool, Barrow-in-Furness, Bolsover, Hastings and Burnley, and a couple of dozen similar areas. Anyone with a rudimentary knowledge of English electoral geography knows that the map resembles, more than anything else, a map of where people are poor, and where most abstain at general elections or vote Labour.

The public sector is proportionately larger in poorer areas. Map 1.6.2 shows the proportion of people aged 16–64 in each district of Britain who are in employment, and who are working in public administration, education and health (a few of the education and health workers will be employed in the private sector). The proportions of people employed in the public sector are highest in Richmondshire with the army base in Catterick (46% of local workers are state employed), in the Scottish islands of Eilean Siar (where a small population requires 43% state employment) and in Oxford (dominated by universities and hospitals, just under 43%). The lowest proportions are in generally well-off, not-too-isolated rural areas, such as Tamworth (15%), Maldon (17%), North Warwickshire (18%) and Melton (19%), and also in Kensington & Chelsea (19%).

The final map referred to in this section, Map 1.6.3, shows the unemployment that would result from massive cuts of a quarter of all public sector jobs. It is drawn by taking current unemployment rates

Map 1.6.1: 2010–11 Reduction in main revenue grant allocations (%), local authorities, England

Reduction in main revenue
grant allocations 2010-11 (%)
- -2.0
- -1.7 – -1.0
- -0.9 – -0.8
- -0.7
- -0.6
- -0.5 – -0.1
- 0.0

and adding to those a quarter of the public sector workforce. This assumes that all those laid off do not get other work or retire or move, but also that their unemployment does not result in knock-on rises in joblessness in their local areas as local services, shops, cafes and amenities (that public sector workers could once afford) close down. Some 407,000 employees, almost 5% of the entire public sector workforce, work in just four cities and make up just under a third of all employees there: Birmingham

(36% of employees), Sheffield (35%), Glasgow (34%) and Leeds (27%). However, these are dwarfed by the public sector workforce of London at 990,000 workers (a 27% share of London's workforce).

We have already seen that the cuts are not to be evenly spread across the country, so Map 1.6.3 may well overestimate the effects of cuts in the South, and underestimate them in the North.

Map 1.6.2: 2009 Proportion of employees in the public sector (%), local authorities, Britain

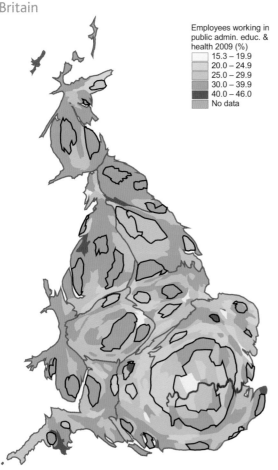

Map 1.6.3: Projection of unemployment rates given a 25% cut in public sector employment, local authorities, Britain

1.7 Where the wealth is: who could afford the cuts?

The final section of this chapter looks at where the monies could be found to pay for debt amassed due to the profligacy of the banking sector. There was an alternative to massive public sector cuts: to reduce the wealth and incomes of those most closely connected to the causes of the crisis. Map 1.7.2 shows figures drawn from the most recent year for which we have data on the income of people who declare themselves self-employed for tax purposes. Many self-employed people are not well paid; they include window cleaners and some hill farmers for instance, but a few are very well paid and in some parts of the country even the average self-employed person is taking home over £100,000 a year (according to their declarations to the tax authorities).

In Kensington & Chelsea the mean income of the self-employed by the 2007/08 tax year had reached £205,000 a year, the next highest was the City of London where that mean stood at £125,000 a year and the next Westminster, at £103,000 (see Map 1.7.2). These incomes are between 10 and 20 times higher than the incomes of the self-employed who live in places at the other end of the income scale, like Hartlepool, Barrow-in-Furness and Copeland (£11,300 a year mean, or £6,970 median).

Comparing 2003/04 and 2007/08 (the widest range of years for which HMRC has released data), average incomes through self-employment in Kensington & Chelsea rose by £145,600 (245%); in the City those incomes rose by 'only' £16,000 (15%), as bonuses within big banks were cut, and in Westminster 'only' by £46,700 (83%) – possibly this high because bonuses in private finance houses cannot be scrutinised as those for big banks can. These rises occurred in just four years. In Copeland in rural Cumbria average incomes of the self-employed over the same four years fell by £2,700 (20%). Map 1.7.1 shows the national picture of those changes in declared self-employed earnings.

Of course, most earnings in Britain are received by people directly employed, not by freelance financiers. Map 1.7.3 shows the national distribution of employees' mean earnings. Again, the impact of the financial sector within London immediately draws

your eye. The district with the highest mean income for all employees (£117,000) is – of course – the London borough of Kensington & Chelsea, closely followed by the City of London (£86,500) and Westminster (£68,300).

Map 1.7.4 shows where the rises in employee average incomes in the four years following 2003/04 have been greatest and again it is the usual suspects. An extra £40,100 was awarded in additional renumeration over just four years for *every* employee paying tax who lived in Kensington & Chelsea, £17,700 for those living in the City and £19,300 for those living within Westminster. Nationally the lowest average wages were found in Penwith, £14,600 a year, down some £200 on four years previously.

In Britain those people working in the sector most responsible for the poor state of the national finances

Map 1.7.1: 2003/04–2007/08 change in mean income of the self-employed (£), local authorities, Britain

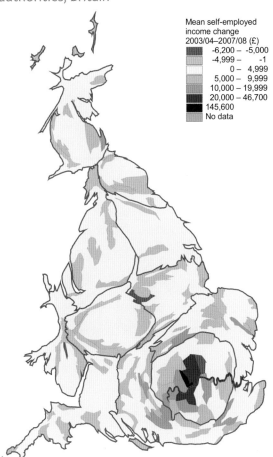

Mean self-employed income change 2003/04–2007/08 (£)

- -6,200 – -5,000
- -4,999 – -1
- 0 – 4,999
- 5,000 – 9,999
- 10,000 – 19,999
- 20,000 – 46,700
- 145,600
- No data

Map 1.7.2: 2007/08 Mean income of the self-employed (£), local authorities, Britain

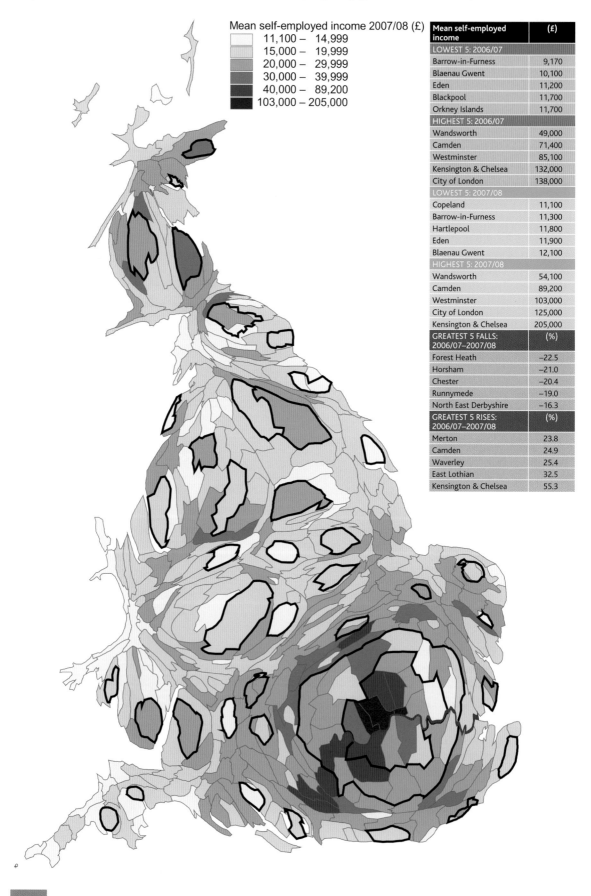

Mean self-employed income 2007/08 (£)

- 11,100 – 14,999
- 15,000 – 19,999
- 20,000 – 29,999
- 30,000 – 39,999
- 40,000 – 89,200
- 103,000 – 205,000

Mean self-employed income	(£)
LOWEST 5: 2006/07	
Barrow-in-Furness	9,170
Blaenau Gwent	10,100
Eden	11,200
Blackpool	11,700
Orkney Islands	11,700
HIGHEST 5: 2006/07	
Wandsworth	49,000
Camden	71,400
Westminster	85,100
Kensington & Chelsea	132,000
City of London	138,000
LOWEST 5: 2007/08	
Copeland	11,100
Barrow-in-Furness	11,300
Hartlepool	11,800
Eden	11,900
Blaenau Gwent	12,100
HIGHEST 5: 2007/08	
Wandsworth	54,100
Camden	89,200
Westminster	103,000
City of London	125,000
Kensington & Chelsea	205,000
GREATEST 5 FALLS: 2006/07–2007/08	(%)
Forest Heath	−22.5
Horsham	−21.0
Chester	−20.4
Runnymede	−19.0
North East Derbyshire	−16.3
GREATEST 5 RISES: 2006/07–2007/08	(%)
Merton	23.8
Camden	24.9
Waverley	25.4
East Lothian	32.5
Kensington & Chelsea	55.3

– the banking sector – continue to receive salaries that were inflated during the boom years, and that have not been dented since. Introducing income taxation which would return levels of take-home pay for these rich people (and others earning like them) to the amounts received by the rich in 2003/04 would raise enough tax for most public sector cuts to be avoided. The instant response to suggestions of this kind is that the banking sector would move offshore. However, it might be worth turning up the pressure to work out at what point that flight really does begin to occur, or to what extent people are crying wolf.

Finally there is another source of finance which the state can turn to rather than behaving as if government were bankrupt: personal wealth. The distribution of national wealth in Britain is even more unevenly arranged than is the distribution of income. High but steadily continuing, even non-

rising, inequalities in income translate into ever-growing inequalities in wealth. Table 1.7.1 shows the most recent estimates of wealth held by individual adults in each region of Britain, sorted from least wealth to most. It is in Yorkshire & Humberside that the least wealth is held by the average adult. In Yorkshire & Humberside mean wealth per adult is 'just' £289,000. However. the poorest of the richest 10% of Yorkshire & Humberside people have recourse to wealth of more than twice that (£710,000) while the richest of the poorest 10% of Yorkshire & Humberside's residents have only £9,700, or 73.2 times less wealth. In London that ratio is 273.

Wealth here comprises pension rights, traditional financial assets and housing equity. One part of that wealth that it would be possible to tax with absolutely no fear of it fleeing overseas is land ownership. A land-value tax could replace regressive

Map 1.7.3: 2007/08 Mean income of employees (£), local authorities, Britain

Mean employment
income 2007/08 (£)
14,600 – 19,999
20,000 – 29,999
30,000 – 39,999
40,000 – 49,999
50,000 – 117,000
No data

Map 1.7.4: 2003/04–2007/08 change in mean income of employees (£), local authorities, Britain

Mean employment
income change
2003/04–2007/08 (£)
-1,400 – -1
0 – 2,999
3,000 – 4,999
5,000 – 9,999
10,000 – 40,100
No data

taxes such as the council tax. Every individual who owns land could be taxed a proportion of its value a year. If they could not pay they could sell a portion of their land. For most households a land-value tax would be much lower than the current council tax which it would replace. A few very wealthy individuals would lose out, of course – but they could most afford to. Again, most public sector cuts could be avoided. It is clear from Table 1.7.1 that there is a great deal of money in Britain.

Perhaps it is because Britain is seen as bankrupt in so many other ways than purely financially that we remain so impotent to solve our own problems and pay off the national debt with the national wealth? The rest of this book concerns a selection of those other kinds of bankruptcy.

Table 1.7.1: 2006/08 Mean, median, decile point and ratio of wealth in Britain by region

GB, 2006/08, Total wealth	Wealth held by individuals (£)				
Country/Region	Mean	10th	Median	90th	90:10 ratio
Yorkshire & Humberside	289,287	9,700	172,727	710,000	73.2
North East	301,117	7,900	169,548	704,890	89.2
North West	311,168	7,790	168,197	764,590	98.2
West Midlands	323,307	9,000	187,664	737,760	82.0
Scotland	339,873	7,600	150,629	710,065	93.4
East Midlands	341,727	13,481	213,690	807,133	59.9
Wales	355,452	8,400	205,544	751,700	89.5
London	371,034	3,420	173,393	933,563	273.0
South West	402,249	14,570	277,684	897,274	61.6
East of England	416,505	15,000	241,259	911,443	60.8
South East	494,338	15,201	287,892	1,104,502	72.7

Chapter 2 Residentially bankrupt

Introduction

Britain is home to a greater concentration of dollar millionaires than anywhere else in the world. Western Europe has the most millionaires in the world[1] and it is within Britain, especially in and around London, that the greatest cluster of the richest people on earth live and, at least for part of the time, are housed. In this chapter we show how, despite the economic crash, the housing wealth of the very richest continues to climb at ever increasing rates.

Over time in recent decades a greater and greater share of total housing, of floor-space, of bedrooms and of gardens, has been acquired by a small but increasingly affluent group of people: the rich. The rich have become much richer in Britain and were best placed, initially, to weather the arrival of economic hard times. Some have picked up great bargains. Residentially the rich have done well out of the crash, they have seen the value of their homes rise while most others have fallen.

Beneath the rich are the affluent, who have tended to copy the rich but on a smaller scale. Some have sought to buy more than one home. Many are concerned over the rate of inheritance tax and worry that the value of their property might at some point exceed the inheritance tax threshold and that they will be taxed on a proportion of that wealth at death.

Britain has had enough housing for all for some time, but every year the homes we have are shared out less and less efficiently as more and more of them are bought and sold through the free market. Even as prices have been falling for most homeowners in recent years, rates of repossession of the homes of those unable to pay their mortgages have been rising.

People who were persuaded to buy homes they can now not afford did so because, as residential inequalities rose, it became more and more vital to pay as much as you could to live as near as you could to the affluent so that you could enjoy their low crime rates, so that your children could mix with their children at school and so that you did not 'waste' your money on rent or on buying a home in an area where prices might not rise quickly. It is for these and similar reasons that so many people in the decade up to 2010 bought homes using interest-only mortgages, hoping that in some other way they would make enough money by later trading down to pay for the actual capital cost of their home.

As more and more people tried to get into the housing market, others bought up holiday homes and second homes, crash pads and country retreats, and so the overall stock of *available* housing decreased despite more houses being built. Many second home owners also engaged in buy-to-let, which should have made these homes available again, but not when empty, and amateur landlords know very little about vacancy rate minimisation. In order to maximise income, private landlords will tend to rent to whoever pays the most, not to who will use the property most effectively.

The growing army of amateur landlords both needed to cover their mortgages and wanted to make a profit on what they considered to be an 'investment'. Thus private sector rents rose despite supply rising as the sector increased rapidly in size. The public sector copied these price rises. Housing became more and more expensive. The size of areas where social security benefits would no longer cover housing costs became larger and larger. The poor were directly excluded from even living near to many affluent areas by these changes, including the policy of the government to move social housing rents towards market rents, but simultaneously not to pay the necessary amount through housing benefit. We map all these recent changes in this chapter.

As the economic crash gathered pace in Britain evictions from both the private and state housing sectors rose. Housing waiting lists grew greatly in length; in places such as Sheffield they reached a maximum of nearly 100,000 families waiting to be housed by 2010. Officially the number of homeless households accepted for housing was falling nationally (and, incidentally, in Sheffield), but that was only as regulations became more draconian and people learned not to apply to be housed unless they were in the very worst of circumstances. In Scotland, where homelessness law is less restrictive, increasing numbers of households were accepted as being homeless as the economic recession deepened. We map the changing geography of homelessness towards the end of this chapter.

The chapter begins with the very richest of homeowners, because the continued protection of their wealth is key to understanding why so many others are still so poorly housed. There are enough homes owned by the rich and the affluent for all to be well housed were we not to continue to ignore the selfish amassing of the best housing assets by the few. The very richest provide the best illustrations of such selfishness and so we start with some of them, but they simply reflect the worst excesses of a system of housing which encourages hoarding and the maladministration of land in general.

In no other large European country is housing as badly distributed as in Britain. In no other similarly affluent country do people live in such cramped and crowded conditions, with so little floor space for most people and so many children sharing a room with a sibling of the opposite sex in their teenage years. Housing in Britain is shamefully poorly used, badly repaired, seen as yet another way to get rich rather than as the means of satisfying everyone's need for a home.

There are many routes to sorting out housing and most of these are easier to implement in a time of economic hardship than when it appears all is going well. Introduction of a land-value tax would curtail the excesses of the super rich, or at least charge them on an annual basis for the flaunting of their excessive wealth. Instigating a right-to-sell that mirrors the right-to-buy would both reduce repossessions in the short term and break up monolithic owner-occupied ghettos in the long term. Repealing section 21 of the Housing Act 1988, which allows tenants to be so easily evicted would discourage Rachman-type landlords as well as the amateur hobbyist.[2] Replicating Scotland's homelessness legislation in England and Wales would make a start on reversing

inequalities in this. All this is already happening elsewhere in the world, but to happen across Britain as a whole we have to first recognise how residentially bankrupt we have become.

2.1   Housing price peaks and multi-millionaires' seats

In the summer of 2007, at the height of the housing boom, there was one constituency where the average price of a home on an average road in an average neighbourhood reached £980,000. That constituency was Kensington. Incidentally, in 2004, the most expensive house ever sold at that time, one of the many homes of Formula One boss Bernie Ecclestone, for £57 million,[3] was located in Kensington Palace Gardens. Surprisingly the crash of 2008 did nothing to bring down the value of all those homes in places like Kensington, but rather, by 2008, the price of the average home there jumped to £1,131,000 and is likely to have continued to increase thereafter.

The map of prices at the height of the boom, shown in Map 2.1.1, reveals how in only nine constituencies in 2007 did average prices exceed half a million. In contrast, in 79 constituencies average prices were less than £130,000 and, in almost all of those places, mean prices fell in the year to 2008. Prices fell in most constituencies, but not in most of those where they had been highest. By 2008 there were 95 constituencies where an average home would cost you less than £130,000; all in places where most people are poor. Figure 2.1.1 shows how house prices fell in most areas in Britain, especially where prices were not already very high.

Map 2.1.1: 2007 Mean housing price (£), parliamentary constituencies, Britain

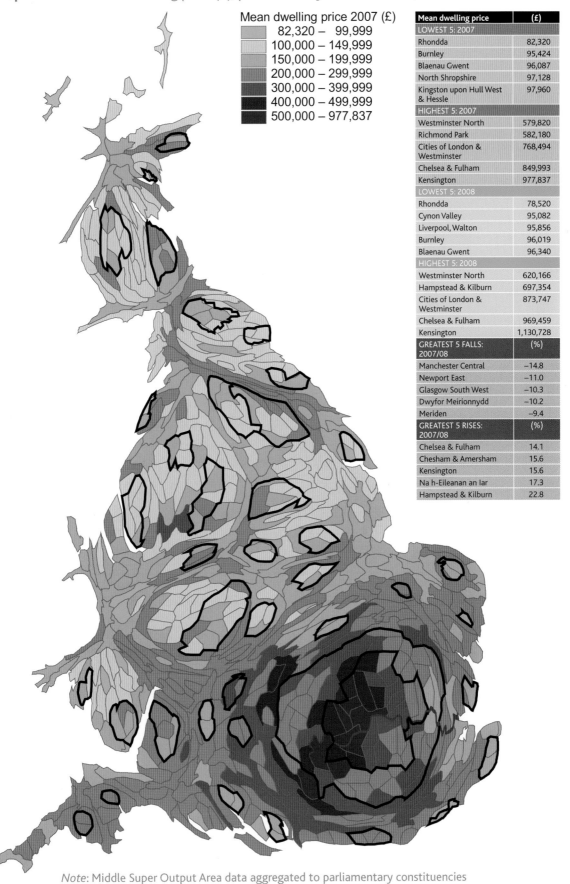

Mean dwelling price 2007 (£)

	82,320 – 99,999
	100,000 – 149,999
	150,000 – 199,999
	200,000 – 299,999
	300,000 – 399,999
	400,000 – 499,999
	500,000 – 977,837

Mean dwelling price	(£)
LOWEST 5: 2007	
Rhondda	82,320
Burnley	95,424
Blaenau Gwent	96,087
North Shropshire	97,128
Kingston upon Hull West & Hessle	97,960
HIGHEST 5: 2007	
Westminster North	579,820
Richmond Park	582,180
Cities of London & Westminster	768,494
Chelsea & Fulham	849,993
Kensington	977,837
LOWEST 5: 2008	
Rhondda	78,520
Cynon Valley	95,082
Liverpool, Walton	95,856
Burnley	96,019
Blaenau Gwent	96,340
HIGHEST 5: 2008	
Westminster North	620,166
Hampstead & Kilburn	697,354
Cities of London & Westminster	873,747
Chelsea & Fulham	969,459
Kensington	1,130,728
GREATEST 5 FALLS: 2007/08	(%)
Manchester Central	−14.8
Newport East	−11.0
Glasgow South West	−10.3
Dwyfor Meirionnydd	−10.2
Meriden	−9.4
GREATEST 5 RISES: 2007/08	(%)
Chelsea & Fulham	14.1
Chesham & Amersham	15.6
Kensington	15.6
Na h-Eileanan an Iar	17.3
Hampstead & Kilburn	22.8

Note: Middle Super Output Area data aggregated to parliamentary constituencies

Figure 2.1.1: 2007 House prices, and falls to 2008 (£), parliamentary constituencies, Britain

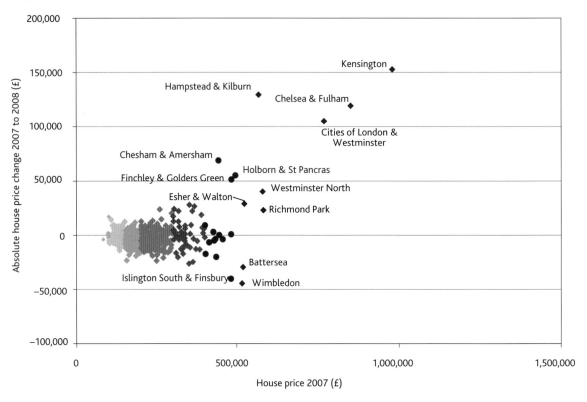

2.2 Housing price change: location, location, location

'Location, location, location' has been the mantra for years: buy in the right place and spend as much as you can, then all will be fine. While this seemed to work for the extremely rich in Kensington, in 2008 and 2009 the affluent in boroughs not very far away watched the value of their homes fall, by a few hundred or by tens of thousands. The reason for this was that they have fewer choices than the rich. For the very wealthy to be truly wealthy, millions of others must not become relatively better-off. If they did the gap would close and the wealthy would become less opulent. One key way in which 'middle income' households are made relatively poorer is that they tend to be behind the trend of the rich in where they invest their far more meagre resources.

They move into stocks and shares when the rich move out, put money into property in areas from where the rich have disinvested.

Those on middle incomes cannot just move their monies around the world at a whim. They do not enjoy non-domiciled tax status. When a market crashes they just have to sit there and take it. As Map 2.2.1 shows, they took it hardest in a ring in England surrounding but extending far out from an apex in Kensington, rippling across Wales and the North. The ripple had not reached most of Scotland by 2008, but it had by 2009. And while the middle-income home buyers were feeling the pinch, the super-rich were continuing to make investments where they thought their money would be safest.

Map 2.2.1: 2007–2008 mean average housing price change (% point), parliamentary constituencies, Britain

Mean dwelling price change 2007–2008 (%)
-14.8 – -10.1
-10.0 – -5.1
 -5.0 – -1.1
 -1.0 –   1.0
  1.1 – 10.0
 10.1 – 22.8

2.3 When the bank takes back your home: repossessions

Most people who buy a home do not buy it outright. The majority of first-time buyers now require help from relatives, but very few parents are rich enough to buy their children homes outright as gifts in Britain, and it is only in very affluent areas that most homes are mainly purchased using inherited money.

Most homes in Britain are not owned by the people living in them, but by the banks who have underwritten loans secured on the property. The bank will let you live in your home for as long as you pay your mortgage. It is a form of rent and an insecure investment. If you default, just a few times, and look as if you may carry on defaulting, then the bank will take back possession of its house. In a recession, such repossessions rise.

Before a bank can repossess your home they need to seek a repossession order from the courts. The rises and falls in the numbers of those orders by region in England and for all of Wales in the year to 2008 are shown in Figure 2.3.1. Not all orders result in repossession, and many mortgage holders give back their home to the bank without a repossession order being made when they cannot continue to pay the

mortgage. The numbers of orders a year may thus be either an underestimate or an overestimate of the numbers of people losing their homes because they cannot pay the banks.

Repossession orders in England and Wales fell to a minimum of 39,000 in 2002, but by 2008 they stood at 111,000 a year, having risen by 21,000 in just one year. Most of that rise in repossessions was in the North of England and London (see Figure 2.3.1). Map 2.3.1 shows the changing rate of repossession orders per thousand households per year. No data for Scotland are included in the maps or the graphs here because none were available. The data for England and Wales are released by the Department of Justice: the part of government concerned with, among much else, protecting private property. In this case it is the property of the banks that government is protecting when (through the courts) it allows people's homes to be seized.

Figure 2.3.1 highlights that, although Map 2.3.1 shows that repossession rates in many parts of London and the South East fell, they also rose greatly in those regions as a whole despite those regions containing some of the more wealthy places least badly affected by the crash. In the poorer parts of the capital and its hinterland, people who had taken out proportionately high mortgages, often those buying

Figure 2.3.1: 2000–08 Annual mortgage possession claims leading to orders, Wales and English regions

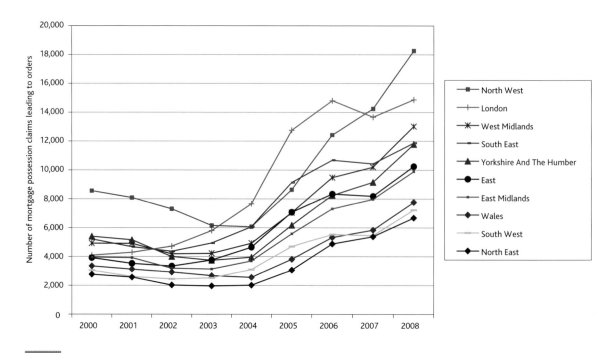

Map 2.3.1: 2007–08 Home repossession order rates (per thousand point change), local authorities, England & Wales

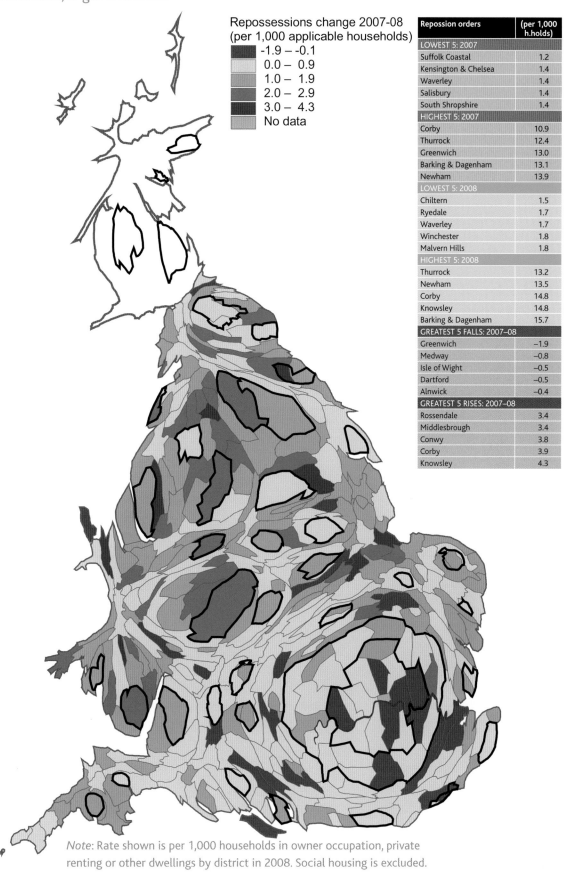

Repossessions change 2007-08
(per 1,000 applicable households)

- -1.9 – -0.1
- 0.0 – 0.9
- 1.0 – 1.9
- 2.0 – 2.9
- 3.0 – 4.3
- No data

Repossion orders	(per 1,000 h.holds)
LOWEST 5: 2007	
Suffolk Coastal	1.2
Kensington & Chelsea	1.4
Waverley	1.4
Salisbury	1.4
South Shropshire	1.4
HIGHEST 5: 2007	
Corby	10.9
Thurrock	12.4
Greenwich	13.0
Barking & Dagenham	13.1
Newham	13.9
LOWEST 5: 2008	
Chiltern	1.5
Ryedale	1.7
Waverley	1.7
Winchester	1.8
Malvern Hills	1.8
HIGHEST 5: 2008	
Thurrock	13.2
Newham	13.5
Corby	14.8
Knowsley	14.8
Barking & Dagenham	15.7
GREATEST 5 FALLS: 2007–08	
Greenwich	−1.9
Medway	−0.8
Isle of Wight	−0.5
Dartford	−0.5
Alnwick	−0.4
GREATEST 5 RISES: 2007–08	
Rossendale	3.4
Middlesbrough	3.4
Conwy	3.8
Corby	3.9
Knowsley	4.3

Note: Rate shown is per 1,000 households in owner occupation, private renting or other dwellings by district in 2008. Social housing is excluded.

some of the cheaper property in the less expensive places, were finding it hardest to cope. Repossessions rose least in absolute numbers in the North East, where more people rent, and in the South West, where the highest numbers own outright.

Map 2.3.2 shows that repossession rates by 2008 were highest in East London and within poorer parts of many cities in the North of England and South Wales. This is where people who buy tend to have the least money behind them, where home 'ownership' rarely means that, and where parents are least likely to help with a deposit. There is a continuum from a little help with the initial deposit, the help most first-time buyers receive now, to parents buying their children a home outright. The further along that continuum you are, the safer

Map 2.3.2: 2008 Home repossession orders (rate per thousand applicable households), local authorities, England & Wales

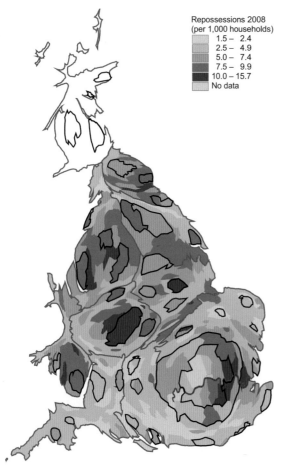

Repossessions 2008
(per 1,000 households)
- 1.5 – 2.4
- 2.5 – 4.9
- 5.0 – 7.4
- 7.5 – 9.9
- 10.0 – 15.7
- No data

Note: Rate shown is per 1,000 households in owner occupation, private renting or other dwellings by district in 2008. Social housing is excluded.

you are in terms of the likelihood of your home being repossessed. However, most young adults in Britain have almost no chance of being able to get a mortgage in the first place. The large and increasing majority of the young – and poorer people who are older – rent.

2.4 Rents: spreading the pain to those who don't gain

By 2010 more people in Britain lived again in housing that was rented. The largest subsection of renting used to be local authority renting; this was the tenure where rents tended to be lowest. But, as Map 2.4.1 shows, that was rapidly changing as the country became poorer. It was not just homeowners and buyers who were feeling the pinch with prices falling and repossessions rising. Those who rented were also seeing their housing costs rise swiftly at a time when wages and benefit uprating were becoming stagnant.

Map 2.4.2 shows that local authority rents tend to be highest in and near to London. Between 2008 and 2009 rents within London rose by more than 5% in Barnet, Hackney, Haringey, Kensington & Chelsea, Lewisham, Merton, Southwark, Tower Hamlets and Wandsworth. They rose between 2% and 5% in another 16 boroughs and fell in only three. Benefit and pension increases and wage claims were all hovering around zero for many people at this time. Thus there were real and serious increases in the cost of renting housing at a time when mortgage costs were falling. Those buying their homes, if they were not falling behind on their payments and living in fear of repossession, were becoming slightly better off again and in doing so moving financially (and usually geographically) even further away from those who were seeing these rent rises.

Data are missing from much of Map 2.4.1 and Map 2.4.2 because in many areas there are almost no council houses left. In London in Bexley, Bromley and Richmond upon Thames the real cost of renting a house from the local authority is incalculably high because either none exist or there are so few you would not imagine being allocated to one. We show just how long you have to wait on average for local authority housing in Section 2.6.

Map 2.4.1: 2007/08–2008/09 Local authority average rent change (%), local authorities, Britain

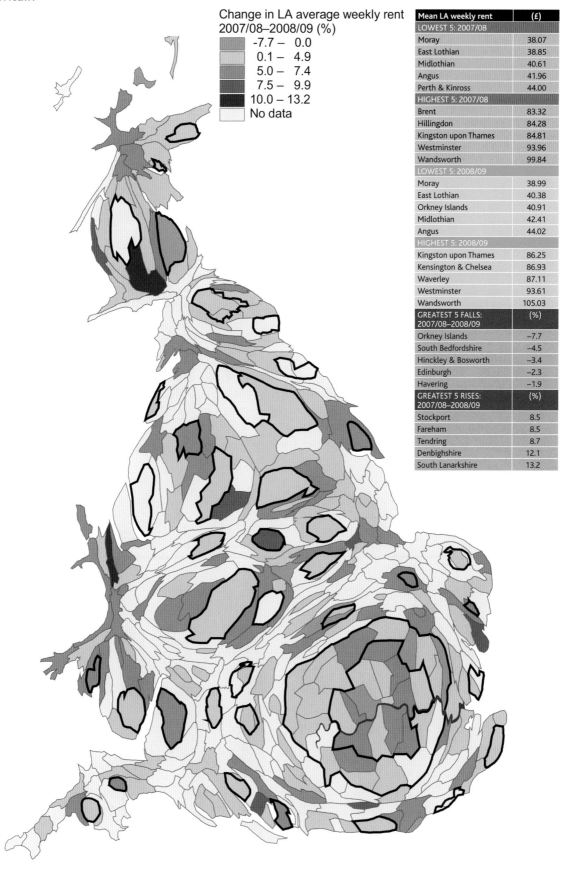

Change in LA average weekly rent 2007/08–2008/09 (%)
- -7.7 – 0.0
- 0.1 – 4.9
- 5.0 – 7.4
- 7.5 – 9.9
- 10.0 – 13.2
- No data

Mean LA weekly rent	(£)
LOWEST 5: 2007/08	
Moray	38.07
East Lothian	38.85
Midlothian	40.61
Angus	41.96
Perth & Kinross	44.00
HIGHEST 5: 2007/08	
Brent	83.32
Hillingdon	84.28
Kingston upon Thames	84.81
Westminster	93.96
Wandsworth	99.84
LOWEST 5: 2008/09	
Moray	38.99
East Lothian	40.38
Orkney Islands	40.91
Midlothian	42.41
Angus	44.02
HIGHEST 5: 2008/09	
Kingston upon Thames	86.25
Kensington & Chelsea	86.93
Waverley	87.11
Westminster	93.61
Wandsworth	105.03
GREATEST 5 FALLS: 2007/08–2008/09	(%)
Orkney Islands	–7.7
South Bedfordshire	–4.5
Hinckley & Bosworth	–3.4
Edinburgh	–2.3
Havering	–1.9
GREATEST 5 RISES: 2007/08–2008/09	(%)
Stockport	8.5
Fareham	8.5
Tendring	8.7
Denbighshire	12.1
South Lanarkshire	13.2

Where there are local authority properties, the highest rents by 2008 were of over £100 a week in Wandsworth. This is the same as many university students pay for the best and most up-to-date en-suite accommodation in 'student villages'. If you have children to clothe, very low income and no wealth, £100 a week is a lot. At the other extreme, £100 a week would not seem much money to you if you were able to buy a house in Kensington Palace Gardens. For the price of that one (£57 million) house you could pay the council house rent for over 13,000 years in the most expensive area in the country. Figure 2.4.1 shows how average local authority rents were rising for people living in Kensington & Chelsea in recent years.

Outside of London, rents are highest in the Surrey districts of Waverley, Guildford, Woking and Runnymede; in Crawley, Wycombe, the New Forest, St Albans and Oxford (£75 a week on average by 2009, up almost £20 in seven years). However, the biggest rises regionally since 2001 have not been in the South East. Regionally, Yorkshire & the Humber has experienced 37% increases in rents since 2001; the Eastern region 36% and the East Midlands 35%. Nowhere has the increase been below 26%. The average incomes of people living in local authority accommodation hardly rose at all over this period. Many groups became poorer, and were made poorer still after having to pay housing costs.

Map 2.4.2: 2008 Mean local authority housing rents (£ per week), local authorities, Britain

LA average weekly
rent 2008/09 (£)

	38.99 – 49.99
	50.00 – 59.99
	60.00 – 69.99
	70.00 – 79.99
	80.00 – 105.03
	No data

Figure 2.4.1: 2001–09 Weekly mean local authority rents (£) in Kensington & Chelsea

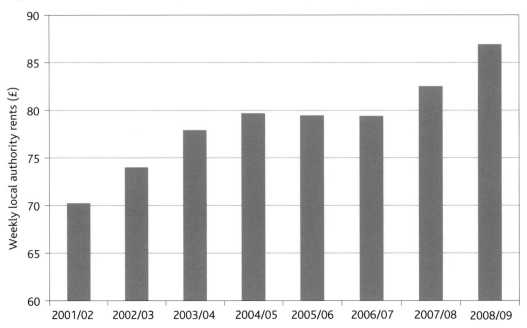

When governments release figures on the proportions of those in poverty before and after housing costs it is before and after having to pay for rent rises such as these that they are talking about. As the formula for rent rises is dictated by central government it is hardly surprising that government does not want to be directly implicated in increasing poverty.

Government did not raise local authority rents because it needed the money: there was an economic boom during most of these years from 2001 to 2008, and the amount raised, from the government's point of view, was trivial. Rents were raised to try to deter people from seeking local authority accommodation in the first place, and to try to drive more and more people into the hands of private landlords. Governments from 1979 to 2009 socially engineered families towards the free market in housing.

We had intended to look at rents in the private sector as well but, regrettably, sufficient data and geographical boundaries of rental areas were not available. Of particular concern is the recent change to local housing allowance, which is the equivalent of housing benefit for those on benefits and low incomes renting in the private rented sector, and which has been reduced from the median to the lowest 30% of rents in a particular rental area and also subjected to a cap. This cap will mean that low-income households will no longer be able to afford to live in many areas of the country.

2.5   Out on the street: landlord evictions

Map 2.5.2 shows the numbers of tenants receiving eviction orders as a proportion of all households living in the local authority area. Not every family and individual that receives an eviction order is evicted. Some may pay the rent they owe and can stay; others may leave before the order can take effect. Some are evicted illegally with no such orders being granted. This map does not include mortgagees evicted from their homes by the banks they owe money to; they are shown in Section 2.3 above. Nevertheless, we chose to use all households as the denominator here so you could see the proportion of households in each area that had been evicted in just the first year of the crash. In 2008 the highest eviction order rates were almost all found in

London. Over 1% of all households were served with an order that year in Brent (1.7%), Haringey (1.5%), Barking & Dagenham (1.2%), Hackney (1.2%), Lambeth (1.1%), Newham (1.1%), Nottingham (1.1%) and Enfield (1.0%).

The information shown here includes tenants of all types of landlord, whether social or private sector, and covers actions made using both the standard and accelerated possession procedures. The accelerated possession procedure is used by landlords in relation to assured shorthold tenancies. Accelerated possession enables orders to be made by the court once the fixed period of tenancy has come to an end, solely on the basis of written evidence and without calling the parties to a hearing. This was made possible by section 21 of the 1988 Housing Act, which undermined the basic right to shelter that had previously been protected under English law.

In the late 1980s shorthold tenancies were mostly associated with people needing accommodation for a fixed period, such as university students, but that quickly changed as these tenancies became the

Map 2.5.1: 2007–08 Change in eviction orders granted (‰ point), local authorities, England & Wales

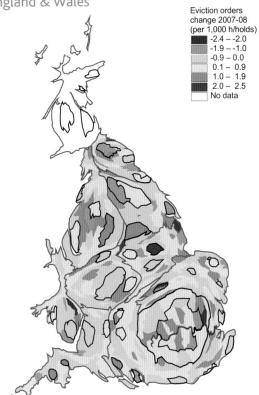

Eviction orders change 2007-08 (per 1,000 h/holds)
- -2.4 – -2.0
- -1.9 – -1.0
- -0.9 – 0.0
- 0.1 – 0.9
- 1.0 – 1.9
- 2.0 – 2.5
- No data

preferred option of private landlords for tenants of all kinds. At the same time, and not least because private landlords were buying up stock, other forms of housing became far harder to acquire. Twenty years after the 1988 Act, assured shorthold tenancies had often become the only housing option for people who could not afford to buy a property or did not qualify for a council home.

This change can be seen reflected in the map which shows where the fastest rises in eviction orders were between 2007 and 2008 (Map 2.5.1). Particular places tell particular stories. It is not just poorer working-class areas which experienced some of the largest increases in the granting of eviction orders between 2007 and 2008, but the subset of those places which had just suffered harder times than most. Luton saw eviction rates rise by an extra 2.1 families per thousand in just the single year shown here, but it had been losing jobs in its car plants for years earlier. Barking & Dagenham is similarly

coloured on the map and tells a similar story of prior job losses. Around this time in Nottingham the electronics firm Ericsson laid off hundreds of workers, again reflected in a later rise in evictions. All this, and a hundred smaller stories of events outside of the control of tenants, affects the map.

Map 2.5.1 only shows where legal eviction orders increased and decreased in number between the height of the boom and the start of the crash. In many places eviction rates fell. Interest rates fell nationally and so landlords' mortgage payments were almost always less difficult to meet in 2008 than in 2007. This may have made landlords slightly less ready to seek eviction of their tenants on late payment of rent. Unemployment had only just begun to rise and so the great rise in tenants being evicted for non- or late payment of rent (that they could not pay because their earnings had ended, and benefits were not enough to compensate) was only just starting during 2008.

Figure 2.5.1: 2003–08 Annual count of eviction orders granted, Kensington & Chelsea

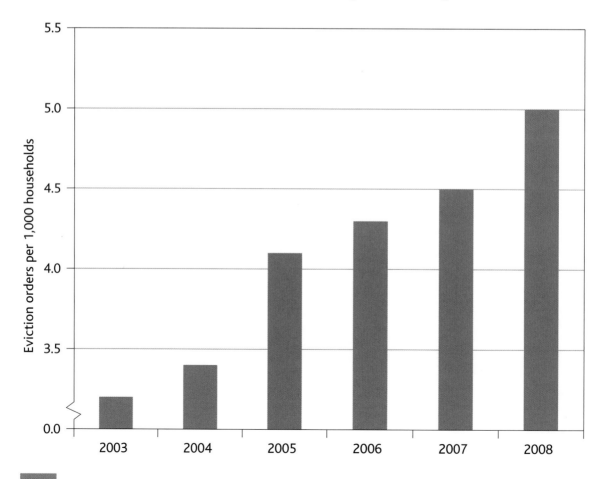

Map 2.5.2: 2008 Eviction orders rate (‰ households, all tenures), local authorities, England & Wales

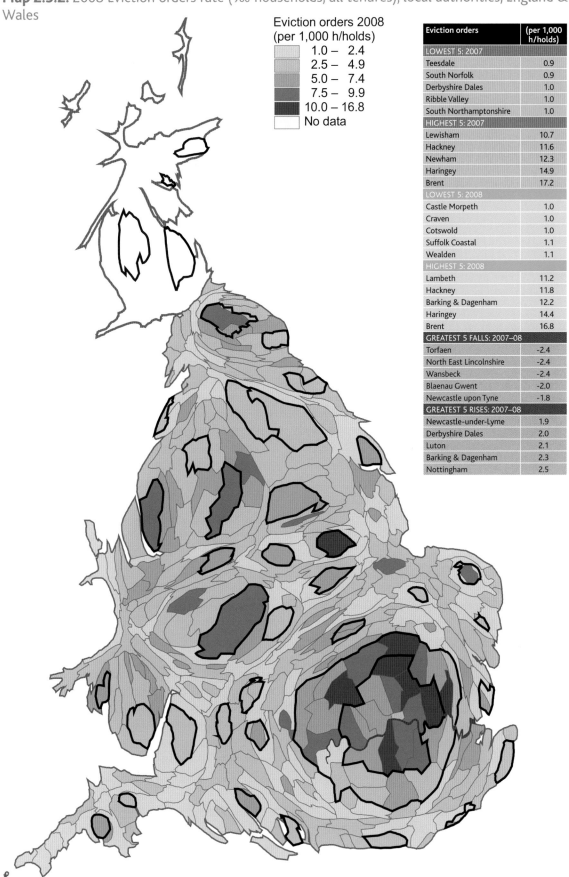

Eviction orders 2008
(per 1,000 h/holds)

- 1.0 – 2.4
- 2.5 – 4.9
- 5.0 – 7.4
- 7.5 – 9.9
- 10.0 – 16.8
- No data

Eviction orders	(per 1,000 h/holds)
LOWEST 5: 2007	
Teesdale	0.9
South Norfolk	0.9
Derbyshire Dales	1.0
Ribble Valley	1.0
South Northamptonshire	1.0
HIGHEST 5: 2007	
Lewisham	10.7
Hackney	11.6
Newham	12.3
Haringey	14.9
Brent	17.2
LOWEST 5: 2008	
Castle Morpeth	1.0
Craven	1.0
Cotswold	1.0
Suffolk Coastal	1.1
Wealden	1.1
HIGHEST 5: 2008	
Lambeth	11.2
Hackney	11.8
Barking & Dagenham	12.2
Haringey	14.4
Brent	16.8
GREATEST 5 FALLS: 2007–08	
Torfaen	-2.4
North East Lincolnshire	-2.4
Wansbeck	-2.4
Blaenau Gwent	-2.0
Newcastle upon Tyne	-1.8
GREATEST 5 RISES: 2007–08	
Newcastle-under-Lyme	1.9
Derbyshire Dales	2.0
Luton	2.1
Barking & Dagenham	2.3
Nottingham	2.5

Eviction order rates fell the most in the year to 2008 largely in those places where they had been unusually high a year earlier due to large numbers of lay-offs in 2007, such as in North East Lincolnshire, in Wansbeck in Northumberland and in Torfaen in South Wales. However, in other places usually assumed to be far more well-heeled, rates were also rising, from quite high levels to begin with. For example, the rate in Kensington & Chelsea rose by 0.5% in just a year, and had been rising steadily for some years (see Figure 2.5.1). The rate in Kensington Palace Gardens is not available, but it is far from impossible that among all these statistics there is also a millionaire or two who fell on hard times.

2.6 Housing lists: waiting a lifetime for a home

We have not got our decimal points in the wrong place in drawing the map shown in Map 2.6.1. There really are a huge number of places where there are more people waiting to be housed than all the local authority housing that exists in a district. In 106 districts of England, in 2010, if everyone who was currently housed by the council were to drop down dead – and all of their homes were suddenly to become available for renting – even then there would not be enough for all applying to be housed and having been accepted as having a (non-priority) need!

Suppose the average family lives in their home for 25 years. At that rate the 2,141 families in South Shropshire who are on the waiting list for one of that district's 108 local authority homes would have to wait, at the longest, 500 years for a home. The waiting list in South Shropshire is almost 20 times the council stock. The reason there are not more than 2,141 families on the waiting list for South Shropshire is because many families do not bother to join the waiting list in places where housing is in such short supply. They move elsewhere or just put up with very cramped conditions such as sharing with another household.

The numbers of local authority tenancies available in 2001 form the best estimate we can make of supply given how housing statistics by area are released. Some of these homes will have been purchased under right-to-buy and will no longer be available

for rent; some will have been transferred to housing associations. Other stock will be available in other forms and some new homes may have been built, although in general the supply of local authority housing has not risen much since 2001, and in many places it has fallen. By 2009 there were more than ten families waiting for every council home that existed in South Shropshire, Christchurch, East Dorset, West Berkshire, Broadland, Epsom & Ewell and Hart.

In the following boroughs there were, by 2009, at least three families applying to be housed for every local authority tenancy that would one day become available: Isle of Wight, Eastleigh, Kennet, Penwith, West Dorset, South Bucks, Surrey Heath, Maldon, Wychavon, West Somerset, Torbay, Swale, Tunbridge Wells, North Dorset, Rushmore, North Wiltshire, Ryedale, Malvern Hills, Stratford-on-Avon, East Hampshire, Spelthorne, Restormel, Vale of White Horse, Cotswold, Basingstoke & Deane, Hambleton, Fylde, South Oxfordshire, West Devon, East Cambridgeshire, Bexley, Windsor & Maidenhead, Eden and South Staffordshire. Nationally in total some 1.7 million households were looking for a home on a local authority waiting list that year. That national total excludes Wales and Scotland, which have different systems and different lists and so are not mapped or counted here.

Almost all of the boroughs with the most acute proportionate housing shortages were in the South West or South East of England in 2009. This is despite the waiting lists being far longer in absolute terms in the North of England (see Map 2.6.2). The longest of all was the 98,000-long list in Sheffield, which had almost exactly doubled from 49,000 in 1997, but still 'only' represented 170% of the 2001 local authority stock by 2009. So, if in Sheffield no one new ever arrives from elsewhere in Britain needing a home, if no young people leave home, if there are no divorces and separations resulting in more housing need, if no one considered vulnerable is found on the streets and has a legal right to a home, then, in around 40 years' time almost everyone on the housing waiting list can be housed!

Proportionately the length of the waiting list is even worse in Bradford, where 51,000 households are waiting (representing 265% of the stock). The worst place in absolute terms in London is Newham

Map 2.6.1: 2009 Households waiting for council housing as a proportion of all council housing stock, local authorities, England

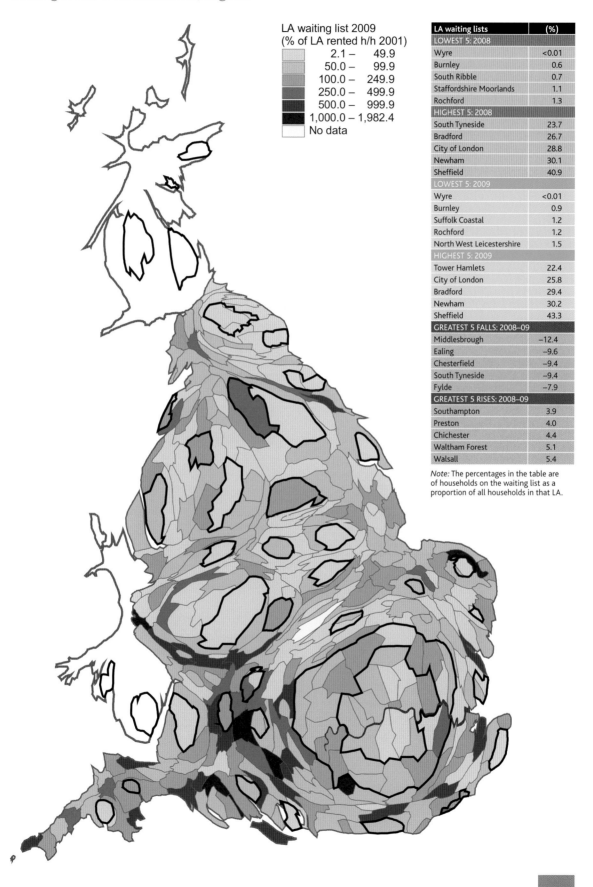

LA waiting list 2009
(% of LA rented h/h 2001)

	2.1 – 49.9
	50.0 – 99.9
	100.0 – 249.9
	250.0 – 499.9
	500.0 – 999.9
	1,000.0 – 1,982.4
	No data

LA waiting lists	(%)
LOWEST 5: 2008	
Wyre	<0.01
Burnley	0.6
South Ribble	0.7
Staffordshire Moorlands	1.1
Rochford	1.3
HIGHEST 5: 2008	
South Tyneside	23.7
Bradford	26.7
City of London	28.8
Newham	30.1
Sheffield	40.9
LOWEST 5: 2009	
Wyre	<0.01
Burnley	0.9
Suffolk Coastal	1.2
Rochford	1.2
North West Leicestershire	1.5
HIGHEST 5: 2009	
Tower Hamlets	22.4
City of London	25.8
Bradford	29.4
Newham	30.2
Sheffield	43.3
GREATEST 5 FALLS: 2008–09	
Middlesbrough	−12.4
Ealing	−9.6
Chesterfield	−9.4
South Tyneside	−9.4
Fylde	−7.9
GREATEST 5 RISES: 2008–09	
Southampton	3.9
Preston	4.0
Chichester	4.4
Waltham Forest	5.1
Walsall	5.4

Note: The percentages in the table are of households on the waiting list as a proportion of all households in that LA.

(at 123% of the stock), where 29,000 are on the books. There are 354,000 households on separate lists across all of London. This pressure for housing creates further housing problems. Waiting lists are an indication of how hard it is to gain a place in local authority housing even if you qualify. In areas where waiting lists are long, households who can only just afford to borrow enough to buy at the bottom end of the market will be more tempted to do so. These households are most likely to borrow very high mortgages in proportion to their incomes, which can create severe difficulties if their financial circumstances change or when house prices fall.

Table 2.6.1 shows that second to the very North of England, it is in Yorkshire & Humberside (where local authority waiting lists are longest) that negative equity is highest. Negative equity means borrowing more than the market value of your home, usually because that value has fallen. If you sell your home you will still have a debt to the bank. Nationally in Britain (and the UK) 4.8% of owner-occupiers held negative equity by 2008. This is as many households again as are on waiting lists for council housing. This count is partly this high because waiting lists for council housing are now so long.

Map 2.6.2: 2009 Households waiting for council housing, local authorities, England

Housing waiting list
2009 (No. h/holds)
- 0 – 4,999
- 5,000 – 9,999
- 10,000 – 19,999
- 20,000 – 29,999
- 50,000 – 97,818
- No data

Table 2.6.1: 2008 Owner-occupiers in negative equity (%), regions and countries, UK

Country/Region	Owner-occupiers in negative equity (%)
Northern Ireland	4.8
Scotland	1.0
Wales	6.1
South West	4.3
South East	5.7
Greater London	6.5
East Anglia	0.9
West Midlands	4.6
East Midlands	5.4
Yorkshire and Humberside	6.7
North West	5.5
Northern	9.2
England	5.2
UK average	4.8

Note: This measure is termed 'relative negative equity', that is, negative equity cases in each region as a proportion of the total owner-occupied housing stock in that region.

2.7 Homelessness: no roots and few rights?

Homelessness legislation is very different in England and Wales compared to Scotland, and hence homelessness statistics are reported in different ways. In Scotland, the aim is for everyone assessed as homeless, whether intentionally or not, to be offered permanent accommodation. According to Shelter, the housing charity: 'Scotland is recognised as having the best homelessness laws in Europe.'[4] In contrast, in England and Wales, it is only those who are unintentionally homeless and in priority need who are likely to be rehoused. Priority need means that applicants have children, are in danger of domestic abuse, suffer from mental illness, or have a disability. Scotland's statistics report on the number of applications assessed as homeless under the Homeless Persons legislation, which includes the various categories reported by England and Wales. These categories are: eligible, unintentionally homeless and in priority need; eligible homeless and in priority need but intentionally; eligible homeless but not intentionally; eligible homeless but not in priority need; and eligible but not homeless. To map equivalent rates across Britain we have summed the England and Wales categories.

During 2008/09 in Britain some 167,000 households had been accepted as homeless (Map 2.7.1). This figure was some 17,000 lower than that of the year before. This fall in homelessness amounts to a reduction of 0.7 households per thousand, as shown in Table 2.7.1. Homelessness appeared to fall almost everywhere in Britain between the two financial years 2007/08 and 2008/09 except across Scotland where it rose by 0.3 households per thousand.

What was occurring? Councils in England and to a much lesser extent in Wales were being told to clamp down on who they accepted as homeless and vulnerable and hence had a responsibility to house, because their normal housing waiting lists had grown so long and because they did not have good homelessness laws or housing allocation methods. Choice-based letting had become a farce. There was enough housing in the country for everyone to have a home with their own bedroom, but many bedrooms were owned by people who did not need them.

Homelessness often appeared to fall the most where waiting lists were rising. Figure 2.7.1 shows where the greatest falls and rises were. In Liverpool the numbers of homeless families accepted as in need rose by 270 in the financial year to 2008/09; the numbers on the waiting lists rose by 4,700. In many other boroughs which may have been stricter in their interpretations of the rules, waiting lists rose despite homelessness acceptances falling. Figure 2.7.1 gives the impression that increased homelessness leads to increased waiting times. This is because one of the nine boxes within the figure is empty. However, this impression is an illusion caused by plotting absolute numbers instead of rates and by only including those places where both numbers are positive, because of the log scales.

When all local authorities are shown and normal (rather than log) axes are used, the distribution forms a cross-shape as shown in Figure 2.7.2. There appears to be no relationship between the numbers of additional households accepted to be homeless in each place and the numbers added to local authority housing waiting lists in the subsequent year. When both those changes are divided by the appropriate denominator then any semblance of a relationship disappears, as the random cluster of points in Figure 2.7.3 demonstrates. Here the changes have been divided first by how many households live in each area and then by how many local authority homes exist. There is no relationship in England and Wales between housing need and the supply of housing or even how many people are on waiting lists.

Table 2.7.1: 2007/08–2008/09 Homeless households (‰ rate and ‰ rate change), regions and countries, Britain

Country/Region	Homeless households 2007/08 (‰)	Homeless households 2008/09 (‰)	Homeless households change (‰)
England	6.1	5.2	-0.8
North East	5.9	4.9	-1.0
North West	6.5	4.7	-1.8
Yorkshire and The Humber	8.5	7.7	-0.8
East Midlands	4.4	3.5	-1.0
West Midlands	7.9	7.2	-0.7
East of England	4.7	4.1	-0.7
London	9.1	8.6	-0.5
South East	3.2	3.0	-0.2
South West	4.5	3.1	-1.3
Wales	10.0	9.9	-0.1
Scotland	17.9	18.2	0.3
Britain	7.4	6.7	-0.7

Note: The denominator is household estimates: 2006 for England and Scotland and 2007 for Wales.

Figure 2.7.1: 2007/08–2008/09 Local authorities where homeless numbers and waiting lists are both rising (counts), England

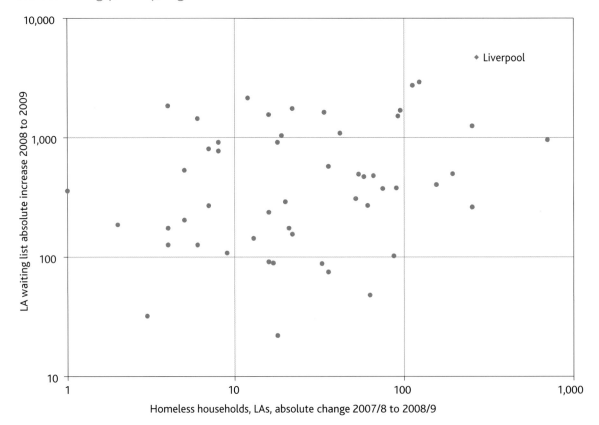

Note: Log scales are used on both axes

Figure 2.7.2: 2007/08–2008/09 Local authorities, homeless number change and waiting lists change (counts), England

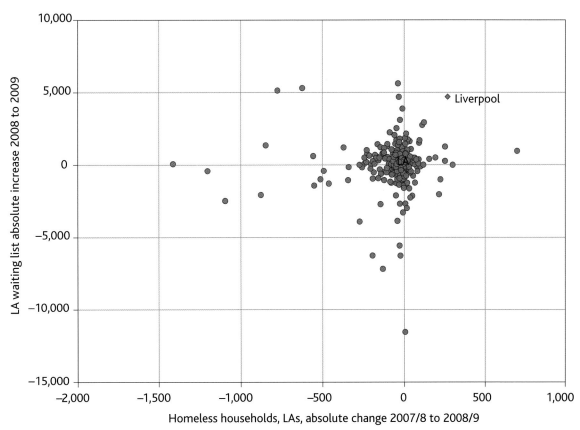

Figure 2.7.3: 2007/08–2008/09 All local authorities, homeless number change and waiting lists change, rate as ‰ households and % stock, England

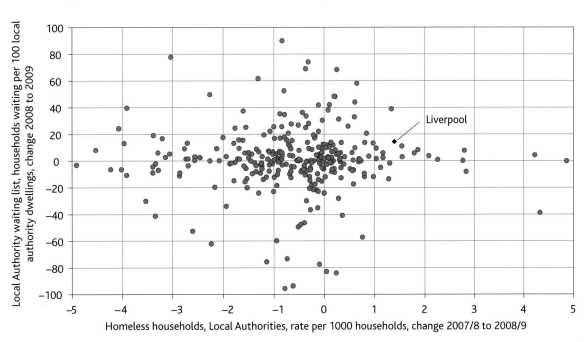

Map 2.7.1: 2008/09 Households accepted as homeless, local authorities, Britain

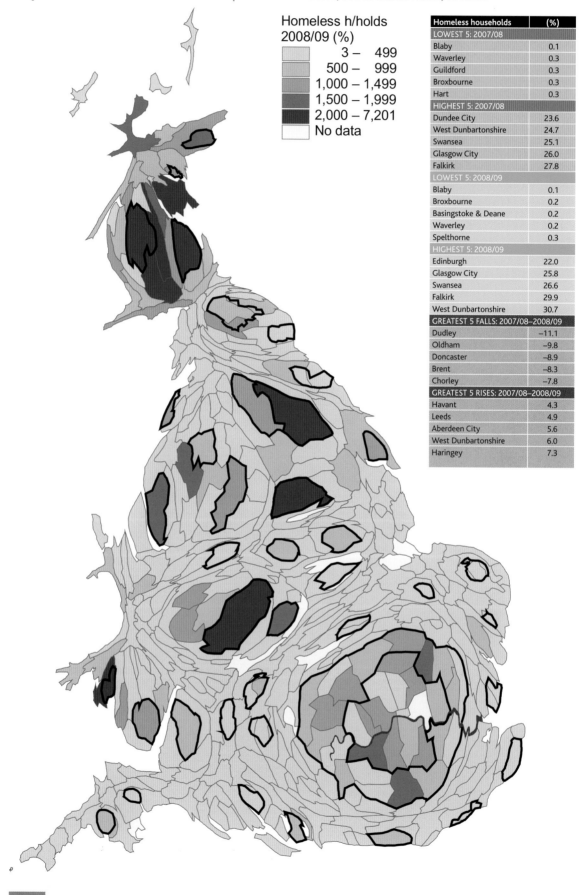

Homeless h/holds
2008/09 (%)

	3 – 499
	500 – 999
	1,000 – 1,499
	1,500 – 1,999
	2,000 – 7,201
	No data

Homeless households	(%)
LOWEST 5: 2007/08	
Blaby	0.1
Waverley	0.3
Guildford	0.3
Broxbourne	0.3
Hart	0.3
HIGHEST 5: 2007/08	
Dundee City	23.6
West Dunbartonshire	24.7
Swansea	25.1
Glasgow City	26.0
Falkirk	27.8
LOWEST 5: 2008/09	
Blaby	0.1
Broxbourne	0.2
Basingstoke & Deane	0.2
Waverley	0.2
Spelthorne	0.3
HIGHEST 5: 2008/09	
Edinburgh	22.0
Glasgow City	25.8
Swansea	26.6
Falkirk	29.9
West Dunbartonshire	30.7
GREATEST 5 FALLS: 2007/08–2008/09	
Dudley	−11.1
Oldham	−9.8
Doncaster	−8.9
Brent	−8.3
Chorley	−7.8
GREATEST 5 RISES: 2007/08–2008/09	
Havant	4.3
Leeds	4.9
Aberdeen City	5.6
West Dunbartonshire	6.0
Haringey	7.3

Chapter 3 Politically bankrupt

Introduction

To try to understand the politics of a country, it helps to understand a little of its political history, and this is particularly so with electoral history. Therefore we begin this chapter by going back almost 100 years and show maps of the last 25 general elections: that is, all those held since the Representation of the People Act 1918, which gave the vote to women in the UK if they were both aged over 30 and occupied premises which had a yearly rateable value of not less than £5 (a large amount back then). It was not until 1928 that the voting age for women was lowered to 21, the same as it was at that time for men. The maps this chapter begins with thus stretch from the end of one period recognised then for being the result of an accumulation of a particular set of corruptions, when Parliament eventually succumbed to the will of the suffragettes, and ends with what could be the end of another such period of rising dissent about the political system, with increasingly loud calls for change and reform.

The voting system prior to 1918 was generally known for how rotten it was. The Reform Act of 1832 had removed 57 rotten boroughs: tiny parliamentary constituencies where a single person could easily buy the vote of a majority of electors. Pocket or proprietary boroughs, larger constituencies but also in effect owned by a single major landlord, were outlawed in the Reform Act of 1867. They had remained for so long because 'Rotten boroughs were defended by the successive Tory governments of 1807–1830 – a substantial number of Tory constituencies lay in rotten and pocket boroughs'.[1] The Tories (who have now become the Conservative Party) did not have a monopoly on being undemocratic. The Liberal Prime Minister Lloyd George pioneered the selling of honours for votes, leading to new laws being enacted. The Representation of the People Act 1949 abolished university constituencies and additional votes which had been granted to the owners of business premises,

and the similarly titled Act of 1969 brought the voting age of men and women down to 18. The Representation Acts of 1985 and 1989 extended these rights to citizens living overseas, as the Tories (who were again in power then) thought they would benefit from this. Thus not all such Acts of Parliament were progressive.

By 2010 the political system was widely regarded as fundamentally corrupt again. The expenses scandal of 2008/09 was the final nail in the coffin of perceived respectability. The aspect of that scandal most amenable to mapping is the amount Members of Parliament claimed for travel allowances, and so we map that later, in Section 3.4.

It was the more esoteric of their claims, the cleaning of a moat (by Douglas Hogg, Conservative), the trimming of a wisteria (David Cameron, Conservative) and the purchase of a duck house (Peter Viggers, Conservative) which most caught the public imagination. However, it was the 'flipping' of addresses to maximise profit on claims for accommodation expenses which involved the greatest sums of money.

But even before the expenses scandal came to light, the government of the day had abandoned a great many of the principles its members had once held. Prominent among these was the principle that you do not go to war for selfish purposes using false information that suggests it is a war of liberation. We map here the results of the 2005 general election in the light of the debate about the war on the people of Iraq. The vast majority who died because of that war were Iraqi citizens. The subsequent British public reaction to that war was severely limited by the political options the public had when it came to voting.

The main opposition party in 2005, the Conservative Party, supported the US-instigated war with Iraq with at least as much enthusiasm as did the Labour Party of government. The third party of British politics, the Liberal Democrats, said they opposed it, but then they said a lot of things about principles while in opposition which they then appeared happy to abandon when coming to share power in the Coalition government formed in the wake of the 2010 election. We show the results of that election, the winners, how much legitimacy they held and how they came to hold it, and then concentrate on the geography of the most recent losers, those who will form the so-called opposition for the near future. We end by looking at how the most recent losers have at least increased their hold slightly on local government, although from a very low base.

Although the present may, in many ways, look similarly corrupt to the past, the future never plays out in quite the same way. This is one reason why the final maps in this chapter concern results of the other elections held on 6 May 2010 – the local government elections – and what configuration of political parties those elections returned to power or in alliance, locally.

Local election results often point to the shape of things to come, the direction in which voters are moving in terms of what they actually want, not what they are told they want in the more media-directed national general election.

In May 2010 many voters returned to support the Labour Party, locally, but this was not quite the same Labour Party as was losing support nationally. The Labour Party was becoming again, locally, in some places, the party that represented people who had the least. In Barking the British National Party lost all of its local councillors to Labour, which now holds all 51 council seats there. In a time of high political corruption, voters, even in the poorest areas, did not turn to that alternative that had been so attractive when the financial crisis was last so severe: the far-right alternative offered by Oswald Mosley's British Union of Fascists in 1932.

Both our politics and our politicians are corrupt in Britain, so much so that we often do not recognise nepotism and cronyism as part and parcel of corruption at home, but readily denounce it abroad. In Britain, people vote in elections where most of their votes will be ignored because of the first-past-the-post system. Any system, which both preserves such unfairness and also results in people

complaining more loudly that a few hundred people could not get to vote (as happened in May 2010) than that millions of votes were routinely wasted by the system of voting, has become politically bankrupt.

Our politicians are corrupted by our system of politics. To win power they must impress local party officials, not voters. In most seats, national and local, the result is a foregone conclusion before the candidate has even been selected by the local party; most seats are not marginal and do not change hands regardless of any national voting swings.

The politicians who got to the very top in May 2010 remain mostly drawn from a tiny number of very selective private schools and, if not from those schools, then from an even tinier number of colleges in just two universities. If you go to the wrong college, never mind the wrong university (or not to university at all), your chances of succeeding in politics are dramatically reduced. There are few signs that the situation is improving very slowly. Slightly fewer Conservative MPs and ministers come from such elitist backgrounds than under John Major's government of 1992; 14 members of the 2010 shadow cabinet had attended a comprehensive school, the highest number ever recorded.

A corrupt, unjust and greatly unequal country will inevitably foster a corrupt politics which tries to dress itself up as principled. In most other more equal affluent countries first-past–the-post elections were removed long ago as archaic. Every vote counts in one way or another in most elections held in most of the affluent world. In countries which are far more economically and hence socially equitable than Britain, politicians are drawn from a much wider cross-section of society, and far fewer people live lives and have expectations and understandings that are so different from most politicians. Only in economically more unequal countries, such as the US and China, is politics more corrupt and the choices presented to electors more limited than in the United Kingdom.

The United Kingdom was disunited back in 1918. Ireland was attempting to escape the clutches of London's control. Today in Scotland there is again serious talk of separation. It would suit the Conservative Party of England if Scotland were to leave the Union; it is only because they are a 'unionist' party that no deal is ever countenanced with the SNP (Scottish National Party). In contrast, politicians in Northern Ireland were hoping for a deal in the wake of a hung parliament and did not get one. However, what now prevents union of Northern Ireland with the Republic is that the Republic, now bankrupt itself, could not support Northern Ireland economically even if Irish reunion became possible politically. Wales has become more divided in recent years, parts of the south of that country swinging towards the Conservatives. And finally, the interests of wealthy Londoners have slowly been pulling away from those of the rest of England, especially the northern cities. The bail-out of banking was a bail-out of wealthy London. Poorer Londoners are beginning to realise more clearly where their interests lie. Locally at least, their votes swung decisively to Labour in spring 2010. When it came to it, Westminster politicians revealed what they cared most about in how they spent most money up to 2010. New Labour spent the most on bankers. The Conservative–Liberal Democrat Coalition will reveal its true priorities in who suffers the most from how they choose to pay for that bail-out.

3.1 A century of first-past-the-post elections, 1918–2010

General elections in Britain are won by the political party that gains the most seats in the House of Commons. Seats are won by winning the majority of votes cast in a constituency. There are many parliamentary constituencies, and their numbers and boundaries change over time. In the not too distant past there were also members elected by some of the most elite universities (they are not shown here). For comparison we show in Map 3.1.1 the results of all of the 25 general elections held between 1918 and 2010, by ancient counties. These are the counties for which, in most cases, lord lieutenants are still appointed to represent the Queen, and each area is now called a lieutenancy. We add up all the votes cast in a county and produce a hypothetical result, showing which party held the majority of votes for that county, whose size is shown as proportional to its current population. We begin in 1918, the first British general election in which women aged 30 and over were permitted to vote.

In the first seven general elections, all those held before the Second World War, there is a smattering of yellow that slowly diminishes. The old Liberal Party, the party that descended from what were called the Whigs, was dying. In the last four general elections of this 92-year period the Whigs reappear in their new Liberal Democrat form, winning a majority of the votes cast in Orkney & Shetland, Ross & Cromarty, Argyll & Bute, Northumberland, Powys, Bristol, Somerset and Cornwall by 2010. Most popular (in general elections) in outlying and out-of-the-way places, if the 2010 general election had not been so evenly balanced between what had become the two main parties, the Liberal Democrats would still not matter.

In 1918 Labour was strongest in the coalfields: it held the majority of votes in Cumbria, Dunbartonshire, Durham, Fife, Leicestershire, Mid Glamorgan and Nottinghamshire. Almost everywhere else then was Tory blue. Although not always obvious from the size of area coloured red, Labour won the general elections of 1945, 1964, 1966, October 1974 and – most decisively – 1997, slipping back a little but still winning in 2001 and 2005, before being routed in 2010. Map 3.1.2 shows in more detail the 2005 general election result by actual parliamentary constituency (in this case projected onto the latest constituency boundaries), and Map 3.1.3 does the same for the 2010 result to allow comparison with the geographically smoothed summary (Map 3.1.1).

The most striking feature of these 25 maps is how blue most of the country was most of the time. The 20th century has been called the Conservative century of British politics for good reason. The Conservatives won the majority of general elections. There are also many counties in which they never failed to win a majority of the vote in all these elections. Across the whole of the south coast of England and wrapping right round London, even in their darkest hour the Tories held a geographical stranglehold around the capital. The Home Counties remain forever Conservative. So too are Gloucestershire, Herefordshire and Worcestershire. It will only be when places like these change colour that the Conservative century will really have ended.

Map 3.1.1: 1918–2010 General election results (notional), ancient counties, Britain

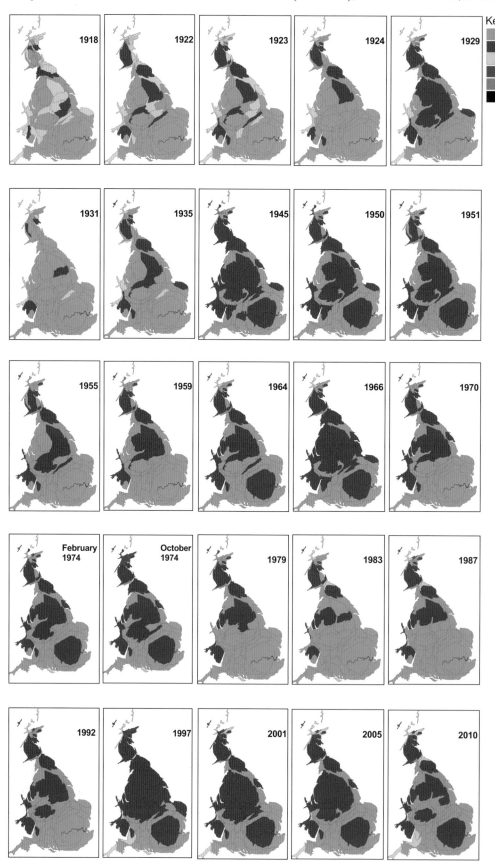

Map 3.1.2: 2005 General election result (notional), parliamentary constituencies, Britain

2005 General Election notional winner
- Conservative
- Independent
- Labour
- Liberal Democrat
- Nationalist
- Respect
- Speaker

Map 3.1.3: 2010 General election result (actual), parliamentary constituencies, Britain

May 2010 General Election winner
- Conservative
- Green
- Labour
- Liberal Democrat
- Nationalist
- Speaker
- Vacant

3.2 A century of losers: who came second, 1918–2010

The changing picture of who comes second over time (Map 3.2.1) is much more interesting in many ways than who comes first. Look at how quickly the picture of runners-up changed between 1918 and 1931. There, under the surface of the winners, is the real volatility of British general elections. First the capital turned red in 1922 (as Labour became the second largest party there), then more blue appeared as areas the Conservatives had previously held were lost, mostly to Labour, particularly in 1929. The map turned red in 1931 as Labour lost across the country, but almost everywhere they were now second; the Liberals would be third for a very long time from here on.

When coloured by runners-up, London turned blue in 1945 and remained blue despite narrow Conservative national victories in 1950 and 1951. London and the south turned red in 1955 and 1959 as Labour was put in second place nationally, but blue again in 1964 and 1966. When Ted Heath won the country for the Conservatives in 1970 he also won London and so the map of second place again saw the capital turn red, and then blue, in both 1974 elections, before turning red again from 1979 to 1992 inclusive, and then blue from 1997 onwards. London became a bellwether for the national swing, its predictive trend only broken in 2010 when the Conservatives did not quite secure enough votes in the capital to win it, and the election as a whole, outright, and so were forced to form a coalition with the Liberal Democrats.

Map 3.2.1: 1918–2010 General election results (runner-up), ancient counties, Britain

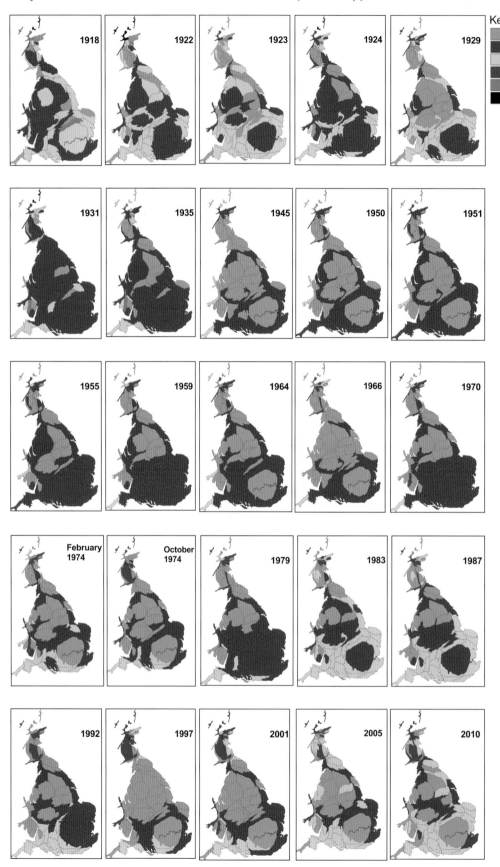

Key
Conservative
Labour
Liberal
Nationalist
Other
Unopposed

Map 3.2.2: 2005 General election result, runner-up (notional), parliamentary constituencies, Britain

2005 General Election notional runner-up
- Conservative
- Labour
- Liberal Democrat
- Nationalist
- Speaker
- Respect

Map 3.2.3: 2010 General election result, runner-up (actual), parliamentary constituencies, Britain

May 2010 General Election runner-up
- Conservative
- Independent
- Labour
- Liberal Democrat
- Nationalist
- Respect
- Speaker
- Vacant

The Liberals/Liberal Democrats, in contrast to Labour, saw their position slowly improve from February 1974 onwards, with some lows in between, but new heights of success at coming second achieved by 2010. Note especially how they almost ring the capital today, only Kent is still standing out in red, with Labour in second place there. Note too the rise of the nationalists, especially in Scotland. The map of who comes second has again become a chequerboard, everything is to play for. Map 3.2.2 and Map 3.2.3 give the detailed picture for the last two general elections and show even more clearly how the sinews of British politics have become so stretched under the surface around the country. It is regarded by increasing numbers of people in Britain that it remains a pity that our political system completely disregards all the votes of all the people who did not vote for the party that happened to come first in the constituency they happened to live in.

Finally, Figure 3.2.1 shows how allegiance has changed over time by plotting the share of the popular vote the Labour Party won in each county in both 1918 and 2010. In 1918 they won 63% of the vote in what is now Mid Glamorgan; by 2010, just under half the vote. By 2010 Labour was most popular in Lanarkshire, where they won just over a third of the 1918 vote. In Berkshire, where their 1918 vote, among agricultural labourers in the main, was similar to Lanarkshire, it is now less than a fifth, and in Rutland it was even higher to begin with and has ended even lower. The changing pattern of the vote is a picture of changing fortunes. As poorer people continued to be forced off the land into the cities and industrial heartlands, the Labour vote moved with them.

Figure 3.2.1: 1918 and 2010 Labour Party share of vote (%), ancient counties, Britain

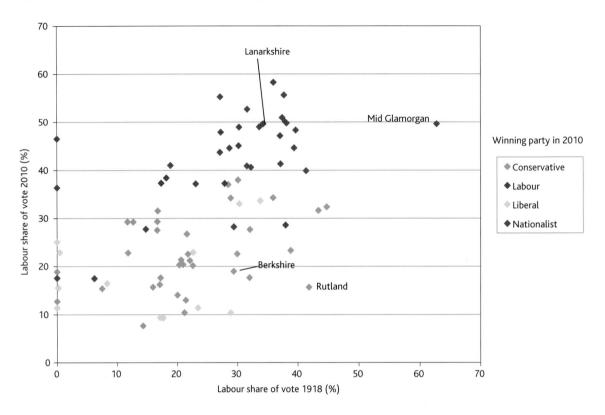

3.3 The 2005 general election: verdict on a war?

The general election of 5 May 2005 was Tony Blair's last general election as Prime Minister and as Labour Party leader. His party had won the previous two elections, first with a landslide in 1997, and then (still very comfortably) in 2001. In 2005, of the 646 constituencies contested across the UK, Labour won 356, Michael Howard's Conservatives won 198, and Charles Kennedy's Liberal Democrats won 62. Respectively these numbers were down 47, up 33 and up 11 on the 2001 result. The 2001 result itself had seen much smaller shifts from 1997, respectively: down 5, up 1 and up 6 seats.

The number of seats being contested changed in 2005, as the Scottish contingent was reduced in number, but this was only a minor influence that aided the acceleration of the swing away from New Labour. There was growing disenchantment at home over Labour's record on inequality (which was growing), but even greater disenchantment over the government's engagement abroad in the illegal war on Iraq, the misleading of both parliament and the people of Britain over Iraq's supposed possession and readiness to use weapons of mass destruction, and the way in which the government ran roughshod over its critics. These critics included many more than the estimated 1.4 million people who took to the streets in protest and the BBC journalists who investigated the lead-up to the war and the reason for the unexpected death of David Kelly (an advisor to the government on weapons of mass destruction whose name was revealed to the press in events which ended in his death. Controversy remains over whether he committed suicide or was murdered.) The BBC saw both its Chair of Governors and Director General in effect pilloried and sacked as a result of the Hutton Inquiry into David Kelly's death, widely regarded, by 2005, as biased (it reported in January 2004). The result was that in the general election of that year only 40.7% of those who chose to vote voted for the party of government. However, that vote was geographically arranged so as to ensure that the majority of seats (55%) were held by Labour.

What would have happened had the 2005 general election been undertaken using the boundaries that were put in place for the 2010 election? The estimated result is shown in Map 3.3.1. The result would have been: Labour 348 seats, Conservatives 210 and Liberal Democrats 62; down 8, up 12 and no change, respectively. The new boundaries created four more seats in England than the old, 650 in all. The result of the election would thus have been only slightly altered if more recent boundaries had been employed. It was not old boundaries that resulted in the Labour Party gaining the majority of seats despite having a significant minority of votes, but an outdated voting system.

Of all the seats Labour would have won in 2005, on the new boundaries, in some 213 of them the Conservatives were runners-up. Most of these were safe Labour seats and, in most that were not, you would have had to vote Conservative to show effective opposition (opposition that might remove an MP). This was not much of a choice, especially if you opposed the war, which both the main two parties supported. Of the remaining 135 seats that Labour notionally won in 2005, the Liberal Democrats were runners-up and were the main, if usually ineffective, opposition. There too a protest vote for any other party was likely to be a wasted vote.

In the seats the Conservatives won the story was even simpler: Labour came second in 129 of them; the Liberal Democrats second in the other 81; and those were the only two combinations which occurred. The map shows all contests that happened that day in May 2005, but it is a map dominated by two shades of light red and two of light blue as a result of how little choice most people in most places really had. Fourteen hundred thousand people marched against the war, but scarcely more than a couple of hundred thousand voters in a few marginal constituencies mattered when it came to voting in the government.

Map 3.3.1: 2005 General election result (notional winner and runner-up), parliamentary constituencies, Britain

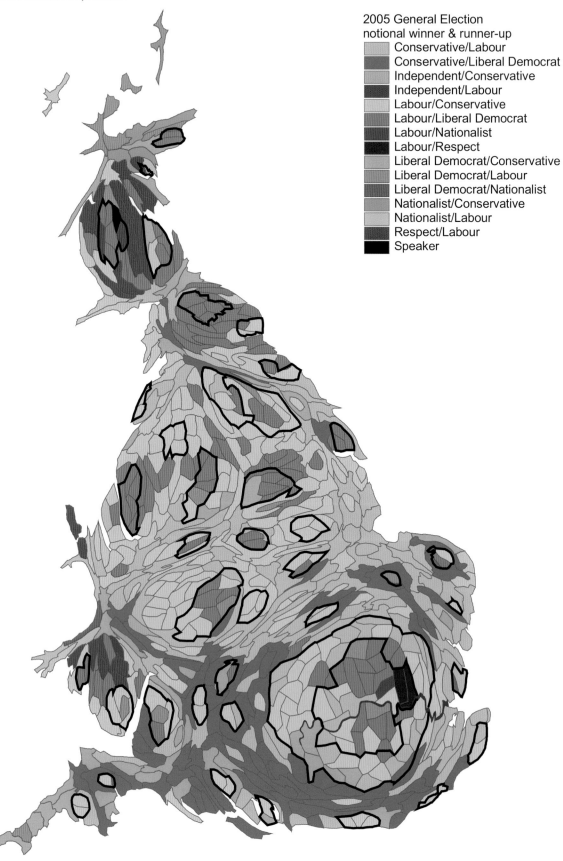

2005 General Election
notional winner & runner-up

- Conservative/Labour
- Conservative/Liberal Democrat
- Independent/Conservative
- Independent/Labour
- Labour/Conservative
- Labour/Liberal Democrat
- Labour/Nationalist
- Labour/Respect
- Liberal Democrat/Conservative
- Liberal Democrat/Labour
- Liberal Democrat/Nationalist
- Nationalist/Conservative
- Nationalist/Labour
- Respect/Labour
- Speaker

3.4 Still fiddling the books? MPs' travel expense claims 2008/09

The 2005–10 parliament will be remembered, above all else, for the MPs' expenses crisis. While the enduring image of that crisis will forever remain the duck house purchased by Peter Viggers, MP for Gosport, accommodation for MPs and their families constituted the greatest of claims made on the exchequer. Often MPs would swap which property they claimed to be their main and second residences to allow them to maximise the amounts they could claim for housing, all of which was property owned by them, even when they were not paying for the mortgage, repairs, decoration or even the gardening. However, it is not easy to determine which MPs' claims were more profligate than others in these cases, as housing in some parts of the country costs more than in others.

One item of MPs' expenses that is amenable to mapping and where comparisons can be made is the costs of their travel, while on parliamentary business within their constituency and to and from Westminster, all of which could be claimed back, and most MPs did claim. Unsurprisingly the five highest

Map 3.4.1: 2008/09 MPs' travel expenses (£ total), parliamentary constituencies, Britain

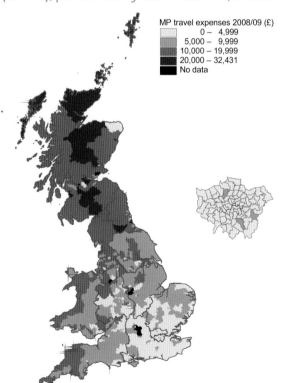

MP travel expenses 2008/09 (£)
- 0 – 4,999
- 5,000 – 9,999
- 10,000 – 19,999
- 20,000 – 32,431
- No data

claimants, claiming between £25,000 and £32,000 a year in travel expenses, were located a very long way from Westminster representing Caithness, Sutherland & Easter Ross; Falkirk; Linlithgow & East Falkirk; Na h-Eileanan an Iar (the Western Isles); and Orkney & Shetland. Map 3.4.1 shows the national picture (excluding Northern Ireland).

Because of the distances between their constituencies and Westminster, those Scottish MPs' travel expenses equate to as little as £31 per kilometre per year for Alistair Carmichael (still Liberal MP for Orkney & Shetland) up to £58 per kilometre per year for Eric Joyce (still Labour MP for Falkirk), and this could be seen as value for money, certainly once you compare their spending per kilometre with that of other MPs.

Working out travel expenses per kilometre from Westminster, the picture inverts (see Map 3.4.2). The highest claims are now made by some of the closest MPs. Claims of between £490 and £1,200 per kilometre per year were made by the representatives of Beckenham; the Cities of London & Westminster; Finchley & Golders Green; Kensington & Chelsea; and Vauxhall. But all these claims are much smaller in terms of monies spent (and the cost of London taxis is high).

How then to compare? The only way is to look at constituencies that lie a similar distance from London. Danny Alexander of the Liberal Democrats and Alex Salmond of the Scottish National Party both represent constituencies between 680 km and 690 km from London. Danny spent £23,400 on his annual travel expenses and Alex some £2,700. But any judgement made might depend on how often they were travelling and for what purpose. Similarly Labour's John Reid, a minister, located 543 km from the capital notched up annual travelling costs of only £4,529, in great contrast to another Labour MP, John McFall, a member of the Public Accounts Committee, located 576 km from the capital, claiming £14,245 in travel expenses over the same period. Closer to London, Phil Woolas, Gerald Kaufman and Richard Caborn (Labour grandees at that time with constituencies in Oldham, Manchester and Sheffield respectively) managed to spend more than £18,600 on travel a year, the highest for any MPs living between 200 km and 300 km from the capital.

Closer to London, among Liberal Democrat and Conservative members, Conservative Caroline Spelman (appointed Secretary of State of Environment in May 2010) spent £10,230 annually travelling in from just 152 km away. At the same time and from the same party, John Gummer spent only £422 travelling in from 133 km away. Even closer, Evan Harris (Liberal Democrat) of Oxford West & Abingdon managed to spend £11,662 a year travelling in from only 86 km away, while Andrew Smith (Labour) of neighbouring Oxford East spent only £2,883.

The levels of expenses alone, however, cannot tell the whole story; it depends on what the travel is used for. To find out how useful each Member of Parliament has been is a far harder job than to find out how much they have claimed. The people of Oxford East voted in greater numbers for Andrew Smith in the 2010 election, held after all these expenses were revealed despite the national mood swinging away from Labour. It is probable that the residents of Oxford West & Abingdon voted Evan Harris out because they wanted to vote a Conservative in, rather than because of his train travel expenses, but had he spent more time in the constituency, would he still have that job? Evan lost by 176 votes.

Map 3.4.2: 2008/09 MPs' travel expenses (£ per km from Westminster), parliamentary constituencies, Britain

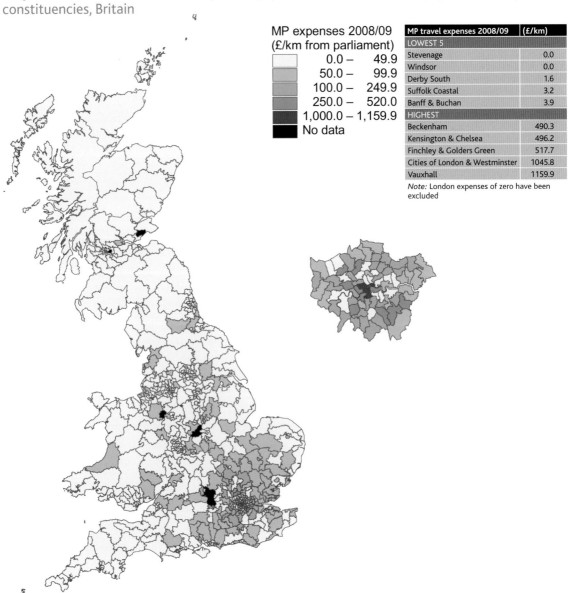

MP expenses 2008/09
(£/km from parliament)
- 0.0 – 49.9
- 50.0 – 99.9
- 100.0 – 249.9
- 250.0 – 520.0
- 1,000.0 – 1,159.9
- No data

MP travel expenses 2008/09	(£/km)
LOWEST 5	
Stevenage	0.0
Windsor	0.0
Derby South	1.6
Suffolk Coastal	3.2
Banff & Buchan	3.9
HIGHEST	
Beckenham	490.3
Kensington & Chelsea	496.2
Finchley & Golders Green	517.7
Cities of London & Westminster	1045.8
Vauxhall	1159.9

Note: London expenses of zero have been excluded

3.5 The 2010 general election result: winners and losers

The general election of 6 May 2010 was Gordon Brown's first and last general election as Prime Minister (and Labour Party leader). The end result was ambiguous over who had won. Of the 650 seats up for grabs, Labour won 258 (down 90 on the notional 2005 result for these new seats), the Conservatives, now led by David Cameron, won 305 (up 95) and the Liberal Democrats, now led by Nick Clegg, won 57 (down 5). To win an outright majority a party needed 326 seats, and the Conservatives were 21 short of that; to have a working minority it was widely considered that somewhere between 310 and 315 were required and, again, they fell short (Labour and the Liberal Democrat vote combined totalled only some 315 seats). After five days of deliberation a Conservative-Liberal Democrat coalition emerged.

Map 3.5.1 shows which party came first and which party second in each seat on 6 May 2010. A little more variety has been added to the key to this map compared with its equivalent five years previously (Map 3.3.1). In one seat the Greens now come first, whereas they had not appeared at all in the key to the 2005 results. Such oddities are interesting, but the overall picture of which large areas swung most to and from Labour was of key importance (Figure 3.5.1).

Swinging towards Labour, by 6%-7% in 2010 as compared to 2005 were the combined constituencies of Renfrewshire, Glasgow and Fife. The next largest swings, of between 4% and 5%, were in Dunbartonshire; Kirkcudbright & Wigtown; Edinburgh; and Caithness & Sutherland. The next largest swings, of between 2% and 3%, were in: Lanarkshire; East Lothian; Ayrshire and Arran; Perth & Kinross and Clackmannanshire; and Midlothian. Scotland swung to Labour.

And the seats which saw the most Labour voters desert the party? Just over 10 extra voters in every hundred did not vote Labour in Northamptonshire (−10.1%), Staffordshire, Kent, Worcestershire, Suffolk and Hertfordshire (−10.4%). And the next ten counties seeing the largest swings away from Labour were: City of Bristol (−8.0%); Cambridgeshire; Lincolnshire; Gwynedd; Buckinghamshire; Wiltshire; Essex; Warwickshire; Rutland; and Norfolk (−9.6%). With one exception they are all in Southern England. In Gwynedd the Labour vote fell because the nationalists increased their vote by 39.4% on 2005. There was no national swing between 2005 and 2010. The country polarised.

Figure 3.5.1: 2005 and 2010 Labour share of vote (%), ancient counties, Britain

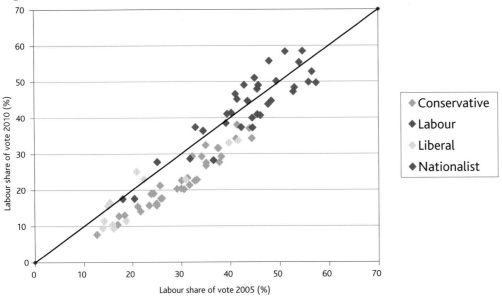

Map 3.5.1: 2010 General election result (actual winner and runner-up), parliamentary constituencies, Britain

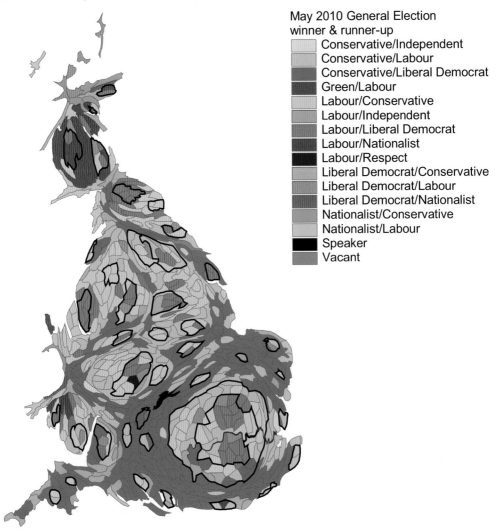

3.6 The 2010 general election result: legitimacy and turnout

Legitimacy is measured here as the proportion of people on the electoral roll who voted for the winning Member of Parliament in each constituency and is shown in Map 3.6.2. Nowhere does any MP elected in 2010 have the support of even half of his or her constituents. The highest legitimacy, 45.6%, is enjoyed by the MP for Westmorland & Lonsdale, Tim Farron (of the Liberal Democrats), who saw his already high vote increase by 14.1%. The lowest legitimacy, of only 17.8%, is held by the MP for Great Grimsby, Austin Mitchell (Labour), who just held on to his seat despite experiencing a 14.4% fall in his vote in 2010. Legitimacy was highest in the

Home Counties where the highest swings to the Conservatives were recorded, usually in seats they already held. It is not just that support for Labour, already low, fell most here, but also that more people voted.

According to the *Guardian*, the Conservatives won some 10,683,528 votes, 36.9% of all votes cast where they stood for election, and some 305 seats as a result (not including the Speaker's seat). Suppose they had won exactly 36.9% of the vote in every constituency they had contested, with the same number of votes overall, but evenly spread. At the extreme, some 14,772 voters would have to be moved into the constituency of Dunfermline & Fife West to ensure that 36.9% figure, but most of those could be found from the 13,815 surplus Tory votes in places like Richmond in North Yorkshire, the seat with the most wasted votes. In return, 13,815 people who abstained would be placed in Richmond from Dunfermline. All this is just part of what would be required to achieve an even spread.

The Conservative vote has been becoming more geographically uneven for years. Some 1,751,646 Conservative voters would have had to move constituencies to ensure an even Tory vote in 2010; 16.4% of their entire vote in the seats where they stood. The proportion is even higher if Northern Ireland and the Speaker's seat are included. In 2005 that percentage was 15.7%, and the last time the Tory vote in Britain was more unevenly spread than in 2010 was way back in 1918. For the Tory vote to become more segregated it must go up the most where it was highest to begin with, and the least, or even decrease slightly, where it was lowest. Even as they were becoming slightly more numerous, Conservative voters were simultaneously becoming more geographically segregated.

The geographical isolation of Conservative voters has been growing steadily since 1979, when their segregation rate was half its current level. After it last reached a maximum, way back in that wartime election of 1918, it then fell, almost continuously, up to 1959 (Table 3.6.1). At the same time the country became generally less socially and spatially polarised. Wealth and health inequalities narrowed, along with those in voting, which became much less of a geographical matter. From 1959 to February 1974,

Map 3.6.1: 2010 General election result disappointed voters (% of vote), parliamentary constituencies, Britain

May 2010 General Election disappointed (%)
- 28.0 – 29.9
- 30.0 – 39.9
- 40.0 – 49.9
- 50.0 – 59.9
- 60.0 – 70.6
- Speaker
- Vacant

Note: Proportion shown is of voters who did not see the candidate they voted for become MP

Map 3.6.2: 2010 General election result legitimacy (% of electorate), parliamentary constituencies, Britain

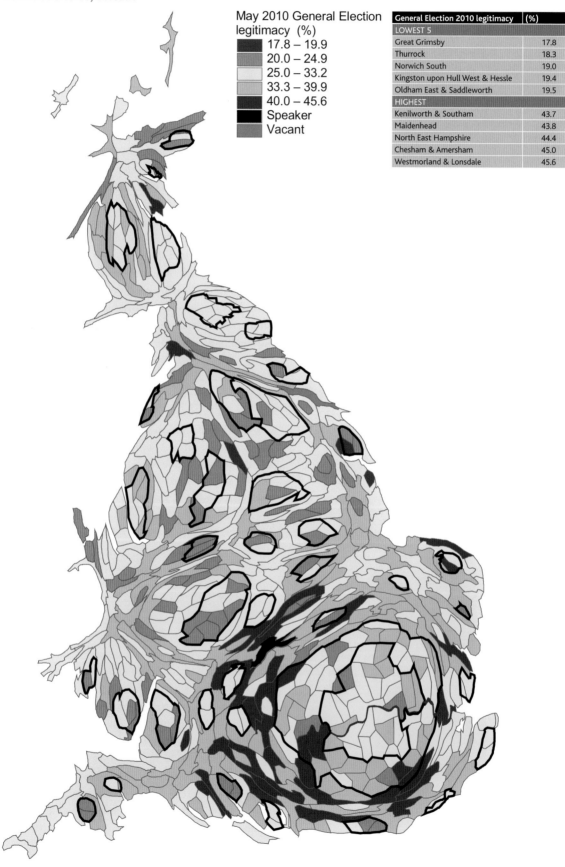

May 2010 General Election legitimacy (%)
- 17.8 – 19.9
- 20.0 – 24.9
- 25.0 – 33.2
- 33.3 – 39.9
- 40.0 – 45.6
- Speaker
- Vacant

General Election 2010 legitimacy	(%)
LOWEST 5	
Great Grimsby	17.8
Thurrock	18.3
Norwich South	19.0
Kingston upon Hull West & Hessle	19.4
Oldham East & Saddleworth	19.5
HIGHEST	
Kenilworth & Southam	43.7
Maidenhead	43.8
North East Hampshire	44.4
Chesham & Amersham	45.0
Westmorland & Lonsdale	45.6

the Tory segregation index remained stable at under 9% of the Conservative vote.

In the 1960s and early 1970s there were Tories everywhere. One-nation Conservatives had support up and down the country. Then, in October 1974, the Conservative segregation index rose to 10.7%. New Conservative voters in the Home Counties swung that party's support heavily southwards, while in the North and West it fell. The Tories might have lost the second 1974 election, but their support had changed geographically and taken the first step on

Table 3.6.1: 1885–2010 Conservative voter segregation index, Britain

Election	Concentration
1885	7.11%
1886	5.53%
1892	5.81%
1895	4.70%
1900	4.39%
1906	6.67%
1910 January	7.91%
1910 December	6.24%
1918	19.30%
1922	14.44%
1923	11.57%
1924	10.62%
1929	9.24%
1931	9.23%
1935	9.65%
1945	7.21%
1950	6.74%
1951	6.77%
1955	6.93%
1959	6.24%
1964	6.51%
1966	7.69%
1970	8.04%
1974 February	8.01%
1974 October	10.72%
1979	9.17%
1983	10.59%
1987	11.84%
1992	11.88%
1997	13.94%
2001	15.05%
2005	15.69%
2010	16.40%

the road towards ever rising political segregation across Britain.

One-nation Tories felt the cold wind of change. Margaret Thatcher was appointed leader of the opposition the following year. In 1979 she secured her first victory and then, in every general election that followed, including 2010, Conservative support overall increased slightly more where it was strongest to begin with, or decreased less there. The segregation index increased the most in 1997, when Tory support fell least where it had been strongest. Wasted votes then, but also the sign of an ever rising segregation, and just one of the many ways in which 1997 was no dramatic break with the past.

What of former periods of political instability? In the two general elections held in 1910 the index dropped on the second occasion, whereas in the latter of the two in 1974 it rose. In May 2010 it was voters in the best-off constituencies who swung most firmly towards David Cameron even though so many there already voted for his party. He failed to secure an overall majority because support for his party was lacklustre in the marginal seats. The last Tory leader to see the segregation of his or her vote fall while in office was Ted Heath. In contrast, in 2010, support swung away from the Tories where it was already lowest in 2005. A politically successful politician sees their share of the vote increase most in those seats where they were previously second placed, so that they achieve a victory.

What does this say for the future? It tells us we are living in remarkable times. The segregation of Tory voters is greater now than it was in 1922, and it has been that high and rising since 2001. To win the largest minority of seats in a general election, despite seeing the greatest increase in your support where you *needed it the least*, is remarkable and perhaps also shows how little empathy many people in Tory shires now feel for those who live in the cities, or the North, or the countries outside of England. And it is in the cities and in the North that most voters were disappointed in 2010. It is here that majorities did not get what they voted for (Map 3.6.1).

3.7 No overall control: local elections and the future

There was another set of elections held on 6 May 2010. The London boroughs had elections for all seats; in all of the metropolitan boroughs, in 20 unitary authorities and in 69 district councils, one third of seats were up for election; and 7 district councils had elections for half of their seats.

Map 3.7.1 shows which political party held control over each local authority after the May 2010 local elections took place. In most cases it was still the Conservative Party, but their hold on local power slipped slightly and fewer councils are coloured blue on the map than had been blue in April 2010, especially in London. In a few cases the Conservatives held power in coalition as a result of the elections. Labour control of local councils is much smaller (after years of contraction), but the picture represents a turnaround for them, with more councils held than before. If the majority party is in coalition this is distinguished on the map.

The Liberal Democrats hold power over even fewer people than Labour but in a greater number of smaller, more scattered areas; the Nationalists fewer still, and they control only one council in Wales. Independents are, in general, even more peripherally arranged than the Nationalists, and finally a swathe of councils across much of Wales and urban Northern England emerged with no party in overall control following these elections. Two other bodies, the Corporation of the City of London (with 25 aldermen and 130 councillors) and the Council of the Isles of Scilly (with 21 councillors), do not fit in any of these classes and, officially, have no political groups: thus they cannot be easily labelled.

The parties which failed to take control of any council, but which put candidates up in many places, winning a very few council seats, included the British National Party, Christian Peoples Alliance, English Democrats, England First Party, Independent Community & Health Concern, the Liberal Party, Mebyon Kernow, People's Voice, residents associations, RESPECT, the Socialist Party, the Scottish Socialist Party and UK Independence Party. Far more councillors were elected purely as Independents. Often in the past this was a label

which really meant Conservative. Nowadays it increasingly does mean independent of party politics.

In recent years local election results have been viewed often as an indicator of how the political winds are changing. The British National Party did badly in local elections in 2010. Labour saw a slight revival in its fortunes, the Liberal Democrats failed in their great attempt at a surge and the Conservatives lost a little ground but remain solidly the party of the English countryside and suburbs. What is not shown in Map 3.7.1 is how many people chose not to vote in May 2010 despite there being both general and local elections, and despite this being one of the closest general elections held for years, an election where the result was far from a foregone conclusion at the beginning of polling day.

Map 3.7.2 shows how many people voted across the country in the general election. In a few parts of Birmingham, Manchester, Hull and Glasgow fewer than half of the registered electorate turned out to vote. Many other eligible adults there will not have been registered. There was little point for many people to vote in many places in Britain where seats were not marginal and especially where none of the three main parties were proposing changes that would benefit people in these poorest of constituencies. Around these cores of resistance to voting are seas of apathy where at least 40% of registered voters did not turn out, and around them are areas where between 30% and 40% of adults who are registered to vote chose not to.

Voting rates are highest in marginal constituencies, and in affluent constituencies where voting is partly seen as an obligation of citizenship. Thus in a belt of constituencies across North Yorkshire, encircling Birmingham and filling in much of the Home Counties over 70% of electors voted. An incredible 84.5% voted in Warwick & Leamington, more than five out of six of the electorate. In a few cases there are suspicions that some extra, illegal, votes were cast by post, inflating these figures for turnout, but these remain some of the highest recorded in recent years. But is this high turnout really impressive?

Compared to other affluent countries, fewer people vote in British local and general elections than in most other places where people have a vote (which is almost all other affluent countries of any size).

Map 3.7.1: 2010 Local election results (council control), local authorities, Britain

Council control May 2010
- Conservative
- Conservative coalition
- Independent
- Independent coalition
- Labour
- Labour coalition
- Liberal Democrat
- Liberal Democrat coalition
- Nationalist
- Nationalist coalition
- No overall control
- Not applicable

Table 3.7.1 shows that the UK ranked 18th out of the 25 richest countries in the world between 1945 and 1998 in terms of the proportion of its population who chose not to vote. Since 1998 even fewer people in the UK have chosen to vote in general, and especially in local, elections. It is disproportionately countries which use first-past-the-post systems which see the lowest turnouts at general elections. At the bottom of the table is the United States.

The great promise of the 2010 general election was of a fairer election system to emerge out of this mess of bankrupt voting. Two of the parties promised this and the party with the largest share of the vote had to make concessions towards a referendum on the issue to be able to form a coalition.

Map 3.7.2: 2010 General election turnout (% of electorate), parliamentary constituencies, Britain

May 2010 General Election turnout (%)
- 44.3 – 49.9
- 50.0 – 59.9
- 60.0 – 69.9
- 70.0 – 84.5
- Speaker
- Vacant

Table 3.7.1: Voter turnout in general elections, 1945–98

Rank	Country	Million person years	%
1	Italy	3,100	91
2	Iceland	22	88
3	Belgium	493	86
4	New Zealand	360	85
5	Australia	695	85
6	Netherlands	1,160	85
7	Austria	586	84
8	Denmark	403	84
9	Sweden	614	83
10	Greece	460	80
11	Germany	5,691	80
12	Norway	325	79
13	Malta	18	79
14	Israel	276	78
15	Finland	394	77
16	Spain	2,285	76
17	Ireland	222	75
18	United Kingdom	3,364	75
19	Portugal	209	75
20	France	2,434	68
21	Japan	4,954	68
22	Canada	1,141	68
23	Switzerland	116	49
24	United States	6,184	48

Chapter 4 Morally bankrupt

Introduction

Morality is a strange recursive concept. It implies 'to do the right thing', but what the right thing might be depends on your view of morality, on what is right and what is wrong. Some rights and wrongs are easier to define than others.

The sexual, physical and mental abuse of children is abhorred by people across the world. Government today accords children special protection when it is thought that they might be at risk of abuse. Formal child protection plans are then made to improve their future safety. When a child is killed who was or should have been identified by the authorities as at risk, there is a great outcry of moral outrage and anger. This anger is not directed only at the killer but also at the authorities who failed to prevent the harm, for example by using a child protection order to allow the compulsory removal of the child from the 'at risk' situation. In the poorest 60 per cent of areas in Britain children are subject to child protection plans in almost direct proportion to their likelihood of living in poverty. The children most likely to be abused are those living in the very poorest neighbourhoods. It does not take a great leap of imagination to extend part of the blame for high and persistent rates of abuse of children in Britain to those, all of us, who allow such high rates of poverty, and the inequality which causes poverty, to continue, and this is especially true when children kill other children.

Children killing other children is extremely rare in Britain. It is much more common in the United States which is, in general, a far more violent society. However, and perhaps partly because of the danger of extreme violence in the United States, bullying between children is recorded as being slightly rarer in the US than in the UK (see Section 4.2). It is the United Kingdom which has been found to have the highest rates of bullying among children in the rich world.

Thankfully, great efforts are now being made to try to control bullying in this country. Cases of bullying are now recorded by schools across all of Britain and almost as soon as such recording begins, rates of bullying tend to fall. Interestingly, it is not in the poorest of places that rates are necessarily highest. They are lowest in many London boroughs. We do not know whether this is because London is more progressive, or because (like the US) the fear of violence escalating results in bullying being more constrained and curtailed within London. In London today knives, and increasingly, guns are carried more often now than was common a few years ago. This caused great fear, at the height of those rises in knife and gun crime, especially among children living in particular parts of London and within the poorest parts of a few other cities. As we write in 2010–11, murder rates in Britain are the lowest for at least a decade, but there is no direct correlation between risk and fear.

There is not necessarily anything particularly immoral about becoming pregnant as a teenager, but teenage pregnancy is often portrayed as a moral issue. Britain is well known for having the highest teenage conception rate in Europe. Although the rate here is much lower than that in the US and also much lower than it has been in the recent past in Britain, it is still very high by international standards, especially for children aged under 16 on whom we concentrate in this chapter.

Sixteen is the minimum age at which children are legally permitted to engage in sex in the UK. Unfortunately there are no systematic estimates made of the number of boys by age and area having sex: all the demographic figures given are for girls and only then for when they conceive and when that conception is either carried through to birth or aborted. Rates of miscarriages and sex not resulting in pregnancy are not known. According to the United Nations report referred to in Section 4.2, some of the highest proportions of young people in the rich world who are unsure of whether or not they had sex on a particular night because they were too drunk to know, live in Britain.

From mid-teenage years to young adulthood, many commentators appear most obsessed with behaviour described as anti-social, that is, acts of petty crime, vandalism, noise, congregating in public spaces, and more dangerous acts that cause fear and lead to mistrust. These anti-social acts include malicious phone calls made to the emergency services and, in particular, the fire brigade. We map these in this chapter because they allow comparisons to be made between areas that cannot be made in a fair way for other anti-social acts. For example, anti-social behaviour orders are issued according to the particular policies of individual local authorities, and so punitive local authorities order far more to be issued than do more lenient authorities. This is why we have chosen to map malicious calls instead. Malicious calls to fire brigades can result in deaths where people are not saved from fires because firefighters are otherwise engaged dealing with hoax calls or fires set deliberately. In recent years in most places such calls have been falling in frequency.

'Crime' is the word reserved for discussing the most serious of behaviour deemed anti-social: that behaviour which has been officially sanctioned as bad. When we map crime of all kinds, we find that in recent years in most areas aggregate rates have been falling. Measuring changes in specific crime rates over time is far from easy. Even a measure as apparently simple as the murder rate in Britain has been swelled by all of Harold Shipman's victims (at least 215), by the 58 Chinese workers found suffocated to death in the back of a lorry in Dover on 20 June 2000, by those other 21 Chinese workers drowned while picking cockles in Morecambe Bay on 5 February 2004, and by the 52 victims of the London terrorist attacks of 7 July 2005. If all those murdered people are included in the murder rate then that rate rose rapidly until recently. If, on the other hand, you count only the number of murderers, then that number has diminished.

Crime, anti-social behaviour and disorder all scare government. Our penultimate example of potential moral bankruptcy and anti-social behaviour in this chapter concerns the exercise of some of those powers that government in Britain has awarded itself since 2000 to allow it to search for what it thinks

might be the anti-social behaviour of others. We plot how often the Regulation of Investigatory Powers Act 2000 (RIPA) was used in 2008/09 and 2009/10 and the places where it was most used. This is the Act that allow local councils to set up covert surveillance to catch people who allow their dogs to foul the pavement or those who 'fly tip' when they leave donations at the doors of charity shops. It also allows the state to use electronic surveillance to spy on its own employees because officials think they might be lying about where they park their cars.

Interestingly, as with crime and anti-social behaviour, and as with teenage pregnancies (most recently), and almost certainly now with bullying and with the number of child protection orders issued in the immediate aftermath of the 'baby Peter' case, *all* these rates indicate that behaviour often labelled as immoral was falling in the last year of the last Labour government. It turns out that Britain was not 'breaking' in spring 2010. However, now, those falls all appear to be reversing again as we write in late 2010, as poverty rises with spending cuts and as the poor are taxed so much more than the rich as a result of the Conservative-Liberal Democrat Coalition's Emergency Budget of June 2010 and Comprehensive Spending Review of October 2010.

This final point brings us to our last example of immoral behaviour: the evasion of tax. It has been estimated that hundreds of times more money is avoided and evaded from legal taxation than is defrauded through the benefit system.[1] The last Labour government made tax avoidance and evasion easier. They did this by dramatically reducing the number of inspectors available, by altering tax laws, and by increasing the minimum level at which couples would be liable to pay inheritance tax.

The incoming Conservative Party of the Coalition government promised to raise the threshold for inheritance taxation even higher, so further cutting tax bills for the very richest in society. We end the chapter by looking at how few people now pay inheritance tax upon the estates of the dead, and at how geographically isolated this small group has become. We live today with a moral bankruptcy among the affluent that our great-grandparents who saw the 1920s would recognise, but which for most of the last century appeared to be on the way out. Today it is back again with vengeance.

4.1   Child abuse, protection and fear

In England moral breakdown is registered most
acutely through the actions of children. It is when
children kill children that the social fabric is seen
to be tearing. From Mary Bell's 1968 trial for
her killing of playmates in Newcastle upon Tyne,
through to one of the killers of James Bulger being
re-imprisoned in 2010 for the alleged possession
and distribution of child pornography, the past half-
century has been punctuated by news stories of the
end of the 'Peter and Jane' lifestyle immortalised in
the Penguin Ladybird reading series that was first
published less than half a century ago, in 1964.

The covers of the Penguin books are of idealised
1950s families showing two young children with
the by-line 'play with us' running along the bottom.
Postwar Britain was just learning about play. The
books featured two children, a boy and a girl,
living in a nuclear family with a full-time working
father and a stay-at-home mother. Nothing bad
ever happened in these books. However, outside of
children's fiction there was a growing awareness that
all was not well within many families that might
have appeared 'Peter and Jane-like' from the outside.

In 1968, even before the Mary Bell trial, the Social
Work Act was passed giving local authorities the
responsibility for investigating child abuse. Mary
had been abused within her home from the age of
four, and the country was still reeling from the 1966
trial of the Moors Murderers Ian Brady and Myra
Hindley. Social services departments were created
by amalgamating other services in 1970, and then a
series of changes to these departments were made
in an attempt to increase protection further. Often
these and later changes were driven by the tragic and
possibly preventable death of a particular child.[2]

As attempts to prevent abuse, injury and the deaths
of children increased, registers of children deemed
to be at risk were established. The latest change to
legislation and practice meant that by April 2008 an
Integrated Children's System was being introduced
across England, phasing out the old child protection
register. Slightly different systems operate in Wales
and Scotland making comparisons between areas and
over time difficult.[3]

In England and Wales children and young people
aged up to and including 18 are included on the
systems. In Scotland only children up to age 15 are
registered in these official statistics.

In the year ending in March 2009 some 547,000
children in England were referred to a social services
department for one reason or another. Some 37,900
became subject to a child protection plan. This
was an increase of 3,900 on the year earlier. Of
the children on a plan, just over one in eight had
previously been the subject of a plan. Furthermore,
during the year ending 31 March 2009, 32,800
children ceased to be the subject of a plan, which
compares to 32,600 by the same point in 2008.[4]
Across all of Britain some 39,322 children were
subject to one of these plans or their equivalent in
March 2009. The locations of these children are
shown, as rates per 10,000 children, in Map 4.1.2.

Map 4.1.1: 2008–09 Change in rate of
children subject to formal child protection
(per 10,000 children), local education areas,
Britain

Child protection
change 2008–09
(per 10,000 children)
- -17 – -1
- 0 – 4
- 5 – 9
- 10 – 19
- 20 – 54
- No data

Map 4.1.2: 2009 Children subject to formal child protection (per 10,000 children), local education areas, Britain

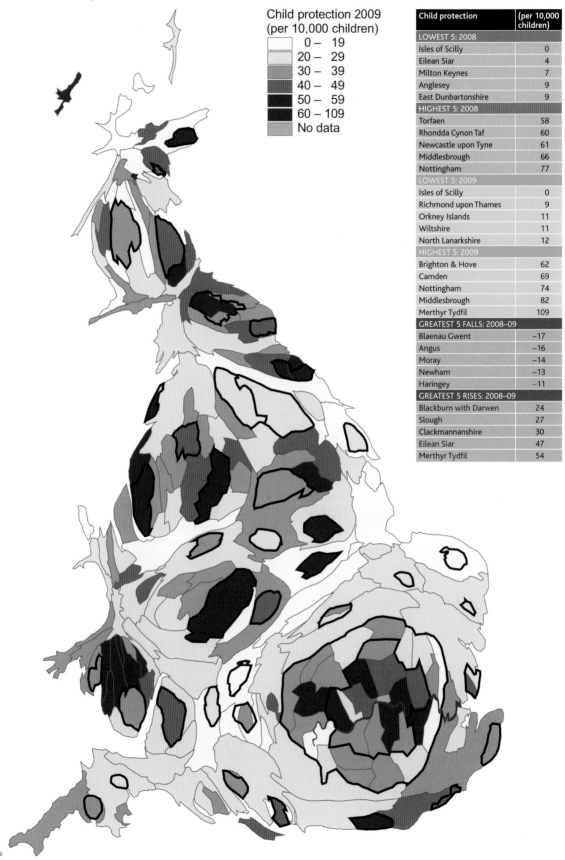

Child protection 2009
(per 10,000 children)
- 0 – 19
- 20 – 29
- 30 – 39
- 40 – 49
- 50 – 59
- 60 – 109
- No data

Child protection	(per 10,000 children)
LOWEST 5: 2008	
Isles of Scilly	0
Eilean Siar	4
Milton Keynes	7
Anglesey	9
East Dunbartonshire	9
HIGHEST 5: 2008	
Torfaen	58
Rhondda Cynon Taf	60
Newcastle upon Tyne	61
Middlesbrough	66
Nottingham	77
LOWEST 5: 2009	
Isles of Scilly	0
Richmond upon Thames	9
Orkney Islands	11
Wiltshire	11
North Lanarkshire	12
HIGHEST 5: 2009	
Brighton & Hove	62
Camden	69
Nottingham	74
Middlesbrough	82
Merthyr Tydfil	109
GREATEST 5 FALLS: 2008–09	
Blaenau Gwent	−17
Angus	−16
Moray	−14
Newham	−13
Haringey	−11
GREATEST 5 RISES: 2008–09	
Blackburn with Darwen	24
Slough	27
Clackmannanshire	30
Eilean Siar	47
Merthyr Tydfil	54

Areas which have a high rate of children subject to protection tend to be urban and poor; areas with the lowest rates tend to be more rural and usually more affluent. Rates of protection depend not just on how many children might require protection, but also on the effectiveness of social workers in offering protection. The rates will be reduced by the degree of resistance to such protection being offered, resistance which might well be higher in more rural and affluent places, where families may be more effectively confident or even litigious in their opposition against attempts by the authorities to intervene. In contrast, more families in poorer areas will be unaware of how to object effectively against child protection measures. Poorer areas also often end up being home to more families which are falling apart emotionally as well as financially.

Rates of child protection changed greatly between 2008 and 2009 (shown in Map 4.1.1). This occured primarily because of the death of one very young child. In August 2007, at the age of 17 months, Peter Connelly (known then as 'baby P'), a child subject to protection plans, was killed through cruelty. The court cases following Peter's death stretched over the subsequent two years, but it became evident that he had been allowed to die despite numerous opportunities for the authorities to intervene. Around the country social workers and other authorities became far more cautious.

In 158 of the areas being studied here, the rate of awarding children protected status rose; in only 44 areas did it fall. Map 4.1.1 shows where those rises and falls occurred. The greatest rises can be seen from the map to have occurred in poorer northern towns and Inner London boroughs. However, analysis of the data shows they occurred only in those parts of those areas where rates were lower than neighbouring places. Authorities were comparing their practice with neighbouring boroughs and districts and increasing the number of protection plans they gave in proportion to the population where the rate was low to begin with.

4.2 Child well-being and bullying

In 2007 the United Nations International Emergency Fund for Children (UNICEF) published

a devastating report on the living conditions of children in affluent nations.[5]

Table 4.2.1: 2010 Local authorities with least and most bullying being reported, England

Rank	Local Authority	Bullying rate 2009/10
1	Isles of Scilly	9.8
2	Kingston upon Thames	19.3
3	Liverpool	19.9
4	Ealing	21.1
5	Camden	21.2
6	Hounslow	21.3
7	Barnet	21.4
8	Brent	21.7
9	Islington	21.8
10	Knowsley	21.9
11	Lambeth	22.6
12	Sutton	22.7
13	Solihull	22.7
14	Wandsworth	22.7
15	Redbridge	23.4
16	Bolton	24.0
17	Enfield	24.0
18	Bexley	24.1
19	Barking & Dagenham	24.2
20	Wigan	24.4
21	Havering	24.4
22	Kensington & Chelsea	24.5
23	Westminster	24.5
24	Haringey	24.6
25	Hammersmith & Fulham	24.9
26	Wokingham	25.0
...		
140	Sunderland	33.3
141	North Somerset	33.4
142	Bracknell Forest	33.5
143	Gateshead	33.5
144	Kingston upon Hull	33.6
145	Bournemouth	34.0
146	Lincolnshire	34.2
147	North East Lincolnshire	34.2
148	Isle of Wight	34.4
149	Bristol	34.7
150	Plymouth	35.2
151	Wakefield	35.2
152	Darlington	37.9

The report found that of the 21 countries surveyed, rates of child well-being were lowest in the UK. Where the children of the UK scored lowest – what caused the country as a whole to rank at the very bottom – was for poor family and peer relationships, and risky behaviour. Younger children were being bullied at home and school more than anywhere else in the rich world, and older children were getting drunk and having sex more often (often having sex while drunk).[6]

Research published in the *British Medical Journal* in the same year showed how the very high rates of inequality experienced by children in the UK predicted very closely just how badly the country did, but it was the bullying that meant it ranked below the US.[7]

> Bullying is repeated behaviour which makes other people feel uncomfortable or threatened whether this is intended or not. There are different sorts of bullying, but the main types are:
>
> *Physical:* hitting, kicking, taking or hiding belongings including money
> *Verbal:* name calling, teasing, insulting, writing unkind notes
> *Emotional:* being unfriendly, excluding, tormenting, spreading rumours, looks
> *Exclusion:* a child can be bullied simply by being excluded from discussions/activities, with those they believe to be their friends
> *Damage to property or theft:* pupils may have their property damaged or stolen. Physical threats may be used by the bully in order that the student hands over property to them
> *Cyber:* cyber-bullying is a more recent problem that has come about through the increased use of mobile phones and the internet. It may include threats or name-calling via the internet chat rooms, web pages, texts or phone calls. It may also involve the misuse of associated technology such as cameras and video facilities.[8]

Using this definition of bullying, the government in Britain surveyed children in schools between April 2008 and the end of March 2010. Children are included as having been bullied whether bullied in school, on the way to or from school, or elsewhere.

Consistent data only exist for local authorities in England and then only for the last year of the period surveyed. This is because in the first year children also included cases of having been bullied in previous years and those episodes could not be excluded from the data to allow for a comparison over time. However, it is very likely that rates will have reduced almost everywhere as the simple awareness and measuring of the abuse at a much more intensive rate than before highlights bullying as unacceptable.

Map 4.2.1 shows the map of where bullying was most and least common in England by the start of 2010. The striking message from the map is how low relative rates of bullying are within most of London. London has tended to be ahead of the times when it comes to progressive civil movements such as feminism, antiracism and rejecting homophobia, and now against the bullying of children in school. Surprisingly, parents in London often talk of how terrible the capital's schools are, despite exam results in London's state schools being much better than across the rest of the country. London is, in many ways, a more interesting place to live as a child or young adult, with more to do and less reason to get bored. Thus, 'Contrary to some expectations, drug use among 16–24 year olds is lower in London (17 per cent) than in the South East (26 per cent) and South West (19 per cent).'[9] It would appear the same is true of bullying. Greater awareness of how bad things can be, and more visible choice may partly explain the different perceptions in London. Table 4.2.1 lists which areas of England had the highest and lowest rates by spring 2010.

The largest recorded falls in bullying were in Kingston upon Thames, Lambeth and Bexley in London, and in Wokingham near London, in all of which less than a quarter of children were being bullied by early 2010. The ten districts with the lowest recorded falls, although all of more than 10%, were: Hackney, Hillingdon, Newham and Tower Hamlets in London; Birmingham and Sandwell in the West Midlands; and Liverpool, Manchester and Knowsley in the North West of England. However, in Liverpool the rate is now extremely low with less than a fifth of children reporting bullying. It must also be remembered that these years are not strictly comparable. Moreover, a number of often more isolated authorities did not collect or process adequate data in the first year. These

Map 4.2.1: 2010 Children being bullied (%), local authorities, England

Children who have experienced
bullying 2009/10 (%)
- 9.8 – 19.9
- 20.0 – 24.9
- 25.0 – 29.9
- 30.0 – 34.9
- 35.0 – 37.9

included: Bedford, Central Bedfordshire, Cheshire East, Cheshire West & Chester, Cornwall, Durham, Northumberland, Shropshire and Wiltshire. In all these cases more than a quarter of children reported still being bullied by 2010. Perhaps that number would have been lower if monitoring had been taken more seriously and had started earlier?

4.3   Conceptions among girls aged under 16

The second reason why the UK ranked the lowest of 21 affluent countries in 2007 when UNICEF assessed children's well-being was the high rate of risk-taking behaviour by children, including having under-age sex. It is illegal for children to have sex in the UK if they are aged under 16. Under English law, penetrative sex below this age is classified as statutory rape as the girl is not deemed able to give permission. In 2006 some 24,921 girls became pregnant as a result of under-age sex, often sex with a boy who was also under age. In 2007 that number rose to 25,500 pregnancies to girls aged under 16. Almost three out of five of all these conceptions will have ended in abortion.

Map 4.3.2 shows the rate of conceptions per 1,000 girls aged 13, 14 or 15 in 2007. In creating the map, numbers for the City of London have been combined with those of neighbouring Hackney, the Isles of Scilly with Penwith, and Rutland with Leicester. Rates were highest in Merthyr Tydfil, with 1.89% of all girls of these ages in that year conceiving. It is worth pointing out that Merthyr Tydfil also had the highest proportion of child protection plans in place in Britain in 2009, at 1.09% of the child population. (In most cases these pregnant girls will not be the same children, although some may have been on a child protection register when they were younger.) It is in places like Merthyr Tydfil where poverty is not sufficiently addressed that people who are more likely to be victims of these outcomes stay or return while others are more likely to move away. When poverty becomes concentrated in an area, people try harder to leave; those young women who do not become young mothers are much more likely to be able to leave than those who do.

After Merthyr Tydfil, the second highest rate of under-age conception was recorded in Dundee City

(1.86%), then the London boroughs of Lewisham, Southwark and Lambeth (1.61%, 1.48% and 1.44% respectively), then Manchester (1.44%) and Hull (1.41%). These places ranked, respectively, 57th, 74th, 11th, 59th, 13th, and 132nd according to how likely children within them were to remain on the child protection register after two years. There is therefore no direct correlation between a high rate of under-age conception and a high rate of child protection. In places like Merthyr Tydfil, Southwark and Manchester both rates are high. In Dundee, Lewisham, Lambeth and Hull under-age conceptions are high but child protection plans are rarer, and in other places, such as Middlesbrough and Nottingham, child protection plans are more common but under-age conceptions rarer.

Under-age conceptions for girls are often rarest in areas which are both affluent and rural. Some ten times fewer girls aged under 16 conceive in the

Map 4.3.1: 2006–07 Change in proportion of girls aged 13–15 becoming pregnant, local authorities, Britain

Change in under 16 conceptions 2006–07 (per1,000)
- -4.8 – -2.0
- -1.9 – 0.0
- 0.1 – 1.0
- 1.1 – 2.9
- 3.0 – 5.9
- Data suppressed

Cotswolds as in Merthyr Tydfil. The Cotswolds recorded the lowest conception rate in 2007 (0.18%) because only eight girls there aged under 16 conceived in that year whereas 10 had a year earlier. A year earlier the lowest rate had been in Craven (also 0.18%, representing six girls there, two more than that became pregnant a year later). Under-age conceptions are so rare in many parts of Britain now that a couple of girls becoming pregnant can alter the rank ordering. Map 4.3.1 shows the geography of these changes. Note again London's unusual position compared to many other English cities.

Commentators on under-age sex often suggest that rates in Britain are high because of some failing of parents or teachers to instruct their children properly, including in the mechanics of sex and contraception.[10]

These commentators tend to routinely ignore the link between high rates of inequality and child poverty in the UK, as compared to countries such as the Netherlands, and the high rates of under-age conception in the UK which result. They might ignore that link because, as we have seen, it is not

Map 4.3.2: 2007 Proportion of girls aged 13–15 becoming pregnant, local authorities, Britain

Under 16 conceptions 2007 (per 1,000)
- 1.8 – 4.9
- 5.0 – 7.4
- 7.5 – 9.9
- 10.0 – 14.9
- 15.0 – 18.9
- Data suppressed

Under 16 conceptions	(per 1,000 girls)
LOWEST 5: 2006	
Craven	1.8
Mid Suffolk	2.2
Cotswold	2.3
Brentwood	2.4
Ryedale	2.5
HIGHEST 5: 2006	
Stoke-on-Trent	14.7
Southwark	15.1
Lewisham	15.2
Dundee City	15.3
Lambeth	15.6
LOWEST 5: 2007	
Cotswold	1.8
Craven	2.4
South Cambridgeshire	2.5
Brentwood	2.6
Hart	2.9
HIGHEST 5: 2007	
Lambeth	14.4
Southwark	14.8
Lewisham	16.1
Dundee City	18.6
Merthyr Tydfil	18.9
GREATEST 5 FALLS: 2006–07	
Wrexham	−4.8
Gwynedd	−3.8
Corby	−2.4
Redcar & Cleveland	−2.4
Rhondda Cynon Taf	−2.4
GREATEST 5 RISES: 2006–07	
Portsmouth	2.6
Boston	2.7
Dundee City	3.2
Torfaen	4.3
Merthyr Tydfil	5.9

obvious for the extreme areas. It is necessary to group areas and to graph the results for the link between poverty and young teenage conceptions to become clear.

The latest data are reported for 2008, when there was a national 3.9% fall in conceptions among those aged under 18.[11]

As yet we have no geographical data on the distribution of this fall.

4.4 Anti-social behaviour: shouting fire

Shouting fire in a crowded cinema is often given as an example of freedom of speech taken too far. It is anti-social behaviour, behaviour likely to cause harm to others, behaviour likely to damage the fabric of society. Most anti-social behaviour is of this kind: people doing things without thinking of the consequences for others. Claiming loudly that benefit claimants are scroungers in a time of economic austerity is not unlike shouting fire in a crowded cinema and causing a stampede. If you claim this and partly as a result benefits are reduced, people suffer. Where poverty rises as a result, a few more children are abused, more young girls become pregnant in their early teens, bullying rises in general and more lives are cut short. The most damaging anti-social behaviour in Britain is of this kind, but unfortunately it is not widely recognised as such. Studies have shown that an extra person commits suicide a day in Britain when more right-wing governments are in power but the link between that outcome and the anti-social behaviour, and the rhetoric of such governments, remains to be proven.[12]

Anti-social behaviour is usually seen as being almost exclusively the behaviour of children and young adults: graffiti, bad language, petty theft, minor violence, drunkenness in public and vandalism. All these blight people's lives, and so anti-social behaviour orders are issued against thousands of children and young adults in attempts to reduce such behaviour. The government even appointed a 'yobbery tsar', Louise Casey, to oversee the issuing of such orders, and to introduce the shaming in public of young people convicted of criminal offences by

making them wear orange jumpsuits on community payback schemes.

We do not map these anti-social behaviour orders here because their distribution reflects far more the zealotry of different local authorities, rather than the extent of such behaviour. What we can measure, directly, are the numbers of people who falsely and maliciously call the fire brigade. In 2009 some 17,000 malicious false alarms were raised annually in England by spring 2009, a 21% fall on a year earlier.[13]

Map 4.4.2 shows where the most and fewest malicious calls to the fire brigade were made in the year ending in March 2009. Across all of Britain some 22,267 calls were made. Such calls were most common in Scotland, almost one being made a year for every 100 people living in Central Scotland, Strathclyde and Lothian. In contrast, in more rural

Map 4.4.1: 2007/08–2008/09 Change in rate of malicious fire alarm calls made per 10,000 persons, fire service areas, Britain

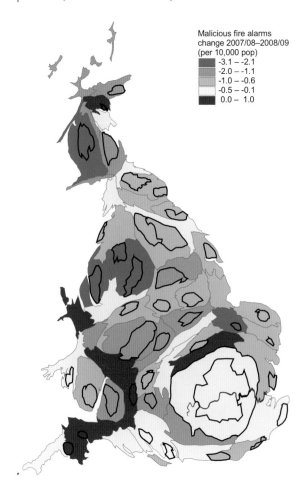

Malicious fire alarms
change 2007/08–2008/09
(per 10,000 pop)
-3.1 – -2.1
-2.0 – -1.1
-1.0 – -0.6
-0.5 – -0.1
0.0 – 1.0

Map 4.4.2: 2008/09 Malicious fire alarm calls made per 10,000 person, fire service areas, Britain

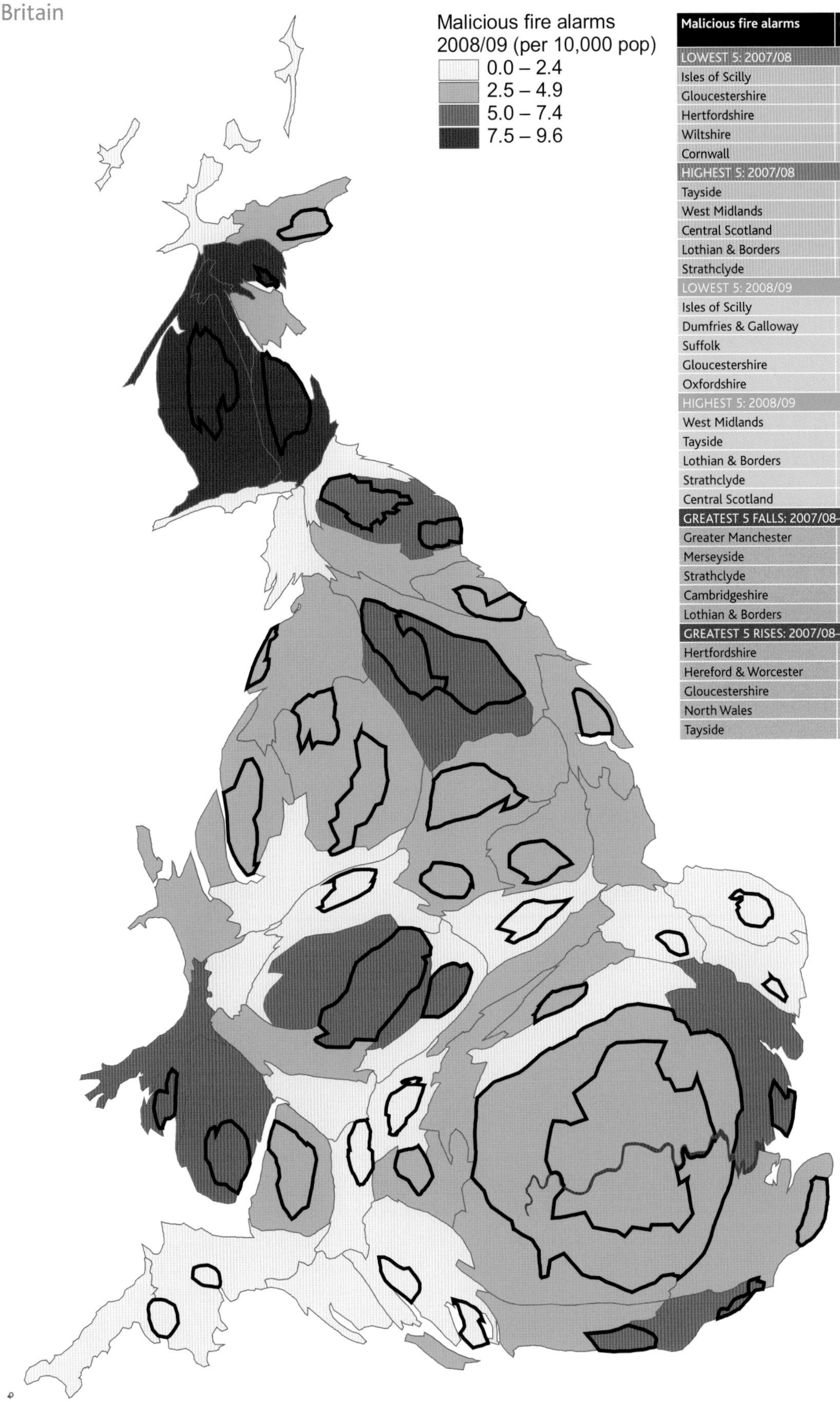

Malicious fire alarms
2008/09 (per 10,000 pop)

- 0.0 – 2.4
- 2.5 – 4.9
- 5.0 – 7.4
- 7.5 – 9.6

Malicious fire alarms	(per 10,000 persons)
LOWEST 5: 2007/08	
Isles of Scilly	0.0
Gloucestershire	1.0
Hertfordshire	1.5
Wiltshire	1.6
Cornwall	1.9
HIGHEST 5: 2007/08	
Tayside	6.7
West Midlands	8.3
Central Scotland	10.7
Lothian & Borders	11.1
Strathclyde	12.2
LOWEST 5: 2008/09	
Isles of Scilly	0.0
Dumfries & Galloway	0.8
Suffolk	1.0
Gloucestershire	1.2
Oxfordshire	1.3
HIGHEST 5: 2008/09	
West Midlands	7.1
Tayside	7.7
Lothian & Borders	9.1
Strathclyde	9.5
Central Scotland	9.6
GREATEST 5 FALLS: 2007/08–2008/09	
Greater Manchester	–3.1
Merseyside	–3.1
Strathclyde	–2.7
Cambridgeshire	–2.6
Lothian & Borders	–2.0
GREATEST 5 RISES: 2007/08–2008/09	
Hertfordshire	<0.05
Hereford & Worcester	0.1
Gloucestershire	0.1
North Wales	0.2
Tayside	1.0

Warwickshire, Cumbria, Leicestershire, Shropshire, Northumberland and Devon & Somerset, as few as one malicious call per 500 people was then being made a year. For the fire service a malicious call in a more rural area usually results in a far longer wasted journey. The statistics shown here do not include the vast majority of false alarms, which are not malicious. Of the 396,000 false alarms called across the whole of the UK each year, some 264,000 are due to faulty apparatus;[14] these calls are annoying but not malicious.

The greatest falls in malicious calls made per person have been in Greater Manchester and Merseyside; both areas saw a fall of 3.1 per 10,000 persons, resulting in roughly half as many calls being made in both conurbations one year as compared to the previous total (2,506 calls in the earlier year falling to 1,304 in the later year across both areas combined). It is thus possible to experience rapid falls in anti-social behaviour in particular localities that are much greater than across the country as a whole. There is nothing inevitable about bad behaviour rising but its falling is rarely reported. Map 4.4.1 shows the overall map of change, which is mostly a map of recent improvements. In Manchester the local newspaper uploaded the voices of people making malicious calls to its website in March 2006. It would appear that this and the related publicity about the costs of such calls in lives and money can have a huge effect.[15]

It is interesting to note that it was in more leafy counties where we find most of the areas where the amount of anti-social behaviour rose, as indicated by rising numbers of malicious calls to the fire brigade. In England, Devon & Somerset, Wiltshire, Hertfordshire, Hereford & Worcester, and Gloucestershire were the five areas registering no improvement or an actual rise when measured on a per capita basis. Often the increase was of just a small number of calls but set against large national falls in rates, the records of these areas do not look good. When this is coupled to the higher rates of drug use mentioned above and more common bullying (Section 4.2), you begin to wonder whether rural life is that idyllic for the young, where many complain of boredom.

4.5 Criminal behaviour of any kind

When it comes to the anti-social behaviour that causes most concern it is actual criminal behaviour that usually tops the list of our fears: the fear of being pickpocketed, mugged, burgled, attacked in our own homes or, at worst, murdered. Crimes come in all shapes and sizes: from the criminal damage of scratching your name on a school desk, to a single act resulting in the multiple killing of the innocent. Each of these actions often counts as a single crime, and what is a crime depends on when and where you live. If a previously legal activity is criminalised you create more crime. If more police officers are employed, almost inevitably more crimes are recorded. If police officers are instructed to record fewer situations as criminal, then crime falls.[16]

The picture of crime for 2008/09 shown in Map 4.5.1 seems to show a country awash with crime, in which a few areas are plagued by very high crime rates. Almost everywhere there are around 10 crimes committed for every 100 people living in a place. However, 100 instances of graffiti sprayed on 100 walls could be counted as 100 crimes, one crime, or – more often – no crime at all. The map of crime partly reflects how crime is recorded in each place. Experience of crime is measured in an annual survey of people as victims, but it is too small to allow mapping.

The map of crime looks better if you compare it to the map for the previous year, 2007/08 (Map 4.5.2). A year earlier there were 5.3 million crimes recorded across Britain. In the latest year there were 5.0 million. That is a rapid fall but, given how flexible the decisions to record crime are, it is hard to be sure of how much of that fall is real. In a way appropriately, in both 2007/08 and 2008/09 the highest rates of crime were recorded for the City of London. In the City almost as many crimes were being committed in a year as there were people living there. The place where crime is next most common is Westminster, where there are 27 crimes recorded each year for every 100 residents living there. These high rates reflect the very high numbers of people coming into these areas to work every day and the relatively low resident populations on which the statistics are calculated.

Map 4.5.1: 2008/09 Crimes committed and recorded per 10,000 persons, local authorities, Britain

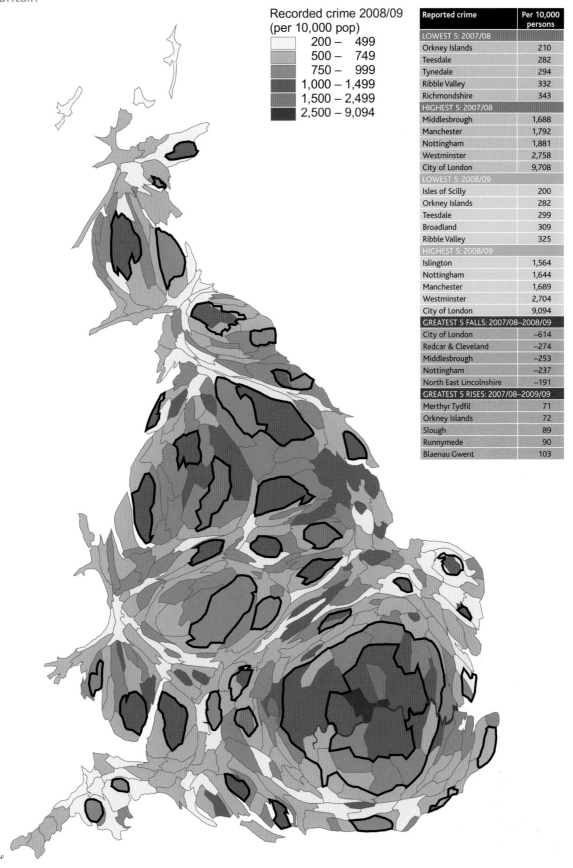

Recorded crime 2008/09
(per 10,000 pop)
- 200 – 499
- 500 – 749
- 750 – 999
- 1,000 – 1,499
- 1,500 – 2,499
- 2,500 – 9,094

Reported crime	Per 10,000 persons
LOWEST 5: 2007/08	
Orkney Islands	210
Teesdale	282
Tynedale	294
Ribble Valley	332
Richmondshire	343
HIGHEST 5: 2007/08	
Middlesbrough	1,688
Manchester	1,792
Nottingham	1,881
Westminster	2,758
City of London	9,708
LOWEST 5: 2008/09	
Isles of Scilly	200
Orkney Islands	282
Teesdale	299
Broadland	309
Ribble Valley	325
HIGHEST 5: 2008/09	
Islington	1,564
Nottingham	1,644
Manchester	1,689
Westminster	2,704
City of London	9,094
GREATEST 5 FALLS: 2007/08–2008/09	
City of London	−614
Redcar & Cleveland	−274
Middlesbrough	−253
Nottingham	−237
North East Lincolnshire	−191
GREATEST 5 RISES: 2007/08–2009/09	
Merthyr Tydfil	71
Orkney Islands	72
Slough	89
Runnymede	90
Blaenau Gwent	103

By looking at the changing rate of crime per person, the effect of the uncertain population base can be removed as that effect will be similarly uncertain for both years. When this is done, recorded crime is found to have risen most quickly in downmarket Blaenau Gwent – with 102 more crimes per 10,000 people in 2008/09, but the second highest rise is in upmarket Runnymede – with 99 more crimes per 10,000 residents. Map 4.5.3 shows the map of change and there are clear geographical patterns to be seen in where recorded crime has risen and fallen most. The processes behind these patterns will reflect a mixture of neighbouring areas copying each other's changing recording practices and also a genuine change in the persistence of crime. Note how crime rates appeared to be rising in outer eastern and southern London boroughs as the recession hit, with crime also rising to the west of Birmingham, in Oxford and in Southampton, and in distinct parts of Wales, Scotland and the North.

One way to achieve an overall picture of where crime has been rising and falling most is to sort all these areas into ten large groups, with the groups based on the earlier crime rates in 2007/08. We can then see what has occurred for these large groups of places, places which are not often geographically contiguous, so not clearly visible on any map. The results, shown in Figure 4.5.1, are remarkable. In every set of these decile areas crime fell, but it fell the most in those areas where it had been highest to begin with. You might have thought the Labour government would have announced this as a success, but the government of the time did not do this analysis, and debates on crime were partly overshadowed by debate over whether the figures were reliable, and, even more so, by wider debates of the first decade of the 21st century on morality in general.

Map 4.5.2: 2007/08 Crimes committed and recorded per 10,000 persons, local authorities, Britain

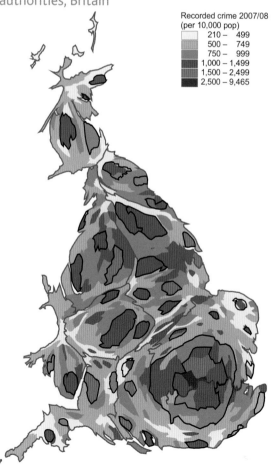

Recorded crime 2007/08
(per 10,000 pop)
210 –   499
500 –   749
750 –   999
1,000 – 1,499
1,500 – 2,499
2,500 – 9,465

Map 4.5.3: 2007/08–2008/09 Change in crimes recorded per 10,000 persons, local authorities, Britain

Recorded crime
change 2007/08–2008/09
(per 10,000 pop)
-371 – -100
-99 –   -50
-49 –   -1
0 –   49
50 – 102

'Britain is witnessing a growth in an underclass whose lifestyles affect everyone,' said the man put in charge of morality by the Conservative Party when in opposition – former Tory leader Iain Duncan Smith,[17] who worked with former prisoner Jonathan Aitken and with Labour MP Graham Allen on his 'Broken Britain' agenda. He went on to concentrate on the cases of baby P and Shannon Matthews in

that same article when talking about crime. So, when the recorded rates of crime were falling fastest in the worst-off areas, when the numbers of people committing murder were falling (if not the number of murders), and when those types of anti-social behaviour that could be consistently recorded was falling, the debate was skewed by talk of a growing criminal underclass.

Figure 4.5.1: 2007/08 to 2008/09 Fall in crime per 10,000 people by deciles of 2007/08 rate, local authorities, Britain

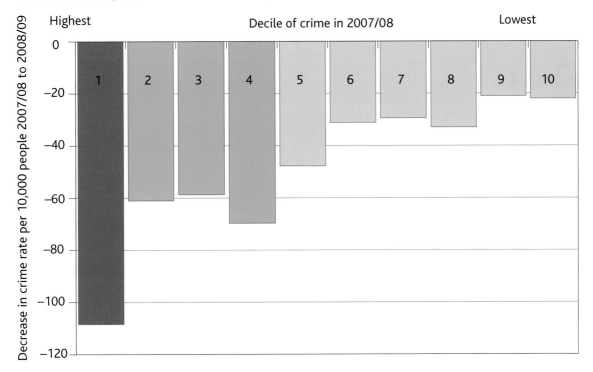

Note: The ten deciles are combinations of local authority areas ranked by the rate of crime in 2007/08 as mapped in Map 4.5.2. The highest crime areas are labelled 1 and those recording the least crime per person are labelled 10. The rate shown for each group of areas is the change in the crime rate per 10,000 people of all ages. In all area groups the recorded crime rates fell between 2007/08 and 2008/09. The bars are shaded using the same colours as the key to Map 4.5.3.

4.6 Legalising formerly criminal behaviour: RIPA

The Regulation of Investigatory Powers Act (RIPA) is an Act of Parliament passed in the millennial year 2000 seen through by Jack Straw, Home Secretary at the time. This Act is ominous because its powers are so far reaching. RIPA is now the law:

regulating the powers of public bodies to carry out surveillance and investigation, and covering the interception of communications. It was introduced to take account of technological changes such as the growth of the Internet and strong encryption. RIPA can be invoked by government officials specified in the Act on the grounds of national security, and for the purposes of detecting crime, preventing disorder, public safety, protecting public health, or in the interests of the economic well-being of the United Kingdom. [18]

RIPA was basically an Act enabling surveillance activities which might otherwise be considered illegal.

As a response to RIPA being introduced into UK law, civil rights groups established Big Brother Watch which reported on actions authorised under RIPA and tallied them up as their use was disclosed by individual local authorities. The rates at which RIPA was invoked in each place from 2008 to 2010 are shown in Map 4.6.1 and Map 4.6.2. Big Brother Watch reported in 2010 that, during these years, local councils were carrying out 11 surveillance operations a day using this Act and they listed a number of specific cases of surveillance. Here is the list of some

Map 4.6.1: 2008/09 RIPA surveillance operations per 10,000 persons, local authorities, Britain

Map 4.6.2: 2009/10 RIPA surveillance operations per 10,000 persons, local authorities, Britain

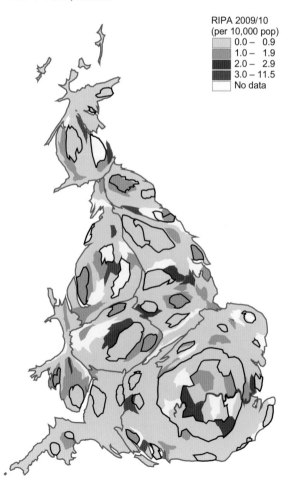

RIPA 2008/09
(per 10,000 pop)
- 0.0 – 0.9
- 1.0 – 1.9
- 2.0 – 2.9
- 3.0 – 6.6
- No data

RIPA 2009/10
(per 10,000 pop)
- 0.0 – 0.9
- 1.0 – 1.9
- 2.0 – 2.9
- 3.0 – 11.5
- No data

of the things RIPA has been used for recently and where:

- Newcastle-upon-Tyne is the worst local authority in the country for RIPA investigations, having spied on their residents 231 times in two years
- Authorities have used covert surveillance to spy on their own employees – because they thought they were lying about their car parking (Darlington), work times (Exeter), sick pay (Hambleton, Hammersmith and Fulham) – or to spy on the wardens they employ to spot crime (Liverpool)
- Over a dozen authorities have used RIPA to spy on dog owners to see whose animals were responsible for dog fouling
- Five authorities have used their powers to spy on people suspected of breaking the smoking ban
- Suffolk County Council used RIPA powers to make a test purchase – of a puppy
- Bromley Council spied on a charity shop to see people 'fly tipping' donations at their door.[19]

The authorities that take most advantage of these powers, including county councils in the rankings, are listed in Table 4.6.1. This list shows how surveillance was often greater in councils where the Liberal Democrats hold power or are in coalition. Thus, Labour brought this illiberal law in, but politicians from all the major parties appear often to have had a predilection to use these powers. Map 4.6.3 shows how the use of RIPA has spread out across the country, sometimes from city to countryside but in other places from the country into the city.

The number of times RIPA has been used in these recent years has been falling, but the Act remains law; the new Coalition government appears to have very little wish to fully repeal it. At present use of the Act is restricted, but at present we are living through relatively peaceful times. Try to imagine how RIPA might be used in times of civil strife: if public sector workers were striking against their employers, might employers who have recourse to this legislation use it to spy on their own workers?

RIPA was introduced by one of the most authoritarian administrations to have ruled Britain in recent years. Its introduction pre-dated the 11 September 2001 atrocities. The secret services already had powers far in excess of those included in RIPA and, although their use of those powers may not always have been lawful, the service was secret. What RIPA does is to legitimise spying in the public realm. It makes explicit the belief that people cannot be trusted, that we live in a society where others cannot be trusted to behave well. No other affluent country has surveillance powers as great as the UK now gives its local and national government. In almost all other affluent countries in the world people trust their

Table 4.6.1: 2008/09–2009/10 Most RIPA surveillance operations, local authorities, Britain

Rank	Local Authority	RIPA authorisations 2008/09	RIPA authorisations 2009/10	Total number of uses of RIPA 2008/09–2009/10
1	Newcastle upon Tyne	183	48	231
2	West Berkshire	54	174	228
3	Walsall	119	96	215
4	Oxfordshire	80	112	192
5	Birmingham	81	95	176
6	Bromley	78	72	150
7	Salford	81	68	149
8	Hampshire	82	55	137
9	Kent	75	61	136
10	Sandwell	64	71	135
11	Durham	30	36	124
12	Wandsworth	51	69	120
13	Surrey	67	38	105
14	Camden	79	25	104
15	Liverpool	49	52	101

Map 4.6.3: 2008/09–2009/10 Change in RIPA surveillance operations per 10,000 persons, local authorities, Britain

RIPA change 2008/09–2009/10
(per 10,000 pop)

- -4.9 – -1.1
- -1.0 – -0.1
- 0.0 – 0.9
- 1.0 – 7.9
- No data

RIPA change 2008/09–2009/10	Per 10,000 persons
GREATEST 5 FALLS	
Newcastle upon Tyne	−4.9
Hastings	−2.5
Camden	−2.4
West Oxfordshire	−2.1
West Lindsey	−2.0
GREATEST 5 RISES	
Epsom & Ewell	1.4
Hammersmith & Fulham	1.5
Rotherham	1.6
Fareham	1.8
West Berkshire	7.9

neighbours more than they do in the UK.[20] Perhaps it would be better to build trust rather than mount more surveillance cameras?

4.7 Legalising tax evasion on inheritance

Citizens have a moral duty to pay tax. Tax provides the funding that the state requires to run government, to prevent people starving, to give all citizens an education and a health service. It is the money that stops us descending into anarchy and helps to create the society in which we live. When businesses do not pay their full taxes they secure an unfair advantage over other businesses. Because of this, the last government set up a telephone hotline: 'The Tax Evasion Hotline has been set up to make the most of vital information from YOU – the public and the business community. It deals with Income Tax, Corporation Tax, Capital Gains Tax, Inheritance Tax and National Insurance.'[21] Unfortunately the number (0800 788 887) was not advertised widely, despite tax evasion costing the state hundreds of times more than benefit fraud.

Many citizens try to avoid paying inheritance and other taxes through exploiting loopholes. When this tax avoidance exceeds legal action it is called tax evasion. Evasion can be made legal, and become avoidance, by changes to the law. The law on inheritance tax is being changed to allow the small number of people rich enough for their estates to be liable for inheritance tax to avoid a large part of their share of that tax. Map 4.7.1 shows the rate of payment of inheritance tax per 1,000 deaths in 2007/08. Currently, only about 7% of people have sufficient wealth to have inheritance tax levied on their estates. Half of those people avoid the tax, at least in the short term. In the majority of cases the tax is delayed because a surviving spouse has inherited and the tax applies only upon that spouse's death, and then with a threshold of double the individual allowance. In 2007/08 only 22,210 estates in Britain were found to be eligible for inheritance tax; some 557,499 people died in the calendar year 2007 (which ended a few months before that tax year), thus inheritance tax was payable on the estates of only around 3.98% of people who died in Britain in the latest year for which data exist.[22]

Rich people often spend a lot of money on legal advice and the setting up of trusts to enable them to avoid paying inheritance tax. Figure 4.7.1 shows on how many estates tax was paid by region in the latest year for which we have data. The vast majority of people are not wealthy enough to be liable for inheritance tax.

More than 68,000 people died in one year in the 80 areas shown in the box below. The highest number, over 2,500, were in Hull. In each of these places fewer than 20 people left estates large enough to be liable for inheritance tax; in some of these areas, probably no one will have paid, because almost no one is wealthy. We are almost all victims of tax evasion, but these are the places where the greatest victims of tax evasion, the poor, are most concentrated.

Kingston upon Hull, Caerphilly, Falkirk, Neath Port Talbot, North Ayrshire (mainland), Knowsley, East Ayrshire, Middlesbrough, Redcar & Cleveland, Blackburn with Darwen, West Lothian, Barking & Dagenham, Telford & Wrekin, Halton, Ashfield, West Dunbartonshire, Nuneaton & Bedworth, Ipswich, Great Yarmouth, Tower Hamlets, Chesterfield, Easington, South Holland, Inverclyde, Torfaen, South Bedfordshire, Hartlepool, Derwentside, Burnley, Sedgefield, Gravesham, West Lindsey, Cannock Chase, Blyth Valley, Blaenau Gwent, Bolsover, Lincoln, Pendle, Hyndburn, Slough, Midlothian, Kettering, Wear Valley, Barrow-in-Furness, Copeland, Selby, East Northamptonshire, Boston, Blaby, Durham, Crawley, Wansbeck, Stevenage, Wellingborough, Rossendale, Merthyr Tydfil, Harlow, North Warwickshire, Redditch, Rushmoor, Tamworth, Ross & Cromarty, Caithness & Sutherland, Chester-le-Street, Forest Heath, Corby, Clackmannanshire, Melton, Oswestry, Eilean Siar, Alnwick, Berwick-upon-Tweed, Helensburgh & Lomond, Orkney Islands, Teesdale, West Moray, Shetland Islands, Lochaber, Skye & Lochalsh and Badenoch & Strathspey.

Note: The box is ordered from the greatest number of deaths to the least.

In contrast to the 80 areas above, where, for all recorded purposes, practically no one is rich enough to have inheritance tax levied upon death, Table 4.7.1 lists the 42 areas where the highest proportions of people had inheritance tax levied on their estates, some 5,390 estates in all. These areas account for just 8% of deaths in Britain, and yet some 24% of estates

Figure 4.7.1: 2007/08 Inheritance tax-paying estates, numbers, regions and countries, Britain

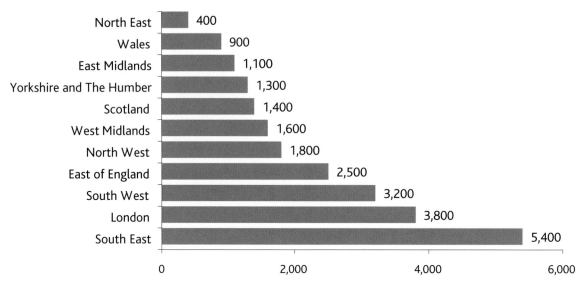

paying inheritance tax can be found in these areas, three times what would be expected were wealth equally spread around the country. The share of inheritance taxation requisitioned from these places will be far higher still because a few people in the wealthiest areas on this list are among the wealthiest people in the country and the world. Map 4.7.2 shows these numbers on the map, but the numbers are deceptive as death rates vary. In Edinburgh tax was found to be due on some 290 estates, for example, but over 4,300 people die each year in Edinburgh, so with only 6.7% paying in the Scottish capital, there are many areas of England where far more are richer and thus even the wealthiest part of Scotland does not feature in this list.

People in Britain are beginning again to wake up to the immorality of extreme wealth. When the man the government appointed to run the nationalised bank RBS, Philip Hampton, tried to defend the astonishingly high pay of top RBS staff there was a great public outcry; simultaneously, the president of Barclays bank, Bob Diamond, 'was described by Lord Mandelson ... as "the unacceptable face of banking" after earning £63 million last year....'[23] Philip Hampton, chairman of RBS, approved of the pay of his chief executive, Stephen Hester, at £4.8 million a year. In comparison to £63 million this is paltry; in comparison to the pay of almost anyone else, it is a fortune. In future, as inheritance tax minima have been raised, the rich will be able to legally pass on to their offspring even more of the wealth they have amassed. This will continue to occur until the law is changed again, and until the law is properly enforced, but most importantly it will continue while paying tax is seen as an unfair burden rather than a civic duty.

Map 4.7.1: 2007/08 Inheritance tax-paying estates per 1,000 persons dying, local authorities, Britain

Taxpaying estates 2007/08
(per 1,000 deaths)
- 5.6 – 24.9
- 25.0 – 49.9
- 50.0 – 99.9
- 100.0 – 149.9
- 150.0 – 176.1
- Data suppressed

Inheritence tax paying estates 2007/08	Per 10,000 deaths
LOWEST 5	
North Lanarkshire	5.6
Sandwell	6.4
Newcastle-under-Lyme	7.5
Rhondda Cynon Taf	7.5
Oldham	9.1
HIGHEST 5	
Richmond upon Thames	143.2
Epsom & Ewell	145.2
South Bucks	151.2
Elmbridge	160.3
Kensington & Chelsea	176.1

Table 4.7.1: 2007/08 Inheritance tax, highest rates, local authorities, Britain

Map 4.7.2: 2007/08 Inheritance tax-paying estates, numbers, local authorities, Britain

Local Authority	Number of taxpaying estates 2007/08	Number of people dying in 2007	Rate per 1000 deaths
Lewes	100	1,056	94.7
Eden	50	527	94.9
Mid Sussex	120	1,258	95.4
Oxford	90	936	96.2
Hertsmere	90	927	97.1
Bromley	270	2,758	97.9
South Oxfordshire	110	1,123	98.0
Rother	130	1,327	98.0
Windsor & Maidenhead	110	1,120	98.2
New Forest	200	2,015	99.3
Wandsworth	170	1,707	99.6
Merton	130	1,285	101.2
East Dorset	100	988	101.2
Hart	60	592	101.4
Hammersmith & Fulham	100	968	103.3
Camden	130	1,252	103.8
Reigate & Banstead	130	1,233	105.4
Tandridge	80	752	106.4
East Hampshire	110	1,030	106.8
Sevenoaks	110	1,030	106.8
Horsham	130	1,209	107.5
Three Rivers	80	739	108.3
West Dorset	130	1,198	108.5
Winchester	120	1,089	110.2
Chiltern	80	723	110.7
Wokingham	110	965	114.0
Cotswold	100	857	116.7
South Hams	110	928	118.5
Chichester	170	1,429	119.0
Guildford	120	990	121.2
Harrow	180	1,464	123.0
Westminster	140	1,127	124.2
Mole Valley	110	840	131.0
Barnet	320	2,374	134.8
Kingston upon Thames	150	1,111	135.0
St Albans	140	1,006	139.2
Waverley	150	1,073	139.8
Richmond upon Thames	170	1,187	143.2
Epsom & Ewell	80	551	145.2
South Bucks	80	529	151.2
Elmbridge	180	1,123	160.3
Kensington & Chelsea	150	852	176.1

Taxpaying estates 2007/08 (number)
- 20 – 49
- 50 – 99
- 100 – 149
- 150 – 199
- 200 – 320
- Data suppressed

Chapter 5 Emotionally bankrupt

Introduction

In this chapter we consider mental (and physical) health and well-being. We begin by looking at how the answers to the first ever official large-scale happiness survey varied across the country in which it was trialled: England. We find that reported levels of happiness appeared highest in the south of England, but this was mainly when happiness was reflected through the answers people gave to a question about their subjective views on their state of health. In responding to this question people took into account issues such as how age affects health, thus the survey is not about their actual, physically measurable, state of health but is much more subjective, about how they feel. It sometimes does not correlate well with actual health statistics for each area.

Subjective health and well-being questions in effect measure how people feel on a scale that includes 'mustn't grumble' and 'bloody awful'. And what determines people's average answers to these questions appears to be how deprived they and their area are, or how fortunate they feel given what they know of others' circumstances. The formula for happiness that we describe below is that the percentage of people in an area who are happy approximates to 82%, less three tenths of the official deprivation score. What is then of interest is where people are happier or less happy, given their lot in life, or the variation from this trend line. We suggest that in London, possibly because of its high rate of in-migrants, optimism is more common. In contrast, factors such as not attracting enough immigrants, insularity, and having to make long commuter journeys can be guessed at as possible explanations for the disparate collection of places where fewer people are happy than we might otherwise expect.

We next find that, conversely, children's emotional health appears to be worse in just those places where that of adults is best, all else considered. Very possibly children detest being moved between cities and countries almost as much as many adults enjoy it. Thus within London are found the highest proportions of children whose emotional health is said to have been damaged by lack of friendships and lack of people to confide in. In contrast, in some of the most deprived parts of the country, where on the plus side as a child you are likely to have been born rather than to have moved there, friendships are more solid and emotional health appears better; but much more is going on than this. Everywhere in Britain between autumn 2008 and 2009 the emotional health of children worsened. Children appeared to be picking up on the heightened economic, societal and maybe even political concerns of their parents and of society as a whole. Many more children in 2009 appeared to have concerns which they could not address or find someone close to talk over with, compared with a year earlier.

Emotional bankruptcy is a state a nation approaches when the mental health and well-being of both adults and children appears to be deteriorating rapidly. Among children it might be expected that this might express itself in heightened under-age alcohol consumption, illegal drug use and the abuse of other legal but potentially harmful substances. However, when we look at the geographical patterns of such abuse we find no easy correlations with high local levels of emotional vulnerability. The highest use is not found where you might expect, nor is there any simple pattern of change over time, but there is an interesting set of patterns nevertheless. Sadly the patterns shown here will be the last for some time, as the survey about children's use of substances and their emotional health that these statistics come from was itself being cut during autumn 2010.

Statistics of how many antidepressants are dispensed to adults and a few older children are likely to continue for some time (as the state has to pay much of the immediate bill). Dispensing rates are highest within parts of Wales, where previous research found reported levels of limiting illness were highest in comparison to mortality rates.[1] We speculate that there will be comparably sized areas within Glasgow where the rates of prescription will be even higher. What we do know is that, everywhere in Britain where antidepressant use was measured in a consistent way between 2007 and 2010, use was found to be rising. The same finding is replicated when rates of dispensing prescriptions for any medicines are considered. Again rates of use are highest in Wales, in those places where needs are most acute, but again this suggests we should consider why people are in need of so many more medicines everywhere. It is not simply that the population is ageing or that more drug treatments are becoming available. People are also becoming sicker as a whole, most quickly in the poorest areas. Something about the way we live is making more of us feel ill everywhere, and more mentally ill than physically ill. The geographical ubiquity of very poor mental health resulting in the need to use acute services (discussed in Section 5.6) adds weight to the various arguments, growing in strength recently, that the way we live is making us ill.

The main palliative on offer from the new government of 2010 was the 'Big Society': volunteering or getting involved in the community, they suggest, should be enough to get us through tough economic conditions, improving our overall well-being along the way. To investigate this we end this chapter by looking at the geographical patterns to volunteering and civic participation in Britain and England, and find them to be very different from each other as there are very different ways in which people can get involved in society. We also find that some of the areas in which the lowest levels of both volunteering and civic participation are found are also some of the places where adults find the most time to talk to their children and where children are most likely to have friends (in what could be called the 'Little Society'). For instance, Sunderland – which we discover here to be one of the areas with the highest childhood emotional well-being – is in the bottom five for both civic participation and volunteering. Perhaps adults were spending too long with their children here to be 'doing good' for others. Perhaps some ways of doing good are good, and others are more annoying. It is even possible that a society that moves more towards seeing charity as the answer to social ills is becoming a society in which more and more people become ill as a consequence of the insecurity that relying on charity instils.

5.1 The 'happiness survey': adult subjective health and well-being

Map 5.1.1 shows how many people replied 'very good' or 'good' to the question 'How is your health in general? Would you say it is ... very good, good, fair, bad or very bad?' when surveyed in England between 1 January and 31 December 2008. Figure 5.1.1 shows the exact wording of the question. The question is as much about well-being as health: someone who is feeling upbeat is more likely to reply positively to the question. The Place Survey was cancelled in August 2010. This seems a curious decision in light of the Coalition government's intention to measure happiness in the UK.

Figure 5.1.1: 2008 The Place Survey overall health/well-being question

Q29	How is your health in general? Would you say it is......
PLEASE TICK ✓ ☒ ONE BOX ONLY	

Very good	Good	Fair	Bad	Very bad
☒	☒	☒	☒	☒

We have included this map at the start of this chapter because it is the first ever official 'happiness map' of a nation within Britain. The map excludes Scotland and Wales because this was an initiative of the Department for Communities and Local Government (DCLG), whose remit only covers England. Look closely at Map 5.1.1 and notice just how smooth the geographical patterns are. Very large numbers of people have been asked about their general state of health in each place, and when you ask such large numbers of people a question such as this and average the responses, you iron out almost all of the variation that chance produces. The questions cannot all have been asked on a particularly sunny day in each place, nor been asked of a small and unrepresentative group of people. That is not to say idiosyncrasies will not remain: why should more people report good health in Bradford than in Leeds, for instance? However, when asking such questions of particular areas it is worth remembering such facts as that the administrative boundary of Bradford extends right up into what might otherwise be called North Yorkshire, and people in North Yorkshire do not appear to fare badly. Neither is this map of health/well-being simply a map reflecting old age. If it were, North Yorkshire people would

Map 5.1.1: 2008 Overall health and well-being (%), by local authorities, England

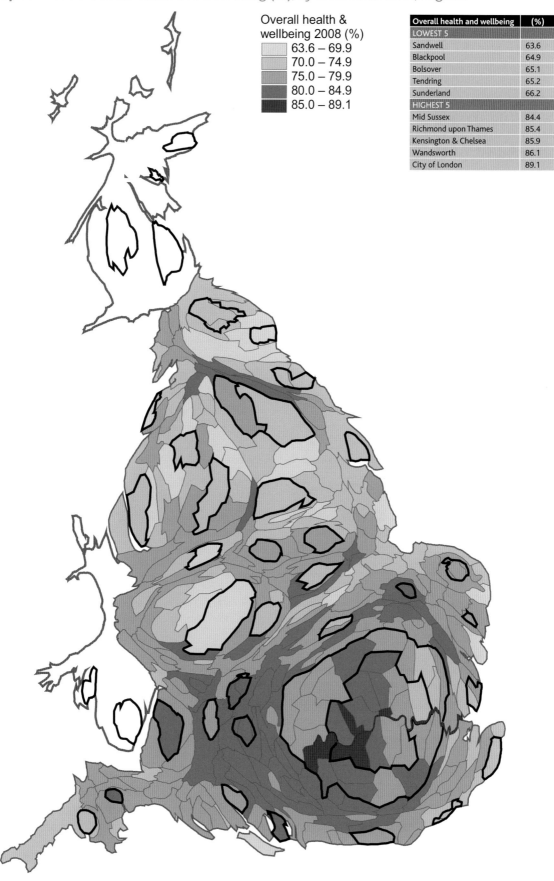

Overall health &
wellbeing 2008 (%)

	63.6 – 69.9
	70.0 – 74.9
	75.0 – 79.9
	80.0 – 84.9
	85.0 – 89.1

Overall health and wellbeing	(%)
LOWEST 5	
Sandwell	63.6
Blackpool	64.9
Bolsover	65.1
Tendring	65.2
Sunderland	66.2
HIGHEST 5	
Mid Sussex	84.4
Richmond upon Thames	85.4
Kensington & Chelsea	85.9
Wandsworth	86.1
City of London	89.1

be complaining more because of the creaks in older joints, and all the other ailments that come with age generally.

What the answers to the question mainly reflect are local levels of deprivation. The simplest of linear regression models explains the bulk of the variance. We've drawn a line in the graph in Figure 5.1.2 to show this linear regression model. This line shows the level of well-being as approximately 82% minus three tenths of the official deprivation score (IMD, ranges between 4 and 47). The average district level of well-being ranges from 64% to 89%. The graph show how closely deprivation and individual subjective well-being relate (the correlation is −0.62).

Figure 5.1.2: 2008 Health/well-being by deprivation, local authorities, England

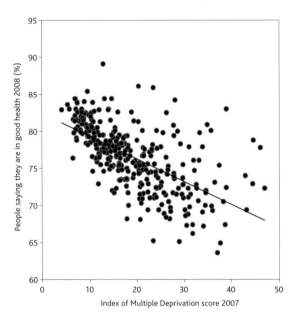

Self-reported health/well-being levels were good or very good for 89.1% of those surveyed in the City of London, officially the best place for general health/well-being in Britain in 2008. In its penultimate year in office New Labour really did ensure that bankers were happier than anyone else! So, although our regression model says that the best level you can ever achieve is 82% of people reporting their health/well-being as good or very good, with models there is always a slight error. It is more accurate to say the proportion with good health/well-being tends to be $82.411\% - 0.307 \star \text{IMD} +/-$ up to 6%, except in the dozen areas listed in Table 5.1.1 as those where

more people reported good or very good levels of health/well-being than would be predicted given the local levels of deprivation and those where fewer did.

The table shows that in Islington, for example, one in eight more people than you would expect (given local levels of deprivation) report good or very good levels of health and well-being. Apart from Bristol, all of these 'better than expected' areas are in London. Bristol stood out as being more optimistically inclined in the original work on a 'misery index' undertaken by researchers in the University of York many years ago.[2] However, now, right across London, including in the second and third poorest boroughs in the country (Hackney and Tower Hamlets), far more people report good health than would be the case if it were just deprivation that mattered. What all these areas, including Bristol, benefit from is an influx of immigrant optimists. By contrast, the most deprived district in England, Liverpool, sees 4.3% less people reporting good or very good health than would be expected from local levels of deprivation. However, Liverpool does not even make it into the top 12 cities shown in Table 5.1.1 as having unusually low rates of well-being (given their 'lot'). What this may partly reflect is the leaving of that city over many years of those looking for better lives.

There are all kinds of reasons why places might rank in the bottom dozen places. One or two may be there by chance, with surveyors having selected a particularly gloomy sample, and the result would not be confirmed on a repeat survey. An area where people are less aware of how much worse things could be will probably also return a lower score. Notably many areas in the bottom 12 have particularly low immigrant populations. Conversely an area which is more acutely aware of how much better things could be would also tend to score badly: the opposite of the residents of Kensington & Chelsea thinking, rightly or wrongly, that 'it can't get better than this'.

What does not kill you might in certain circumstances make you stronger, but it might also make you a little more bitter. Similarly, almost unbounded optimism that tomorrow will be better may make it easier to get through today in some of the roughest parts of London, but faith and hope alone will not make life better. It is not good to feel more down than you need to, but also not always good to feel too positive either, if there are good reasons not to be so cheerful. We can be emotionally bankrupt by having a deficit of understanding and a surplus of optimism, just as much as by having too much pessimism or *schadenfreude*.

Table 5.1.1: Local authorities in England where health/well-being levels are most different from those predicted by deprivation rates

Rank	Place	IMD score	Healthy (%)	Residual (%)	IMD rank
Areas where more extra people report good health/wellbeing than deprivation rates predict:					
1	Islington	39.0	83.0	12.5	8
2	Kensington & Chelsea	23.5	85.9	10.7	101
3	City of London	12.8	89.1	10.6	252
4	Hammersmith & Fulham	28.1	84.2	10.4	59
5	Tower Hamlets	44.6	78.8	10.1	3
6	Wandsworth	20.3	86.1	9.9	144
7	Hackney	46.1	77.8	9.5	2
8	Lambeth	34.9	80.9	9.2	19
9	Haringey	35.7	80.1	8.7	18
10	Westminster	26.3	82.5	8.2	72
11	Southwark	33.3	79.8	7.6	26
12	Bristol	27.8	80.8	6.9	64
Areas where fewer people report good health/wellbeing than deprivation rates predict:					
12	Wigan	26.9	68.2	−5.9	67
11	Blackpool	37.7	64.9	−6.0	12
10	Corby	26.2	68.4	−6.0	75
9	Kettering	15.1	71.7	−6.1	214
8	Waveney	22.3	69.4	−6.2	114
7	Sunderland	31.8	66.2	−6.5	35
6	Amber Valley	18.1	70.0	−6.8	159
5	Sandwell	37.0	63.6	−7.4	14
4	Isle of Wight	20.7	68.1	−8.0	134
3	Bolsover	28.9	65.1	−8.4	55
2	Wellingborough	17.8	68.2	−8.8	168
1	Tendring	23.4	65.2	−10.0	103

5.2 Children's emotional health

In the very same years that the DCLG surveyed a very large group of adults (the Place Survey) in England to determine their well-being, the then Department for Children, Schools and Families was arranging to survey very large numbers of youngsters to try to gauge their emotional health and how it was changing in the annual TellUs survey: 'TellUs is a representative sample of pupils in School Years 6, 8 and 10 in maintained schools, including academies and pupil referral units (PRUs), in a local area. Tellus4 survey took place in schools in autumn 2009'.[3] Note that 'maintained schools' means state schools, including church schools.

According to this 'TellUs' survey, a child is said to have good emotional health if they answered 'true' to having one or more good friends and to at least two of three statements about being able to talk to their parents, friends or another adult. These statements were:

- 'When I'm worried about something I can talk to my mum or dad.'

- 'When I'm worried about something I can talk to my friends.'

- 'When I'm worried about something I can talk to an adult other than my mum or dad.'

The options given to answer these questions in autumn 2009 were: 'True/Neither true nor not true/Not true/Don't know', the same as in the

TellUs3 survey in autumn 2008, and so the statistics are comparable over time for these two years. The results, shown in Map 5.2.1 imply that everywhere children's emotional health was becoming worse between autumn 2008 and autumn 2009. Figure 5.2.1 shows the exact form of the questions asked.

The largest falls in children's emotional well-being were recorded in generally affluent Poole (14.3% fewer doing well), and the next largest in much poorer Hackney (down 13.8%). The only place where there was no rise in poor emotional health was in Bromley, where the proportion stayed at exactly 54.6% being able to answer 'yes' to having friends and being able to talk to them and an adult about worries. So even in Bromley 45.4% of children aged 11 to 15 could not do this. The smallest increases were in Shropshire (1.3% more unhappy); Warwickshire (1.2% more); Gloucestershire (1.2% more), Wiltshire (0.7% more) and Bedfordshire (0.6% more).

In great contrast to adults, the lowest levels of good emotional well-being in children were found within London by 2009. The lowest levels in the country[4] were in Hackney (just 49.4% happy); Richmond upon Thames (49.6%); Brent (49.7%), Newham (49.8%) and Lambeth (49.9%). In all these boroughs a majority of children said they either had no good friends or that they could not talk to a friend or adult over worries. It is possible that the very things that make adults in many of these areas more optimistic than most – for example, being a new arrival – make children lonelier.

Figure 5.2.1: Question on children's emotional health from TellUs survey

16. Please read each sentence below and tick the box next to it to show if it is true for you or not true for you.

Where we mention your mum and dad, we mean either your parents or the person/people, such as step parents, carers or grandparents who you live with and who look after you most of the time.

PLEASE TICK **ONE** BOX ON EACH LINE

	True	Neither true nor not true	Not true	Don't know
I feel happy about life at the moment	O	O	O	O
I have one or more good friends	O	O	O	O
When I'm worried about something I can talk to my mum or dad	O	O	O	O
When I'm worried about something I can talk to my friends	O	O	O	O
When I'm worried about something I can talk to an adult who isn't my mum or dad	O	O	O	O

Map 5.2.1: 2008–09 Children's emotional health change (% point), local authorities, England

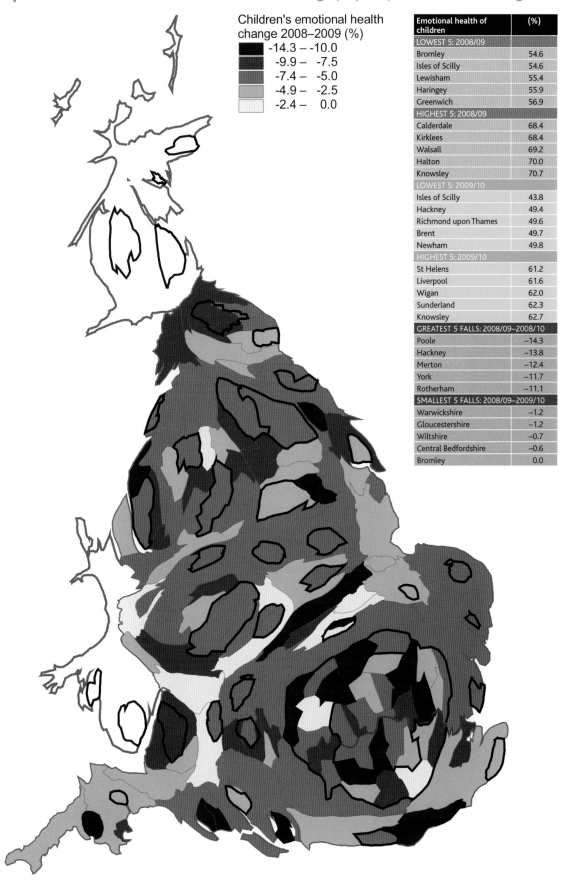

Children's emotional health change 2008–2009 (%)

- -14.3 – -10.0
- -9.9 – -7.5
- -7.4 – -5.0
- -4.9 – -2.5
- -2.4 – 0.0

Emotional health of children	(%)
LOWEST 5: 2008/09	
Bromley	54.6
Isles of Scilly	54.6
Lewisham	55.4
Haringey	55.9
Greenwich	56.9
HIGHEST 5: 2008/09	
Calderdale	68.4
Kirklees	68.4
Walsall	69.2
Halton	70.0
Knowsley	70.7
LOWEST 5: 2009/10	
Isles of Scilly	43.8
Hackney	49.4
Richmond upon Thames	49.6
Brent	49.7
Newham	49.8
HIGHEST 5: 2009/10	
St Helens	61.2
Liverpool	61.6
Wigan	62.0
Sunderland	62.3
Knowsley	62.7
GREATEST 5 FALLS: 2008/09–2008/10	
Poole	−14.3
Hackney	−13.8
Merton	−12.4
York	−11.7
Rotherham	−11.1
SMALLEST 5 FALLS: 2008/09–2009/10	
Warwickshire	−1.2
Gloucestershire	−1.2
Wiltshire	−0.7
Central Bedfordshire	−0.6
Bromley	0.0

Unless you bear the importance of making and being able to keep friends in mind, then the five areas with the highest levels of child well-being in 2009 might be a little unexpected. Remember that adults were more likely even than their general levels of deprivation would suggest to report low levels of health/well-being in Liverpool? Well, the five areas of England where children had the best emotional health were: St Helens (61.2%), Liverpool (61.6%), Wigan (62.0%), Sunderland (62.3%) and Knowsley (62.7%). None of these are affluent places, but they are all places where children are much more likely (than is common in England) to both have friends and to be able to talk to them or an adult about their worries.

Map 5.2.2 and Map 5.2.3 show the distributions of childhood emotional well-being across England at both dates. For any particular borough, the rate going up or down in just one year may not be very meaningful; it is the wider patterns that are more striking. Four of the five districts with the lowest levels of child well-being in 2008 were in London; and among the areas at the other end of the scale, where well-being was greatest, all were still poorer parts of the North of England. Knowsley was the place that rated the best.

Nationally, across all of England 62.6% of children were doing well in autumn 2008, which fell to 56.0% by autumn 2009. As mentioned earlier, there will be no opportunity to compare results for autumn 2010 or subsequent years as the TellUs Survey has now been cancelled.

Map 5.2.2: 2008 Children's emotional health (%), local authorities, England

Children's emotional health 2008 (%)
54.6 – 59.9
60.0 – 64.9
65.0 – 69.9
70.0 – 70.7

Map 5.2.3: 2009 Children's emotional health (%), local authorities, England

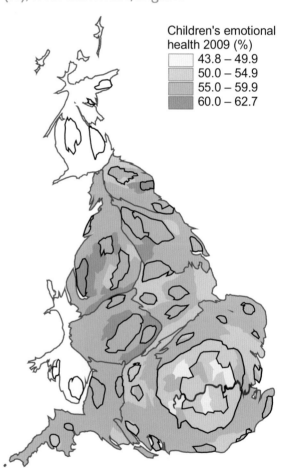

Children's emotional health 2009 (%)
43.8 – 49.9
50.0 – 54.9
55.0 – 59.9
60.0 – 62.7

5.3 Children using drugs, alcohol and/or volatile substances

A small number of children frequently misuse drugs, volatile substances (such as sniffing glue) and/or alcohol, or even use all three, and admit to this in surveys. Because the same questions were asked for huge numbers of school children in England in autumn 2008 and autumn 2009 we can produce Map 5.3.1, which shows how the rates of substance abuse have been changing in recent years. Because the TellUs survey that recorded these reports was disbanded so abruptly during summer 2010 we will not be able to draw similar maps to these again or to know whether it is unusual to have so many children using particular substances in one place or another, to be able to sense whether something is changing, not based on anecdote, but on the systematic collection of data.

The five largest increases in the reporting of substance abuse between autumn 2008 and autumn 2009 occurred in local authorities as disparate as Bristol (up 5.6%), the Scilly Isles (up 5.5%), the unitary authority of Thurrock (up 5.4%), the county of North Yorkshire (up 4.8%) and the London Borough of Croydon (up 4.5%). Substance abuse is thus not something which only occurs in the urban ghettos of the poor. A great many children and parents live in the areas where, in just one year, an extra five or six children in every hundred (two more in every classroom) were reporting using drugs, alcohol or other hallucinogenics as compared to the numbers of children sitting in those very same seats a year earlier. Note that in the survey the year 6 children (aged around 11) are not asked about drug abuse, just about abuse of the other two substances.

The five largest falls in the year 2008–09 were in similarly disparate places: in Darlington (3.8%), Oldham (4.1%), Bromley (4.4%), St Helens (5.4%) and Reading (7.2%). Again, these places of extreme change are spread right around the country. If you compare the maps of children's emotional health shown in Section 5.2 with these maps of their substance abuse you will see that at the geographical level there appear to be no strong connections. We cannot predict from other data why these rates rise or fall as they do. Why have the falls generally been greater east of the Pennines, for example? There could have been more effective programmes in Hull to prevent shops selling alcohol to under-age people, or the regulations there on buying products you can sniff might have been better enforced in 2009 as compared with 2008.

Map 5.3.2 shows levels of reported substance abuse in 2008, Map 5.3.3 those levels in 2009. In 2008 substance abuse was most common in the metropolitan districts of Barnsley, St Helens and Wakefield, where between one in six and one in seven children reported substance abuse during their later school years. Contrast this with Bracknell Forest, Tower Hamlets and Haringey, where fewer than 3% of all children reported such substance abuse. Perhaps the children of these boroughs are a little too streetwise to report their behaviour in a survey? By 2009 two of these three districts were still among the ten areas with the lowest rates in the country. Either children in different year groups were colluding over a 12-month period to deceive us, or this survey really was telling adults something they didn't know about children growing up in very different parts of England.

Map 5.3.1: 2008–09 Change in reported substance misuse by young people aged 11–15 (% point), local authorities, England

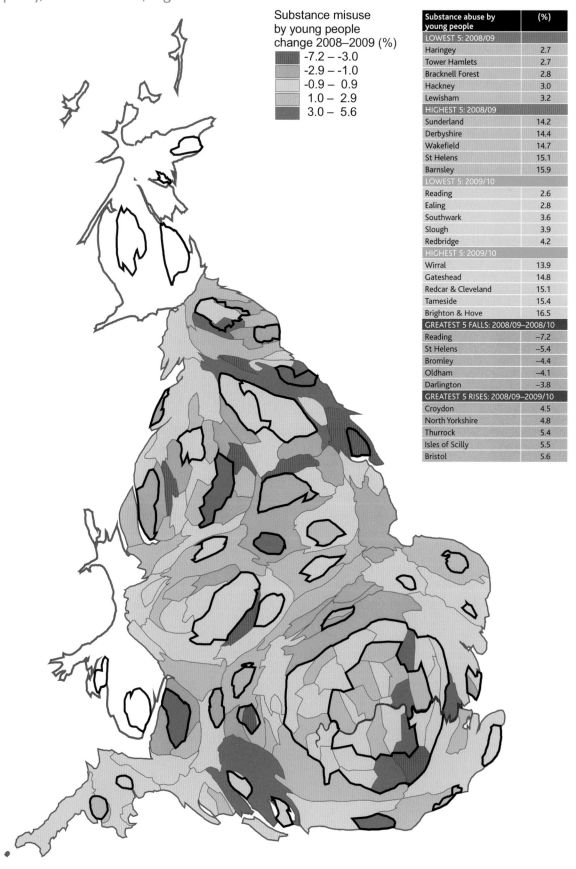

Substance misuse
by young people
change 2008–2009 (%)

- -7.2 – -3.0
- -2.9 – -1.0
- -0.9 – 0.9
- 1.0 – 2.9
- 3.0 – 5.6

Substance abuse by young people	(%)
LOWEST 5: 2008/09	
Haringey	2.7
Tower Hamlets	2.7
Bracknell Forest	2.8
Hackney	3.0
Lewisham	3.2
HIGHEST 5: 2008/09	
Sunderland	14.2
Derbyshire	14.4
Wakefield	14.7
St Helens	15.1
Barnsley	15.9
LOWEST 5: 2009/10	
Reading	2.6
Ealing	2.8
Southwark	3.6
Slough	3.9
Redbridge	4.2
HIGHEST 5: 2009/10	
Wirral	13.9
Gateshead	14.8
Redcar & Cleveland	15.1
Tameside	15.4
Brighton & Hove	16.5
GREATEST 5 FALLS: 2008/09–2008/10	
Reading	−7.2
St Helens	−5.4
Bromley	−4.4
Oldham	−4.1
Darlington	−3.8
GREATEST 5 RISES: 2008/09–2009/10	
Croydon	4.5
North Yorkshire	4.8
Thurrock	5.4
Isles of Scilly	5.5
Bristol	5.6

Map 5.3.2: 2008 Reported substance misuse by young people aged 11–15 (%), local authorities, England

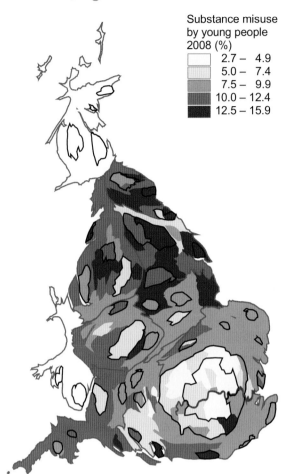

Substance misuse
by young people
2008 (%)
2.7 – 4.9
5.0 – 7.4
7.5 – 9.9
10.0 – 12.4
12.5 – 15.9

Map 5.3.3: 2009 Reported substance misuse by young people aged 11–15 (%), local authorities, England

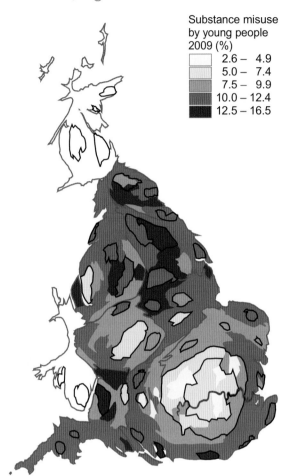

Substance misuse
by young people
2009 (%)
2.6 – 4.9
5.0 – 7.4
7.5 – 9.9
10.0 – 12.4
12.5 – 16.5

5.4   Adults popping pills to ward off ills

Children are far from alone in seeking out substances that help them to escape reality. Adults abuse far greater quantities of alcohol and drugs than children ever physically could withstand, or could afford to pay for. Such behaviour when undertaken by adults is often referred to as 'self-medicating'. Alcohol far outstrips any other legal or illegal drug in terms of how much is consumed by adults in Britain.

In different parts of Britain the differing national agencies record information on the prescriptions of antidepressant drugs in very different ways, release the data at different times, and have done so for differing year definitions – calendar or financial. The only year for which we can draw a map of all of Britain is the 2008/09 financial year shown in Map 5.4.1 and even then we can only use the crude measure of items prescribed. We have combined these with population data to best estimate where the fewest and most people aged 15 or over who were taking antidepressants were. Private prescriptions are not included here, nor medication secured over the internet, or acquired in other ways. Note that in England, the areas reported are Primary Care Trusts, in Scotland, NHS boards, and in Wales, Local Health Boards.

When measurement is simply by the number of items dispensed, the highest rates of antidepressant use are found in Wales. Rates are highest in Bridgend, Torfaen and Blaenau Gwent, where across all the population more than 1.5 items were prescribed per person in the 2008/09 financial year. This average includes a few people who were prescribed many items while a majority would have had none. The highest rates in England were recorded for Blackpool (1.23 per person in that year), Salford (1.14) and Gateshead (1.08). The highest rates in Scotland were for Greater Glasgow & the Clyde (1.09), Dumfries & Galloway (1.06) and Lanarkshire (1.04 per person per year when averaged out). Note that Glasgow is a far larger area than any of the Welsh or English districts mentioned above. Within Glasgow there will almost certainly be some areas with populations the size of Blackpool and Bridgend where the prescription rate is even higher than in those towns, but the statistics within Scotland are not further disaggregated.

On the map, rates are lowest within London and in parts of Birmingham. The lowest rates in England (three to four times lower than the highest) were recorded in Kensington & Chelsea, Ealing and Redbridge (but remember that private prescriptions were not included in this dataset). It is very probable that people are likely to have to leave London if they fall ill and become depressed for any great length of time. Those who are finding life hard are much more likely to leave or move home than are people living elsewhere in Britain. Blackpool, Bridgend and Glasgow are often places where people end up after having fallen down on their luck elsewhere.

The problem of simply comparing items prescribed is that different items of medicine can contain different numbers of pills meant to be used over differing time periods and are often of varying strengths. Outside of England this issue has been addressed. Map 5.4.2 shows how the prescription and dispensing of comparable defined daily doses of antidepressants changed in Wales and Scotland from 2007/08 to 2008/09; we have no figures yet of this measure for 2009/10. We do know that before then everywhere rates of use rose. This is true whether we are counting items or doses, but precisely where the rises were greatest and least depends on how we count the drugs that are thought to work.

Item use rose the most in: Torfaen, Merthyr Tydfil and Rhondda Cynon Taff, with an extra item being prescribed a year for every ten people living there. A single item can, of course, constitute enough pills for a course of treatment, or just enough for a week. The smallest increases in items prescribed were in Lothian, Grampian and Flintshire. By defined daily dose, use increased the most in two different parts of Wales, and one that featured in the list above. In 2008/09 in Blaenau Gwent, Neath Port Talbot and Merthyr Tydfil, an extra eight to ten comparable doses a day were being prescribed for every 1,000 residents aged 15 or over. Thus in these places the average extra item contained more doses than elsewhere. The smallest increases by this measure were not in Scotland but in Wales – in Denbighshire, Monmouthshire and Pembrokeshire – of only an extra one or two doses per 1,000 people per day. Still there were *no falls*. But in these more rural parts of Wales, people visit the pharmacist more often to get less each time, whereas in more urban areas counting by item underestimates dosage. All this is worth

Map 5.4.1: 2008/09 Antidepressants prescribed (number of items per person aged over 15 years), primary care trusts/health boards, Britain

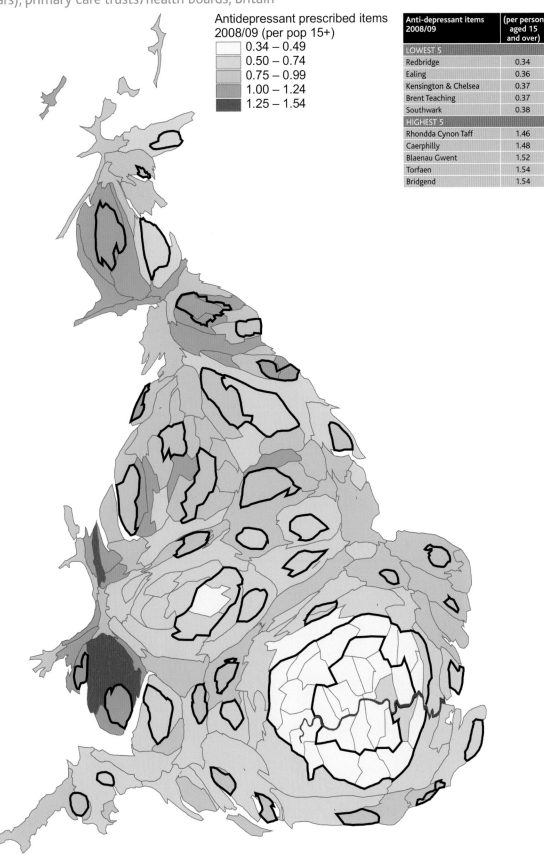

Antidepressant prescribed items
2008/09 (per pop 15+)

0.34 – 0.49	
0.50 – 0.74	
0.75 – 0.99	
1.00 – 1.24	
1.25 – 1.54	

Anti-depressant items 2008/09	(per person aged 15 and over)
LOWEST 5	
Redbridge	0.34
Ealing	0.36
Kensington & Chelsea	0.37
Brent Teaching	0.37
Southwark	0.38
HIGHEST 5	
Rhondda Cynon Taff	1.46
Caerphilly	1.48
Blaenau Gwent	1.52
Torfaen	1.54
Bridgend	1.54

bearing in mind when considering the picture of change in England where all we can count are items.

Map 5.4.3 shows how many more items were being dispensed in each part of England in 2009/10 as compared with 2008/09; the most recent figures for items in Scotland and Wales were not released at the time of writing. The 12 largest rises per capita were all in areas in the North, in order: Gateshead (up 0.14), Blackpool, Redcar & Cleveland, Sunderland, County Durham, Barnsley, Knowsley, North Tyneside, Middlesbrough, Salford, South Tyneside and Newcastle (up 0.10). The next largest rise was in Swindon (where many jobs had very recently been lost). *Nowhere in England were any falls recorded.*

Everywhere emotional bankruptcy was on the rise. The half dozen lowest rises were in: Brent (0.03), Sutton & Merton, Harrow, City & Hackney, Camden and Lambeth (0.02). Worse still, note that the rises here may appear lower partly because more is now being dispensed per item in London than was the case a year earlier.

Figure 5.4.1 shows how the recent slowdown in prescribing in Scotland, which was prompted by a target to try and maintain prescription at 2006 levels,[5] has subsequently ended. With the current recession, prescriptions are rising rapidly again in Scotland, as no doubt would be found across the UK were comparable statistics available.

Map 5.4.2: 2007/08–2008/09 Change in defined daily doses of antidepressants prescribed (per 1,000 population aged over 15 years), health boards, Scotland and Wales

Map 5.4.3: 2008/09–2009/10 Change in antidepressants prescribed (number of items per person aged over 15 years), primary care trusts, England.

Figure 5.4.1: 1992–2009 Antidepressant doses dispensed by NHS per 1,000 persons per day, Scotland

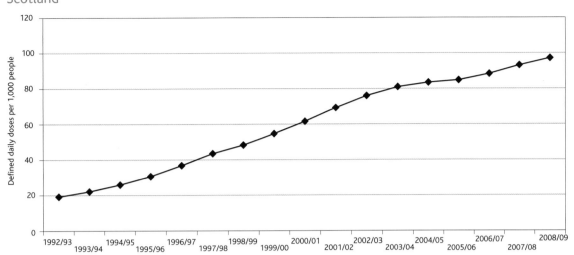

5.5 Taking medicines for any ills at any age

The rise in prescriptions of antidepressants partly reflects a rise in the prescriptions of medicines in general. The highest rises in the latest period we have data for, 2007/08 to 2008/09, were found in the North East of England and especially along or near the East Coast main-line in Darlington, Peterborough, Sunderland, Middlesbrough and Redcar & Cleveland. Here, by the second 12-month period, an extra two or more items were being prescribed per person as compared with the earlier 12 months. These areas are among those where rates of antidepressant prescriptions have also been shown to be very high and where antidepressant use was found to have had the greatest increase recently. Map 5.5.1 shows just how strongly clustered changes in overall prescription levels are. They react to changing local circumstances: rising despair, ageing and other causes of increased need among patients. Nowhere have prescription rates fallen over this period. The smallest rises, all of at least a fifth of the largest above, were recorded in Islington, Grampian, Southampton City, Mid Essex, Kensington & Chelsea and Camden.

Numbers of prescriptions being given for medicines are rising everywhere because almost everywhere the population is ageing, because more treatments become available over time and because in particular places people's health is deteriorating, not least as rates of depression increase.[6] As Figure 5.5.1 shows, rates for the dispensing of medicines have traditionally been higher in Wales, because people there have tended to suffer more illness due to the industrial past of that country, but also because more of the illnesses suffered in Wales have not resulted in higher rates of premature death. Rates in Scotland have been lower, and have fallen in comparison to Wales, almost certainly because significant numbers of people in Scotland are, on average, not seeking as much help for ailments as they should. One reason for this might have been that, although the prescription fee in Scotland has been reduced since 2008, in Wales prescriptions have been free since April 2007. Rates of dispensing are slightly lower in England, but they are following the trend of Wales; this is despite there still being a fee for prescriptions in England. Of course, certain groups of people, such as children, those over the age of 60 and those in receipt of certain benefits, are exempt from prescription charges.

The statistics being shown here are simply items dispensed for England and Scotland, but for Wales they are items prescribed, so to allow comparison we have applied the national rate at which prescriptions become medicines dispensed at each point (about 95%). Map 5.5.2 and Map 5.5.3 show the national distribution of where the most and least items were dispensed in both 2007/08 and 2008/09. The two maps are very similar because the patterns of need by area do not change rapidly over time. In 2008/09 Blackpool just beat former leader, Bridgend, to top

Figure 5.5.1: 2002–09 Prescription items per person per year (national averages), countries

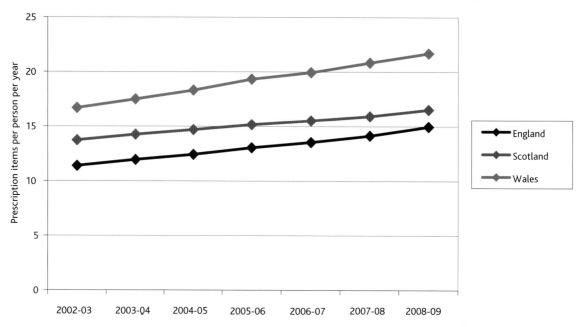

place, with an average of 25 items being prescribed per person per year in both areas. Merthyr and Blaenau also swapped third and fourth places but Ceredigion remained in fifth (23.5 per person per year). At the bottom of the table the three lowest dispensing areas remained the same at 11, 9 and 8 items per person per year being dispensed respectively in Buckinghamshire (generally affluent), Camden (often transient) and Kensington & Chelsea (occasionally super-rich).

We end with an extract from a newspaper report written recently by a pharmacist based in Cardiff on why it is so much better for prescriptions to be free to all:

It was extremely difficult for a pharmacist to be put in a situation where a patient who had been prescribed three items by a GP could only afford to buy two of them.

In this situation a pharmacist had to work out, in partnership with the patient, which item they should leave behind. When all the prescribed items were important to the patient's health this was an impossible situation. It was clear to any pharmacist put in this situation that prescriptions charges were a barrier to better health. For pharmacists – who have always been uneasy about their role as tax collectors for the government – the advent of free prescriptions has made their lives and the lives of their patients so much easier. Patients no longer need to complete complicated declaration forms written in small print on the back of prescription forms before they receive their medication and the administration processes in pharmacy and in the pricing bureau have been made so much easier.[7]

Prescription charges only save money in the very short term and in a very small-minded fashion.

Map 5.5.1: 2007/08–2008/09 Change in all prescriptions dispensed (per person per year), primary care trusts/health boards, Britain

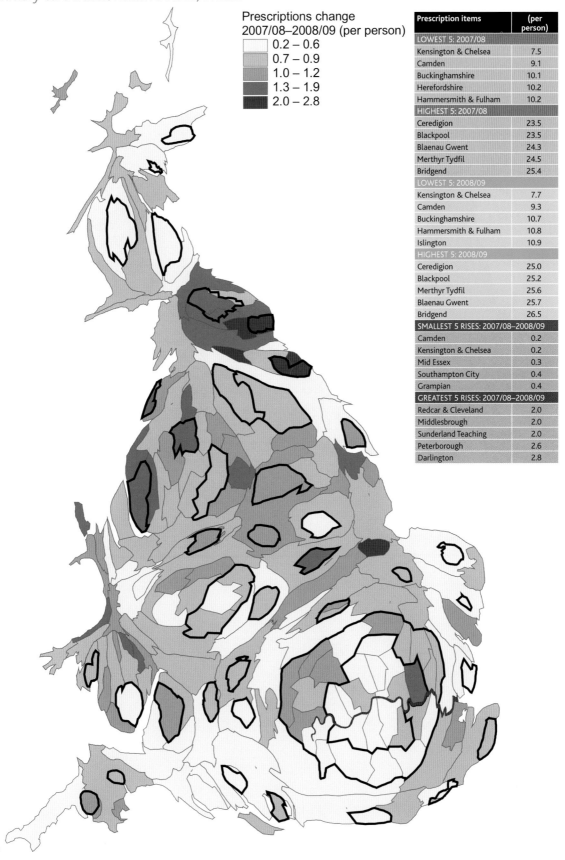

Prescriptions change
2007/08–2008/09 (per person)

- 0.2 – 0.6
- 0.7 – 0.9
- 1.0 – 1.2
- 1.3 – 1.9
- 2.0 – 2.8

Prescription items	(per person)
LOWEST 5: 2007/08	
Kensington & Chelsea	7.5
Camden	9.1
Buckinghamshire	10.1
Herefordshire	10.2
Hammersmith & Fulham	10.2
HIGHEST 5: 2007/08	
Ceredigion	23.5
Blackpool	23.5
Blaenau Gwent	24.3
Merthyr Tydfil	24.5
Bridgend	25.4
LOWEST 5: 2008/09	
Kensington & Chelsea	7.7
Camden	9.3
Buckinghamshire	10.7
Hammersmith & Fulham	10.8
Islington	10.9
HIGHEST 5: 2008/09	
Ceredigion	25.0
Blackpool	25.2
Merthyr Tydfil	25.6
Blaenau Gwent	25.7
Bridgend	26.5
SMALLEST 5 RISES: 2007/08–2008/09	
Camden	0.2
Kensington & Chelsea	0.2
Mid Essex	0.3
Southampton City	0.4
Grampian	0.4
GREATEST 5 RISES: 2007/08–2008/09	
Redcar & Cleveland	2.0
Middlesbrough	2.0
Sunderland Teaching	2.0
Peterborough	2.6
Darlington	2.8

Map 5.5.2: 2007/08 Prescriptions dispensed (per person per year), primary care trusts/ health boards, Britain

Map 5.5.3: 2008/09 Prescriptions dispensed (per person per year), primary care trusts/ health boards, Britain

Prescriptions 2007/08
(per person)
| 7.5 – 9.9 |
| 10.0 – 12.4 |
| 12.5 – 14.9 |
| 15.0 – 17.4 |
| 17.5 – 19.9 |
| 20.0 – 25.4 |

Prescriptions 2008/09
(per person)
| 7.7 – 9.9 |
| 10.0 – 12.4 |
| 12.5 – 14.9 |
| 15.0 – 17.4 |
| 17.5 – 19.9 |
| 20.0 – 26.5 |

5.6   Mental health service users

The National Health Services Mental Health Minimum Dataset (MHMDS)[8] for the 2008/09 annual return is the first to have been extracted to produce statistics on the incidence of people aged 18 and over using mental health services in each local authority area of England. The documentation surrounding the data is meticulous. For instance, in the footnotes of the file in which this data is disseminated it is stated that the totals in the dataset as a whole for England include some 17,029 people 'for whom information about Government Office Region, but not Local Authority, was available. Of these, gender was unknown for 86'. For those people whose area of residence could be determined, some 1,165,000 were users of mental health services during this year, 2.88% of the adult population.

The areas where rates of use were highest are very likely to be places where there are specialist facilities which result in unusual numbers of people with poor mental health living nearby. More than 5% of the population of the following four districts used mental health services in 2008/09: Walsall, Harrogate, Brighton & Hove, and Lincoln. The lowest rates of service use, where less than 1% of the population used the services available, occurred in Winchester, the Isle of Wight, Eastleigh, and Test Valley. It can be assumed that in most of these areas fewer services are available. We do know from the footnotes with the data release that the Isle of Wight did not record the gender of the few users of its services. This suggests that mental health provision was not especially carefully monitored on the island at this time. The documentation with the data says that the 72 users there for whom gender is known were residents of the island treated by services based elsewhere.[9]

Map 5.6.1 shows the national distribution of people who used mental health services in 2008/09, the first year for which such use was tabulated geographically within England. Recorded use tends to be lower in the Home Counties and in more rural areas, and higher within cities and much of the North, but also higher around some of those four areas of very high use identified above. Quite why the distribution of users should be like this is not well known, not least because the geographical data have only so very recently been released. The causes of so many people having such acute needs are not well known either, nor are the causes for the much greater numbers having needs that result in the prescription of antidepressants and other drugs but who are not referred to mental health services.

In 2006, research groups such as those of Richard Layard, the economist and government advisor based at the London School of Economics and Political Science, found that around one in three families in the UK contained a member who was suffering from one or more problems of poor mental health.[10] In 2007 and 2008 clinical psychologist and author Oliver James documented why this appeared to be occurring, in great detail, both in a work written for the general public and in a more specialist volume.[11] A year later, in 2009, working for the World Health Organisation, Lynne Friedli, mental health promotion specialist and author, identified more formally that it is the way we currently live, particularly in a country as unequal as the UK, that is fundamentally at fault.[12] In 2010 the data shown in Map 5.6.1 were released, revealing for the first time just where the most acute need was concentrated and how very poor mental health is geographically widespread. Thankfully, at the aggregate rather than the individual level, mental health is one area of health in which our understanding is more rapidly changing and improving than in many others. The prescriptions that are increasingly being suggested as most appropriate are not individual but society-wide.

The emotional bankruptcy of Britain is largely a result of how unequal our lives are and the multiple consequences of that.[13]

Map 5.6.1: 2008/09 Mental health service users (‰), local authorities, England

Mental health service
users 2008/09
(per 1,000 adults)

	3.7 – 19.9
	20.0 – 29.9
	30.0 – 39.9
	40.0 – 49.9
	50.0 – 54.9

Mental health service users 2008/09	(per 1,000 adults)
LOWEST 5	
Test Valley	3.7
Eastleigh	6.7
Isle of Wight	7.0
Winchester	7.3
New Forest	10.1
HIGHEST 5	
Bury	49.6
Lincoln	50.3
Brighton & Hove	51.4
Harrogate	51.8
Walsall	54.9

5.7   Foot soldiers of the Big Society

Taking part in what is called 'formal volunteering' means giving unpaid help, through groups, clubs or organisations which support social, environmental, cultural or sporting objectives, at least once a month, every month in the 12 months before the date the question is asked. In the Department for Communities and Local Government's survey of volunteering in England in 2008 and 2009 respondents were asked:

Please think about any group(s), club(s) or organisation(s) that you've been involved with during the last 12 months. That's anything you've taken part in, supported, or that you've helped in any way, either on your own or with others. For example, helping at a youth or day centre, helping to run an event, campaigning or doing administrative work.

Please exclude giving money and anything that was a requirement of your job.

Overall, about how often over the last 12 months have you given unpaid help to any group(s), club (s) or organisation(s)?

Please only include work that is unpaid and not for your family.

- At least once a week…
- Less than once a week but at least once a month…
- Less often…
- I give unpaid help as an individual only and not through groups(s), club(s) or organisation(s)…
- I have not given any unpaid help at all over the last 12 months…
- Don't know…

In the Scottish Household Survey, respondents aged 16 and over were asked if they had given up time to volunteer in the previous 12 months.

Map 5.7.2 shows the proportion of people who said they volunteered in this way. Helping out in church on just one Sunday in four would count, as would being a member of almost any committee that required answering one email a month. Across the country as a whole, just over a quarter of people claimed to volunteer in such ways in 2008. The map suggests it was in the leafy suburbs and Home Counties where such volunteering was most common. In Scotland 16- and 17-year-olds were included in the survey too, and some data from 2007 as well as 2008 were involved, but these things make little difference to the patterns shown. It is the kind of question asked that alters what people say. This kind of volunteering is least common in South Tyneside, Sunderland, Knowsley and Kingston upon Hull.

Contrast the pattern for volunteering shown in Map 5.7.2 with that for participation derived from the Citizenship Survey, shown in Map 5.7.1. In this face-to-face survey, civic participation is defined as the '… proportion of the adult population who say they have in the last 12 months participated in a group which makes decisions that affect their local area'.

Map 5.7.1: 2008 Civic participation (% engaged in), local authorities, England

Civic participation 2008 (%)
- 7.6 – 9.9
- 10.0 – 13.9
- 14.0 – 16.9
- 17.0 – 19.9
- 20.0 – 25.7

When it comes to volunteering with democratic influence, only 3% of the population answer 'yes'. And they do so with different geographical concentrations and lacunae. Civic participation is least common in Sunderland, Stockton-on-Tees, Cannock Chase and Rochford. Sunderland is the one place which consistently sits towards the bottom of both lists, but as we noted in introducing this chapter, it is also one of the areas where children's emotional health is highest. Civic participation in general is most common not in the leafy suburbs but in cities: most of all in the very different boroughs of the City of London, Camden, Tower Hamlets and Kensington & Chelsea. Map 5.7.1 shows just how much more urban-based (and Cornish!) civic participation is in comparison to volunteering.

Volunteering and civic participation might be very different activities carried out more or less earnestly in very different places, but one thing the two types of activity have in common is that both are in decline. We can only know this nationally. Rates have only been reported at area level for 2008, and for civic participation only for areas within England. Figure 5.7.1 shows how volunteering rates reached a high with the economic boom in 2005, and how civic participation peaked at the verge of the crash in 2007–08. Since then both activities have started to decline rapidly in popularity. The new government of 2010 announced that volunteering and voluntary civic participation (the Big Society) were the way forward just at the point when thousands of citizens decided that such things were not the future for them.

Figure 5.7.1: 2001–10 Volunteering and civic participation, national trends (% adults)

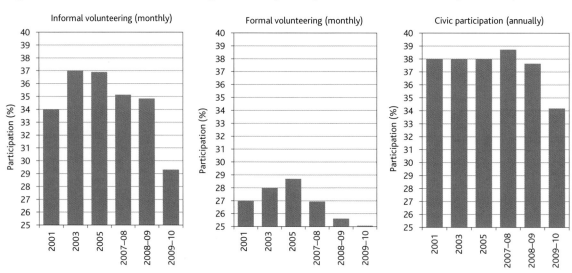

Map 5.7.2: 2008 Adults engaged in regular volunteering (%), local authorities, England and Scotland

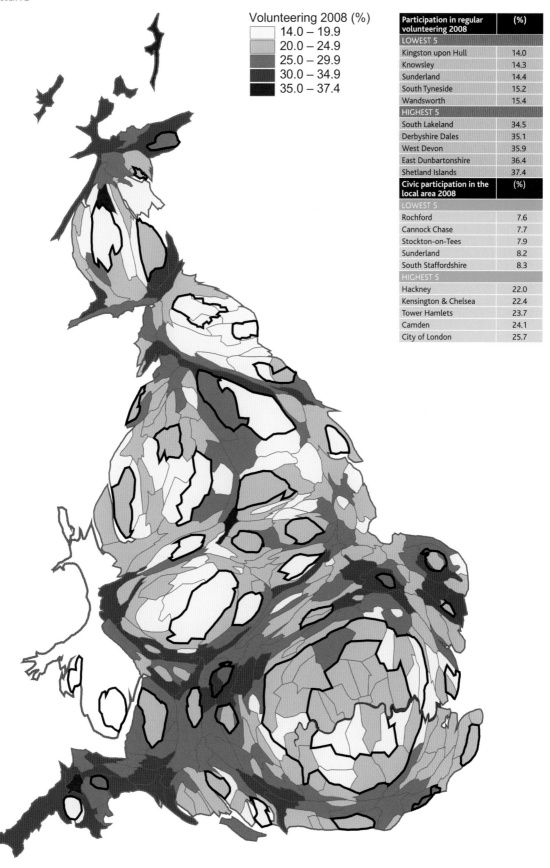

Volunteering 2008 (%)
- 14.0 – 19.9
- 20.0 – 24.9
- 25.0 – 29.9
- 30.0 – 34.9
- 35.0 – 37.4

Participation in regular volunteering 2008	(%)
LOWEST 5	
Kingston upon Hull	14.0
Knowsley	14.3
Sunderland	14.4
South Tyneside	15.2
Wandsworth	15.4
HIGHEST 5	
South Lakeland	34.5
Derbyshire Dales	35.1
West Devon	35.9
East Dunbartonshire	36.4
Shetland Islands	37.4
Civic participation in the local area 2008	(%)
LOWEST 5	
Rochford	7.6
Cannock Chase	7.7
Stockton-on-Tees	7.9
Sunderland	8.2
South Staffordshire	8.3
HIGHEST 5	
Hackney	22.0
Kensington & Chelsea	22.4
Tower Hamlets	23.7
Camden	24.1
City of London	25.7

Chapter 6 Environmentally bankrupt

Introduction

When the financial crisis hit Europe, one wry response from those affected early on in Ireland was to retort: 'That which does not kill you makes you stronger'. There remains a great misunderstanding concerning suffering. In most cases that which harms you, even if it does not kill you in the short term, will tend to shorten your life in the long term and will certainly make it more uncomfortable in the medium term. If it does not harm you it might well harm others, if not now then in the future. This is what is meant by environmental harm – damage being done more widely than to the individual, where the actions of one person curtail the options of others. When the environmental harm which is being committed spirals out of control it is fair to say that people are heading for environmental bankruptcy.

Environmental harms range from the immediate to those repercussions which appear only to threaten us from the far horizon. The most immediate form of harm is that which is (or might be) damaging right now. Drinking water of poor quality or breathing in air that is damaging to our lungs are significant forms of environmental harm, but we contribute to such harms when we add alcohol to our drinks, or cigarette smoke to the air we breathe. The greatest immediate killers of humans are the ways in which we have managed to make our own personal environments much more dangerous than would naturally occur.

This chapter begins with a series of statistics concerning the greatest threats to young people in Britain today. These are introduced by contrasting the different approaches to fatal environmental risk which can be found around the world. For children it is not smoking or drinking which are most harmful, but cars. In Sweden there is now a road accident policy that *all* deaths of children on the roads should be prevented at whatever cost. In

Britain we are now so protective of very young children – those aged 5 to 9 – that more die due to disease today than as pedestrians, which had been the greatest threat for most of the past two decades. However, by age 10, cars are the greatest danger to children when all risk categories are compared. By the onset of adulthood, cars and a small number of cases of suicide together account for half of all deaths at these young ages: nine deaths a week among 17-, 18- and 19-year-olds from these causes alone, almost all due to cars. The numbers of deaths of young adults from such causes continues to rise throughout their twenties, only falling relative to other risks when they reach their late thirties.

Around 30,000 people of all ages are killed or seriously injured on the roads in Britain every year. In 2008 some 27,855,000 cars were registered to be driven on the country's roads. That rose slightly to 27,868,000 during 2009 (partly with government encouragement for buying new cars through a 'scrappage scheme'). Unsurprisingly, more people tend to be killed or seriously injured where more cars are registered. It is also unsurprising that within Britain overall air pollution is worse in the more crowded cities into which more cars are driven, but especially where they are more likely to be driven in congestion. Fine particles in the air capable of getting into the lungs are measured as levels of PM_{10}. PM_{10} air pollution levels are worst of all within the centre of London, and in recent years exposure to nitrogen oxide emissions and benzene pollutants has increased most there and to a lesser extent in a number of smaller urban centres, but with distinct geographical regional variation. Cars and other forms of transport contribute just under a third of all the CO_2 emissions that can be attributed to particular localities in Britain. The car damages our local and our global environments more significantly than any other recent invention.

Considering the other two thirds of CO_2 emissions, domestic emissions are highest from the wealthiest areas of the country and industrial emissions are greatest from poorer areas where industry tends to be located. The good news is that recently, almost everywhere, emissions have been falling, although sadly this is due to the effects of recession, not to collective decisions being made to pollute less. We note later that if such reductions were to be continued without a break for several decades then our overall emissions would quickly reach much safer levels. For that to occur, we would either have to be forced into such action through industrial and economic collapse, or our priorities would have to be changed abruptly. What this chapter shows is that we *can* adapt to sudden reductions in consumption and pollution – we have just done so.

When considering the levels of, and changes in, consumption of electricity and gas resources across the country, we note that to reduce consumption levels further, overall affluence in the richest areas needs also to be reduced. This is because we find that even when overall levels of consumption fall due to price rises, consumption rates still tend to increase in those places where some people are very rich and hence where price rises have the least influence. This is as true for car and petrol consumption as it is for electricity and gas (and also for excess purchases of everyday goods). Numerous complex schemes could be introduced to try to curtail the especially damaging environmental behaviour of the more affluent members of British society. Alternatively, the far simpler policy of advocating greater economic equality to maximise environmental efficiency could be advanced. People with fewer resources tend to spend their money more wisely.

People with fewer resources also tend to waste less as they shop less. A greater amount of their income has to be spent on necessities such as food. Food entails great waste in terms of packaging, overconsumption and 'food miles'. We bring this chapter to an end by looking at the contents of our dustbins: we show how many kilograms a year are now thrown away and what proportion of that is recycled. We reiterate the argument that it is better never to purchase an item in the first place (if it is not really required), rather than to buy and recycle it. And we show how this kind of thinking can be used to suggest that those places which recently recorded the highest rates of recycling are not necessarily the most environmentally minded if initial rates of consumption there are much higher than average.

Nevertheless we end on an optimistic note, seeing how quickly in very recent years our consumption rates and hence waste generation rates have been falling and, simultaneously, how rates of more essential recycling are also now quickly rising. It might be easier to be green in a recession, but the country is not currently heading towards environmental bankruptcy – although more by accident than design. We know that in practice it is possible to reduce waste and pollute far less, and we have started to do that. The question now is: can we plan to do that in future when we have a choice over whether to do the right thing?

6.1   Environments that kill the young

We carry an innate fear for the safety of our children. Children and young adults are our collective future. We seek to make their environments as safe as is possible. However, what is seen as possible varies from place to place. In more fatalistic societies it is more often implied that 'what will be, will be'. Conversely, in some Scandinavian countries and others with a similar philosophy, policies are now being adopted that say that no child should suffer due to the environments we create. In contrast, in many Anglo-Saxon nations in recent years, a different policy has been quietly championed and a price has been put on the life of each child. Cost-benefit analysis is then applied to judge whether particular interventions – for example, the building of a crash barrier between opposing lanes on a country road – are economically worthwhile

In the first few years, and especially the first few weeks of life, children are most likely to die or suffer because of conditions they are born with. Although some of these conditions will be caused or worsened by the external environment the mother experienced while pregnant, most causes of poor health and premature death of the very young in Britain are not directly environmental. That alters when children reach school age. In the years 2006 and 2007 one child aged between 5 and 10 died on average every day in Britain. A very wide range of causes were attributed to these 780 young deaths. Diseases of the nervous system are now the single most common combined cause of death at these ages, accounting for 14% of all such deaths.

Table 6.1.1 shows the total number of deaths of young people in Britain over the two years 2006 and 2007 and the number that were due to external factors.

Table 6.1.1: 2006–07 Numbers of deaths of children and young adults, Britain

Age	Cause of death	Number of deaths
5–10 yrs	All	780
	External	122
11–16 yrs	All	1,392
	External	489
17–19 yrs	All	1,833
	External	1,007
20–24 yrs	All	3,506
	External	1,743
25–29 yrs	All	4,019
	External	1,510

Figure 6.1.1 shows all the causes of mortality of 5- to 10-year-olds drawn in proportion to their frequency during these years. Figure 6.1.2 isolates just those causes directly linked to factors external to the body: environmental factors. Even at these ages, more children die of such external factors combined (16%) than from the most common internal factor (14%). The most dangerous causes of death due to external environmental factors are cars, which cause almost half of external deaths at these ages, mostly of pedestrians. A similar pattern is shown for older, secondary school children, aged 11–16, of whom 17% of those who die are killed by cars, mostly dying as passengers in an accident (see Figure 6.1.3).

However, at these ages suicide and undetermined intent are also beginning to account for significant numbers of deaths (Figure 6.1.4). On average, two children aged 11 to 16 die every day in Britain.

Figure 6.1.5 and Figure 6.1.6 show how, by ages 17 to 19, cars are by far the greatest danger. Along with suicide and undetermined intent, the car accounts for half of all mortality at these ages; three years of life during which 18 young people die a week. These patterns then begin to change in young adulthood. At ages 20–24, death due to the taking of drugs rises in importance (Figure 6.1.7). Almost 34 adults in their early twenties die on average each week in Britain. Cars, suicide and undetermined intent, and to a lesser extent drugs, account for half of all mortality at these ages; only a quarter of all young adult deaths are not attributable to external factors (Figure 6.1.8).

Finally Figure 6.1.9 and Figure 6.1.10 show how the pattern begins to change by the time people reach their late twenties. Some 39 people a week die at these ages, half from the causes we have been highlighting, but now with a few deaths due to alcohol having to be added to account for over half the total. Cars still account for over a tenth of all deaths at these ages, but suicide and undetermined intent are the underlying cause of almost a fifth of all deaths at ages 25 to 29. Many deaths from undetermined intent are probably due to suicide, but some will be due to accidents. Suicide rates vary dramatically country by country.[1] They too are environmentally influenced, although in this case it is the social environment that matters most.

Figure 6.1.1: 2006–07 All causes of death of 5- to 10-year-olds, Britain (%)

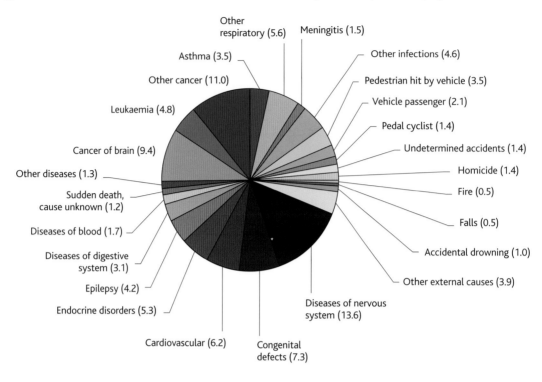

Figure 6.1.2: 2006–07 External causes of death of 5- to 10-year-olds, Britain (%)

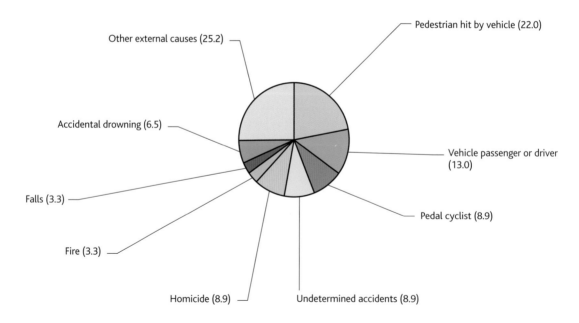

Figure 6.1.3: 2006–07 All causes of death of 11- to 16-year-olds, Britain (%)

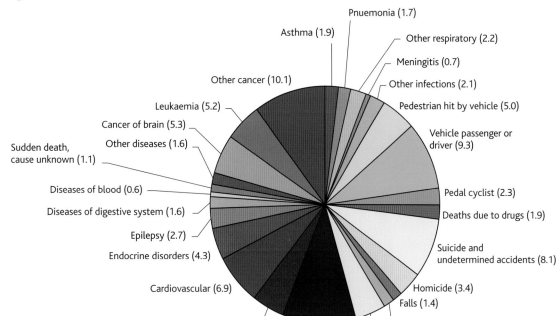

Pnuemonia (1.7)
Asthma (1.9)
Other respiratory (2.2)
Meningitis (0.7)
Other cancer (10.1)
Other infections (2.1)
Leukaemia (5.2)
Pedestrian hit by vehicle (5.0)
Cancer of brain (5.3)
Vehicle passenger or driver (9.3)
Other diseases (1.6)
Sudden death, cause unknown (1.1)
Pedal cyclist (2.3)
Diseases of blood (0.6)
Deaths due to drugs (1.9)
Diseases of digestive system (1.6)
Suicide and undetermined accidents (8.1)
Epilepsy (2.7)
Endocrine disorders (4.3)
Homicide (3.4)
Falls (1.4)
Cardiovascular (6.9)
Congenital defects (4.6)
Accidental drowning (1.5)
Diseases of nervous system (10.3)
Other external causes (4.2)

Figure 6.1.4: 2006–07 External causes of death of 11- to 16-year-olds, Britain (%)

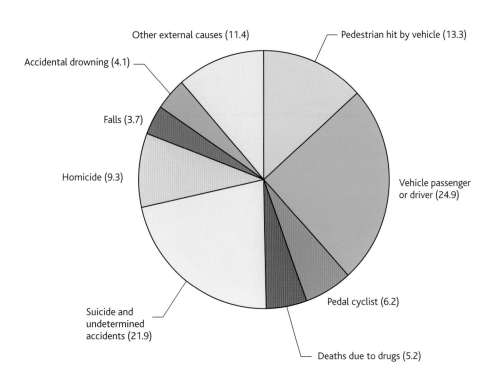

Other external causes (11.4)
Pedestrian hit by vehicle (13.3)
Accidental drowning (4.1)
Falls (3.7)
Vehicle passenger or driver (24.9)
Homicide (9.3)
Pedal cyclist (6.2)
Suicide and undetermined accidents (21.9)
Deaths due to drugs (5.2)

Figure 6.1.5: 2006–07 All causes of death of 17- to 19-year-olds, Britain (%)

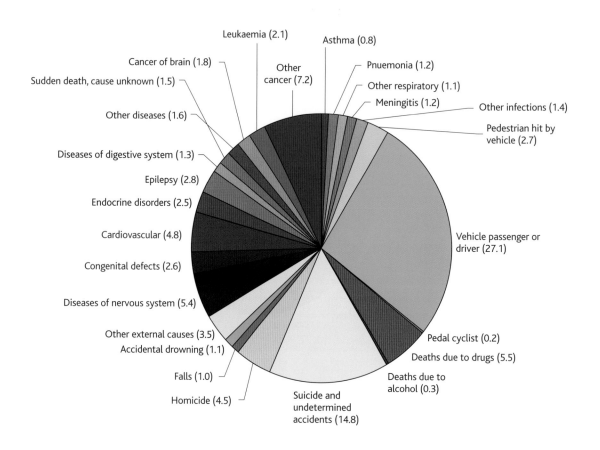

Figure 6.1.6: 2006–07 External causes of death of 17- to 19-year-olds, Britain (%)

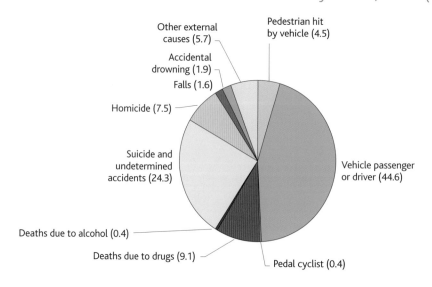

Figure 6.1.7: 2006–07 All causes of death of 20- to 24-year-olds, Britain (%)

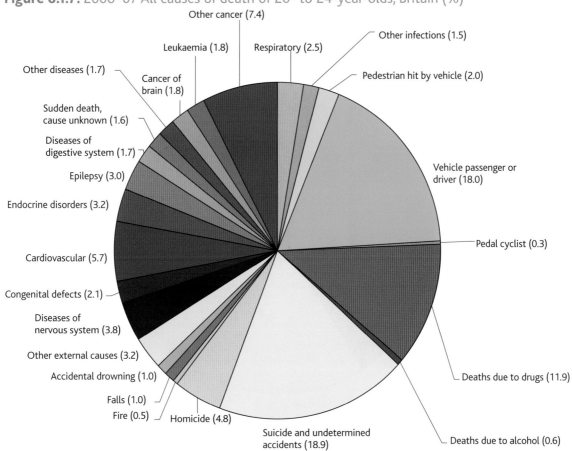

Figure 6.1.8: 2006–07 External causes of death of 20- to 24-year-olds, Britain (%)

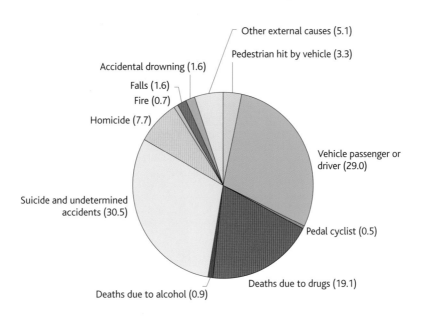

Figure 6.1.9: 2006–07 All causes of death of 25- to 29-year-olds, Britain (%)

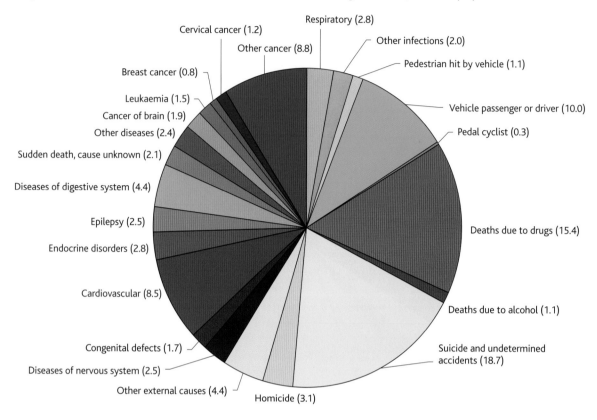

Figure 6.1.10: 2006–07 external causes of death of 25- to 29-year-olds, Britain (%)

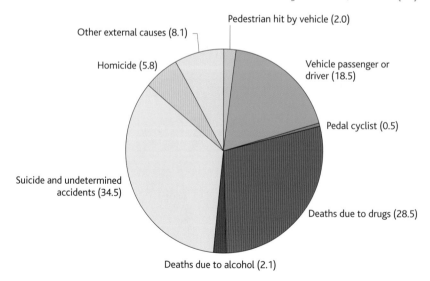

6.2 Cars: the greatest environmental threat

Cars are the most immediate everyday threat to life in Britain. Over the long term the pollution they emit and the wars that are fought to secure the oil to run them, as well as the waste involved in building and maintaining them, are all highly damaging; but it is the everyday practical reality of sharing streets and (because of driveways) pavements with cars that causes the gravest threat.

Some 28,597 people were killed or seriously injured on Britain's roads due to traffic accidents in 2008. Almost 10% of those killed or injured were children. Almost all of these accidents involved cars. The number of deaths and serious injuries had fallen from 30,784 a year earlier, as high oil prices and the onset of recession led to a reduction in driving and also in reported accidents, although fewer cars on

the road do not always mean safer roads, as driving speeds may increase. Map 6.2.3 shows how it is in the countryside that road accident and death rates are highest at all ages, with serious accident rates of more than one person in a thousand a year recorded in Richmondshire, Argyll & Bute, Ryedale, Tynedale, Purbeck, Craven, Aberdeenshire, Daventry, Wealden and Hambleton. The highest recorded rate is in the City of London, and the rate in Westminster also exceeds 1 in 1,000. However, in both these cases it is the high daytime populations of these areas that artificially increase the reported risk. The denominator population is usual residents, so the high accident rates shown within London in Map 6.2.3 reflect high numbers of in-commuters, not more dangerous streets.

For children, the picture, as shown in Map 6.2.1, is a little different. Although the highest rate of those killed or seriously injured is still found in the City

Map 6.2.1: 2008 Children killed or seriously injured by traffic, local authorities, Britain

Map 6.2.2: 2009 Licensed cars (per 100 people), unitary authorities & counties, Britain

Map 6.2.3: 2008 All people killed or seriously injured by traffic, local authorities, Britain

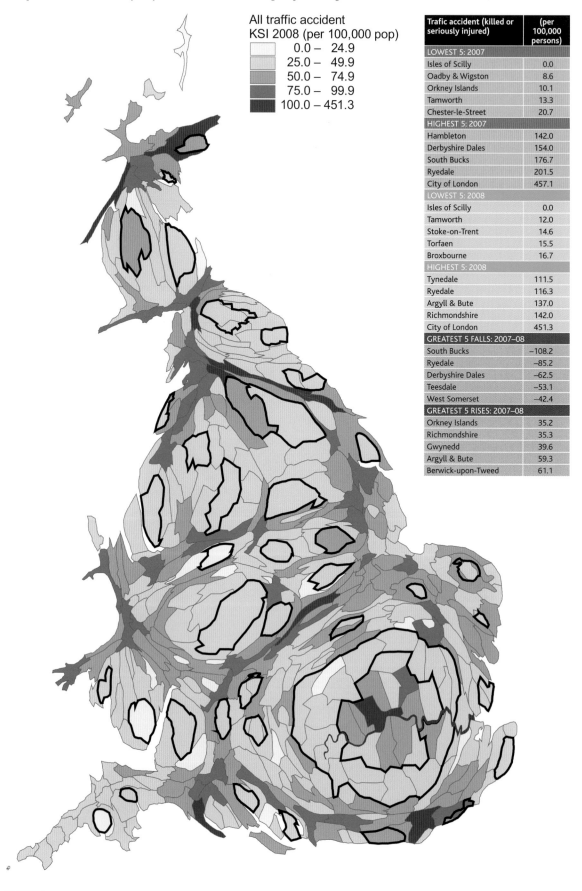

All traffic accident
KSI 2008 (per 100,000 pop)

	0.0 – 24.9
	25.0 – 49.9
	50.0 – 74.9
	75.0 – 99.9
	100.0 – 451.3

Trafic accident (killed or seriously injured)	(per 100,000 persons)
LOWEST 5: 2007	
Isles of Scilly	0.0
Oadby & Wigston	8.6
Orkney Islands	10.1
Tamworth	13.3
Chester-le-Street	20.7
HIGHEST 5: 2007	
Hambleton	142.0
Derbyshire Dales	154.0
South Bucks	176.7
Ryedale	201.5
City of London	457.1
LOWEST 5: 2008	
Isles of Scilly	0.0
Tamworth	12.0
Stoke-on-Trent	14.6
Torfaen	15.5
Broxbourne	16.7
HIGHEST 5: 2008	
Tynedale	111.5
Ryedale	116.3
Argyll & Bute	137.0
Richmondshire	142.0
City of London	451.3
GREATEST 5 FALLS: 2007–08	
South Bucks	−108.2
Ryedale	−85.2
Derbyshire Dales	−62.5
Teesdale	−53.1
West Somerset	−42.4
GREATEST 5 RISES: 2007–08	
Orkney Islands	35.2
Richmondshire	35.3
Gwynedd	39.6
Argyll & Bute	59.3
Berwick-upon-Tweed	61.1

of London, for instance when visiting school trips suffer misfortune, and although rural districts such as South Shropshire, Argyll & Bute and South Ribble show some of the highest rates, it is in northern towns that casualties are most common: Hyndburn, Congleton, Preston, Durham, Burnley and Glasgow were among the top 20 areas in 2008 for child traffic accident casualties and deaths out of over 400 British local authorities. Conversely, those living in the Derbyshire Dales, Surrey Heath, Rugby, Mendip and Bromsgrove (each home to over 10,000 children) encountered some of the lowest risks, but risks were almost as low for children in Kingston upon Thames and Kensington & Chelsea in London. In these areas children are so rarely allowed out on their own (to cycle or even to walk to the nearby home of a friend) that casualties are kept very low.

Map 6.2.2 shows how many cars were licensed per person to be driven in each area in 2009. This is the first year in which figures were released with a detailed enough geographical resolution to compare car registrations with traffic accidents. Slough turns out to be the car capital of Britain. More cars are licensed to be driven in Slough than there are people to drive them. Often cars are licensed by garages selling them, or car factories about to move them, and so we need to be a little wary of imputing where the highest concentrations of vehicles are driven on the public roads, but the overall suburban and rural pattern reflects accidents overall, as do rates of registration generally, being lowest within city centres where, mostly due to speeds being slower, far fewer accidents result in fatalities. Rather than keeping children imprisoned in their homes we would do far better to keep speed limits below 20mph on all residential streets.[2]

6.3   Air quality: how what you breathe varies geographically

Although there are many more car miles driven per person in rural areas, there is also much more space per person and therefore much greater volumes of air. Because of this, car exhaust fumes are dissipated far more widely and quickly in the countryside. In suburbia, pollution from car exhausts, central heating boilers and industrial processes tends to be higher. However, it is within city centres that air pollution levels are usually worst. Map 6.3.1 shows the counts

of PM_{10} particles, almost all of which are pollutants created by human activity. These are particles of a particular microscopic size, small enough to enter our lungs easily and particularly damaging to the lungs of children and babies. Pollution hotspots include Redcar & Cleveland, Southampton, Westminster, Oxford and unsurprisingly, Slough: these are areas where PM_{10} emissions are over one hundred times the lowest rate in Britain, found in Argyll and Bute. Since 2007, PM_{10} emission rates have increased in all of these areas other than Slough. Patterns of change over just one year can be influenced by measurement error, weather conditions and short-term changes in collective human behaviour. Nevertheless, despite the complex causality, short-term fluctuations are in many cases worth monitoring by area. Map 6.3.2 shows the changing geographical distribution of nitrogen oxide (NO_x) emissions. The internal combustion engine of cars is one of the major contributors of these particular pollutants. Between 2007 and 2008 NO_x pollution rates rose even higher within central London. Many factors will have played a part in fuelling this rise, but note how in other areas of the country pollution rates fell. Along the rivers Trent and Humber, coal-powered power stations reduced their emissions over this period as industrial demand for electricity fell with the onset of recession. In contrast, in London, pollution kept on rising, partly due indirectly to the later banking bail-out keeping business there afloat.

How quickly exposure to particular air pollutants can change in a year is most clearly illustrated by Map 6.3.3, which shows how between 2007 and 2008 there was a rapid increase in exposure to benzene in the air in London, Bristol, Birmingham, Liverpool, Manchester, Newcastle, Edinburgh and Glasgow; but a fall across most of Wales, Yorkshire and Lincolnshire. Again, benzene is a health-damaging pollutant. Breathing in large quantities of benzene when there is an accidental industrial release can cause instant death. Again, rates of release are normally very much concentrated within a few major cities (and oil refineries). The most recent increases in pollution per square kilometre – and hence per person living there – have been in the centre of London. The most recent and largest decreases have been where economic activity has slowed down most, to the East of the Pennines.

Map 6.3.1: 2008 Pollution: PM$_{10}$ emissions (per km^2), local authorities, Britain

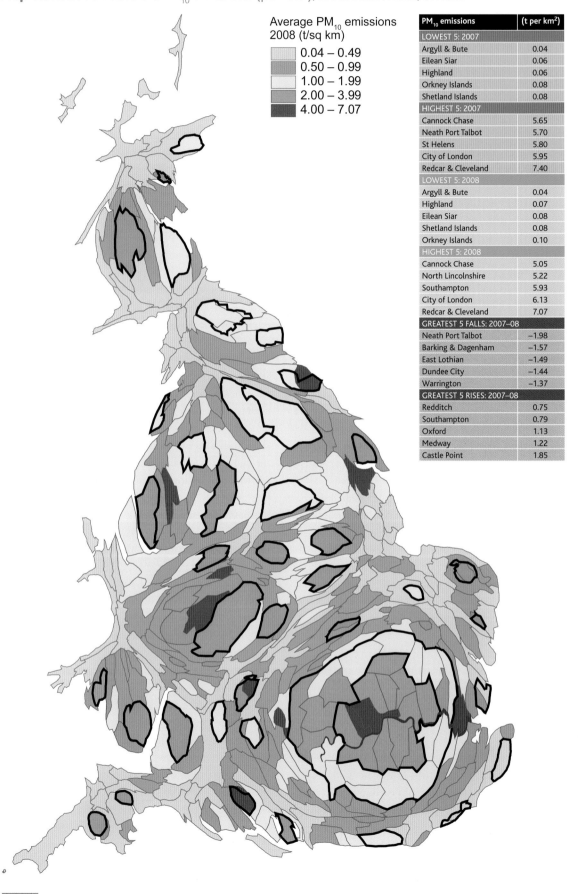

Average PM$_{10}$ emissions 2008 (t/sq km)

	0.04 – 0.49
	0.50 – 0.99
	1.00 – 1.99
	2.00 – 3.99
	4.00 – 7.07

PM$_{10}$ emissions	(t per km^2)
LOWEST 5: 2007	
Argyll & Bute	0.04
Eilean Siar	0.06
Highland	0.06
Orkney Islands	0.08
Shetland Islands	0.08
HIGHEST 5: 2007	
Cannock Chase	5.65
Neath Port Talbot	5.70
St Helens	5.80
City of London	5.95
Redcar & Cleveland	7.40
LOWEST 5: 2008	
Argyll & Bute	0.04
Highland	0.07
Eilean Siar	0.08
Shetland Islands	0.08
Orkney Islands	0.10
HIGHEST 5: 2008	
Cannock Chase	5.05
North Lincolnshire	5.22
Southampton	5.93
City of London	6.13
Redcar & Cleveland	7.07
GREATEST 5 FALLS: 2007–08	
Neath Port Talbot	−1.98
Barking & Dagenham	−1.57
East Lothian	−1.49
Dundee City	−1.44
Warrington	−1.37
GREATEST 5 RISES: 2007–08	
Redditch	0.75
Southampton	0.79
Oxford	1.13
Medway	1.22
Castle Point	1.85

Map 6.3.2: 2007–08 Change in emissions of NO$_x$ (per km^2), local authorities, Britain

Map 6.3.3: 2007–08 Change in emissions of benzene (per km^2), local authorities, Britain

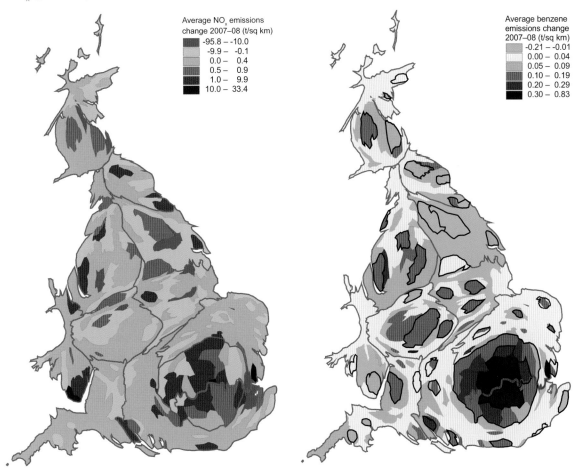

Average NO$_x$ emissions change 2007–08 (t/sq km)
- -95.8 – -10.0
- -9.9 – -0.1
- 0.0 – 0.4
- 0.5 – 0.9
- 1.0 – 9.9
- 10.0 – 33.4

Average benzene emissions change 2007–08 (t/sq km)
- -0.21 – -0.01
- 0.00 – 0.04
- 0.05 – 0.09
- 0.10 – 0.19
- 0.20 – 0.29
- 0.30 – 0.83

Note: The National Atmospheric Emissions Inventory (NAEI) publishes maps of emissions by 1x1 km grid squares for the UK. Each grid square was allocated to its relevant local authority and the mean value calculated.

6.4   Burning up the planet: CO_2 emissions

Recently estimates have been made of how much carbon dioxide (CO_2) pollution has been emitted from each region of Britain from domestic, industrial and transport activities, as well as how much is absorbed by local forestry and other carbon sinks.[3] Industry and commerce produced slightly less CO_2 pollution than did all domestic and road use combined in Britain in recent years, but more than either of these two sources when each is measured alone. These official estimates of CO_2 emissions have been published for the years 2005, 2006 and 2007. Map 6.4.1 shows just one of the many maps that can be produced from this data – the distribution of CO_2 emitted due to road transportation by area in 2007. Geographically, road transportation emissions vary more than those for any other activity, with a twentyfold difference between the most and least extreme local authority areas.

Environmental and political campaigners such as George Monbiot have explained repeatedly – and increasingly convincingly – the argument that we simply should not continue to pollute at the levels we do, especially in terms of how much additional CO_2 we cause to be emitted. This and emissions of other greenhouse gases are harming the environment and contributing to artificial global warming and the exhaustion of limited natural resources.[4]

Just under a third of the emissions that have been measured and attributed to specific areas of the country are due to transportation pollution, mostly from petrol engine exhausts. Up to a further third of emissions are due to domestic pollution, mostly from the heating of homes. Finally, over a third of emissions in almost all areas is due to the activities of industry – again mostly caused by their consumption of energy either from the coal, oil and gas-fired electricity-generating power plants supplying that energy, or directly through the use of such fuels at the industrial plants themselves.

Table 6.4.1 shows the local authorities with the highest and lowest net CO_2 emissions, and also the authorities with the highest and lowest per capita emissions. Note that Argyll & Bute has enough carbon sink capacity to result in negative overall emissions.

Table 6.4.1: Areas with highest and lowest net CO_2 emissions, local authorities, Britain, 2007

Local authority	Total CO_2 emissions 2007 (kt CO_2)	Local authority	Total CO_2 emissions 2007 (t per person)
Argyll & Bute	−331	Argyll & Bute	−3.6
Isles of Scilly	13	Highland	2.7
Alnwick	228	Hackney	4.2
Orkney Islands	241	Waltham Forest	4.2
Teesdale	255	Redbridge	4.2
Oswestry	283	Merton	4.3
Oadby & Wigston	290	Haringey	4.3
Christchurch	298	Lewisham	4.3
Eilean Siar	299	Harrow	4.5
Weymouth & Portland	301	Weymouth & Portland	4.6
...	...	...	...
Wansbeck	3,434	Eden	27.0
Fife	3,587	Ellesmere Port & Neston	27.1
Sheffield	3,694	Rugby	27.3
Glasgow City	3,910	High Peak	31.3
Stockton-on-Tees	4,019	Rutland	35.4
Leeds	5,541	Wansbeck	55.7
Birmingham	6,595	Neath Port Talbot	60.8
Neath Port Talbot	8,357	Redcar & Cleveland	62.5
Redcar & Cleveland	8,707	North Lincolnshire	70.9
North Lincolnshire	11,297	City of London	201.1

Map 6.4.1: 2007 CO_2 emissions due to road transport (tonnes per person), local authorities, Britain

Road transport CO_2 emissions 2007 (t per person)

- 0.5 – 0.9
- 1.0 – 1.9
- 2.0 – 2.9
- 3.0 – 4.9
- 5.0 – 11.4

Road transport CO_2 emissions	(t per person)
LOWEST 5: 2006	
Isles of Scilly	0.5
Lincoln	0.7
Camden	0.7
Barrow-in-Furness	0.8
Islington	0.8
HIGHEST 5: 2006	
Daventry	8.1
City of London	8.3
South Bucks	8.4
Eden	9.2
North Warwickshire	11.2
LOWEST 5: 2007	
Isles of Scilly	0.5
Camden	0.7
Lincoln	0.7
Islington	0.8
Harrow	0.8
HIGHEST 5: 2007	
Daventry	8.0
City of London	8.3
South Bucks	8.7
Eden	9.5
North Warwickshire	11.4
GREATEST 5 FALLS: 2006/07	
Chorley	−0.2
West Devon	−0.2
Brentwood	−0.1
Forest Heath	−0.1
Mole Valley	−0.1
GREATEST 5 RISES: 2006/07	
Sedgemoor	0.2
South Bucks	0.2
Eden	0.3
Epping Forest	0.4
Uttlesford	0.4

6.5 Electricity and gas: changing consumption

Map 6.5.1 reinforces the message that it is easily possible for our overall levels of consumption and hence of waste and pollution to fall quickly. The map shows how electricity consumption fell almost everywhere across Britain as electricity prices rose relative to disposable incomes between 2007 and 2008. When measured per household, electricity consumption calculated in kilowatt hours was found to have fallen the most between these two years in the Shetland Isles and Anglesey, where the cost of supplying power tends to be higher than average due to the remoteness of property and where there is not the alternative of piped gas for heating. In contrast, in just a few London boroughs and other southern districts, consumption actually rose despite those increases in cost, most notably in the already quite high consumption areas of Westminster, Kensington & Chelsea, the City of London and the affluent New Forest and Poole districts. To reduce electricity consumption levels, overall affluence in the richest areas needs also to be reduced. The need to reduce our consumption of electricity and other forms of energy generated by fossil fuels was made crystal clear by Nicholas Stern, former Chief Economist and Senior Vice President of the World Bank, in the official report that bears his name.[5] There is near-unanimity now across the political and social spectrum in Britain, and much of the rest of the rich world, that it is vital that our waste and consumption is rapidly curtailed.

Apart from where there are no piped gas supplies, such as in the far north of Scotland where more electricity is used for heating, the consumption of electricity continues to be greatest per household in those areas where people are wealthier, not where there might be greatest need to consume more electricity, for example, where it tends to be colder. Map 6.5.2 demonstrates this geographically.

Electricity consumption per household was greater than 5,600 kWh in the following 18 areas (not noted for their inclement climate): West Oxfordshire; West Somerset; Stratford-on-Avon; Eden; North Norfolk; Chichester; Restormel; West Berkshire; South Bucks; Mid Suffolk; South Oxfordshire; King's Lynn & West Norfolk; South Hams; South Shropshire; Uttlesford; Cotswold; North Cornwall and Kennet. In contrast, per household over the same period consumption was less than 3,700 kWh in the following 18 areas (mostly not noted for their particularly warm locations): South Tyneside; Blaenau Gwent; Camden; Sunderland; Blyth Valley; Norwich; Wansbeck; Caerphilly; Sedgefield; Torfaen; Rhondda Cynon Taf; Easington; Merthyr Tydfil; Sheffield; Durham; Middlesbrough; Hartlepool and Gateshead. Note that between the most extreme districts here, households are consuming twice as much electricity in Kennet in the South of England as compared to South Tyneside in the far North.

Lastly in this section, Map 6.5.3 highlights how this discrepancy is not caused by there being an abundance of gas to use to heat homes in the north of England and a lack of gas in the south. Gas is used the least within London, where there is the most effective urban heat island in Britain.

Rates of gas consumption are lowest (in fact zero) where there is no mains supply: on the Orkney Islands, Shetland Islands, Eilean Siar and across the Isles of Scilly. After that, due to a combination of urban heat islands and shared dwelling insulation, and poverty (or so much affluence that electricity is used instead of gas), the lowest rates of gas consumption are found within London and a few other, mainly urban, areas. In only Tower Hamlets and Southwark do rates of use fall below 12,500 kWh per household per year. The highest rates of consumption, again roughly twice the amount per household as in the lowest consumption areas, is in places such as South Bucks, Chiltern and East Renfrewshire, where over 23,000 kWh is consumed by each household annually.

Map 6.5.1: 2007–08 Change in electricity consumption (kWh per household), local authority aggregates, Britain

Domestic electricity consumption change 2007–08 (kWh/household)

- -765 – -400
- -399 – -200
- -199 – -100
- -99 – 0
- 1 – 30
- 31 – 150

Electricity consumption	(kWh per household)
LOWEST 5: 2007	
Blaenau Gwent	3,464
South Tyneside	3,520
Camden	3,563
Sunderland	3,695
Torfaen	3,697
HIGHEST 5: 2007	
Highland	7,782
Eilean Siar	8,283
Isles of Scilly	8,575
Orkney Islands	9,515
Shetland Islands	11,349
LOWEST 5: 2008	
South Tyneside	3,362
Blaenau Gwent	3,389
Camden	3,488
Sunderland	3,530
Blyth Valley	3,531
HIGHEST 5: 2008	
Argyll & Bute	7,462
Eilean Siar	7,798
Isles of Scilly	8,383
Orkney Islands	9,259
Shetland Islands	10,584
GREATEST 5 FALLS: 2007–08	
Shetland Islands	−765
Anglesey	−718
Forest Heath	−564
Gwynedd	−522
Eilean Siar	−485
GREATEST 5 RISES: 2007–08	
New Forest	41
Tower Hamlets	60
City of London	66
Kensington & Chelsea	75
Weymouth & Portland	150

Map 6.5.2: 2008 Electricity consumption (kWh per household), local authority aggregates, Britain

Domestic electricity consumption 2008 (kWh/household)
- 3,362 – 3,999
- 4,000 – 4,999
- 5,000 – 5,999
- 6,000 – 6,999
- 7,000 – 10,584

Map 6.5.3: 2008 Gas consumption (kWh per household), local authority aggregates, Britain

Domestic gas consumption 2008 (kWh/household)
- 11,487 – 13,999
- 14,000 – 15,999
- 16,000 – 17,999
- 18,000 – 19,999
- 20,000 – 23,486
- No data

6.6 Waste: measuring how much we buy (given how much we throw away)

In Britain we create and import so much power and so many goods that it is hardly surprising that the vast majority of all this effort is wasted. Only a tiny fraction of the heat we generate to warm our homes actually warms our bodies. Most of it warms furniture, carpets and walls and all of it slowly escapes from even the most well-insulated of properties. It is far more efficient to wear an extra layer of clothing than to turn up the thermostat a degree. Similarly, most of the energy we consume and the travel pollution we create through the journeys we undertake could be greatly curtailed if we didn't take part in the daily rituals of 'the school run' or 'the commute'. If we had to include in our household expenses the full environmental costs of heating our homes and driving our cars then we might behave very differently from how we do today.

The most excessive behaviour we exhibit is in how much rubbish we generate in affluent countries. The main result of shopping is the rapid generation of waste. In Britain the average family currently consumes about *six times* the weight of goods per year consumed by families only one generation earlier.[6] Almost everything we buy from shops is thrown away within in a very short time. Within 24 hours we throw away much of the packaging that comes with most goods. We tend to throw away or otherwise waste as much as half of the food we purchase, by weight. The average item of clothing or pair of shoes purchased is worn very few times, and, because our homes cannot accommodate ever more items, we throw away almost as much as we buy. However, there is hope: that we are just beginning to buy less and hence waste less.

Map 6.6.1 shows how, between the financial years 2007/08 and 2008/09, in 290 of England's 354 local authorities, domestic waste collected per person fell. There is no especially clear pattern over this short time span to explain why in a few places waste levels rose and why in other areas they were reduced. Apparent profligacy may increase as a recycling scheme is introduced in an area, and in this particular map we are including waste that ends up being recycled. However, it is better always to generate less waste by not buying things you don't really need, no matter how good you are at recycling the packaging.

The greatest increase in waste being collected per person between these two years occurred in Lichfield which also saw an extra 29 kg per year (per household) of non-recyclable waste being generated, so this initially green-looking market town would appear to be the least green place in England when it came to change in rubbish generation. In contrast, Tower Hamlets in the heart of London saw the greatest fall in rubbish being generated in England, some 87 kg less per person per year, or some 216 kg less non-recyclable waste per household.

Green campaigners such as Molly Scott Cato, green economist, social innovator and ideas merchant, explain just how urgent and achievable reductions in pollution and the generation of waste are.[7] By 2008/09 each person in Lichfield was generating over 50% more waste than each resident of Tower Hamlets. A year earlier, before the improvements in Tower Hamlets and the regression in Lichfield, that ratio had been only 14% more waste being generated in Lichfield. It is clearly possible to change behaviour in a very short time span. Map 6.6.2 shows how it is possible to throw away far less even than in Tower Hamlets (per person). This has already been achieved in the following areas, where the least rubbish is generated: Weymouth & Portland (290 kg per person), Hyndburn, Oxford, Purbeck, Malvern Hills, Oadby & Wigston, East Devon, Mid Suffolk, South Somerset, Camden, Worcester, Tendring and Taunton Deane. In contrast, in the following 13 areas, almost (and in a few cases more than) twice as much is thrown away per person in municipal wheelie bins: Rutland, Hartlepool, Milton Keynes, Doncaster, Halton, the East Riding of Yorkshire, West Berkshire, North Lincolnshire, Poole, Peterborough, the Isle of Wight, the City of London, the Isles of Scilly (964 kg per person/year). These areas are the extreme places mapped in Map 6.6.1.

Finally Map 6.6.3 shows in which areas the most non-recycled waste is generated (not per person, but per household). Households tend to be smaller where people are older, and so the leaders here are all rural areas where less than 400 kg non-recycled waste per household per year is collected: South Hams (349 kg per household/year), Weymouth & Portland, Cotswold (greatest fall of 216 kg per household per year), South Shropshire, Taunton Deane, Teignbridge, Staffordshire Moorlands, East Lindsey and South Somerset. In contrast, per

Map 6.6.1: 2007/08–2008/09 Change in total domestic waste collected (kg/person), local authorities, England

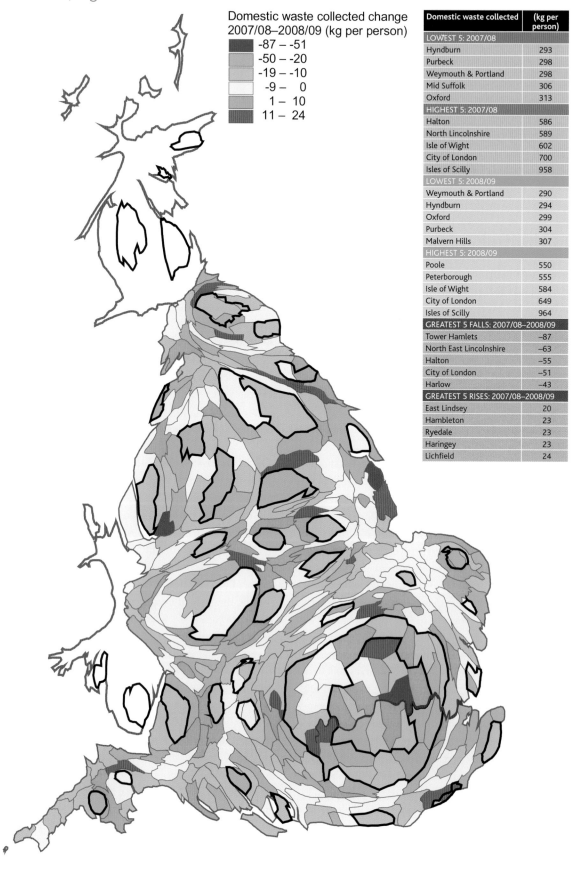

Domestic waste collected change
2007/08–2008/09 (kg per person)

- -87 – -51
- -50 – -20
- -19 – -10
- -9 – 0
- 1 – 10
- 11 – 24

Domestic waste collected	(kg per person)
LOWEST 5: 2007/08	
Hyndburn	293
Purbeck	298
Weymouth & Portland	298
Mid Suffolk	306
Oxford	313
HIGHEST 5: 2007/08	
Halton	586
North Lincolnshire	589
Isle of Wight	602
City of London	700
Isles of Scilly	958
LOWEST 5: 2008/09	
Weymouth & Portland	290
Hyndburn	294
Oxford	299
Purbeck	304
Malvern Hills	307
HIGHEST 5: 2008/09	
Poole	550
Peterborough	555
Isle of Wight	584
City of London	649
Isles of Scilly	964
GREATEST 5 FALLS: 2007/08–2008/09	
Tower Hamlets	–87
North East Lincolnshire	–63
Halton	–55
City of London	–51
Harlow	–43
GREATEST 5 RISES: 2007/08–2008/09	
East Lindsey	20
Hambleton	23
Ryedale	23
Haringey	23
Lichfield	24

household, more than 800 kg of (non-recycled) waste is generated in the following nine areas: North Warwickshire, Slough, Sunderland, Isle of Wight, West Berkshire, Halton, Barking & Dagenham, Newham and Isles of Scilly (1,460 kg).

Map 6.6.2: 2008/09 Total domestic waste collected (kg/person), local authorities, England

Domestic waste
collected 2008/09
(kg per person)
290 – 299
300 – 399
400 – 499
500 – 599
600 – 964

Map 6.6.3: 2008/09 Domestic waste collected and not recycled (kg/household), local authorities, England

Residual domestic
waste 2008/09
(kg per h/hold)
340 –   499
500 –   599
600 –   699
700 –   799
800 – 1,460

6.7 Recycling: if you have to use it, then reuse it

It is better not to consume in the first place anything you do not need to buy. Most of what you need to buy can be recycled. The packaging of the food and drink you buy can almost always be recycled if well made. Better still, packaging can be made which can be reused without recycling.

From compost toilets to bottle banks, across almost all of England and Wales, recycling is becoming more and more commonplace.

As yet Scotland does not provide disaggregated statistics for households, just for municipal waste; therefore it could not be included here, nor in the previous Section 6.6, on waste generated.

The only domestic statistics Wales provides by area are recycling rates, and so Welsh districts can be included on two of the maps shown here. It is worrying that some parts of Britain still do not count waste carefully, as the more carefully we count, the less we are likely to waste in the future.

Map 6.7.1 shows how recycling rates have been rising in the most recent years we have data for in all but 51 of the 376 local authorities in England and Wales. A high recycling rate is not necessarily ideal if all it reflects is very high overall consumption of easily recycled packaging. Similarly, a huge increase in the local recycling rate is not so great if it merely indicates the introduction of a recycling scheme which should have existed before. Thus the increase in the proportion of rubbish recycled in Cotswold from 43% to 61% in one year is more impressive than Rochford's larger jump from 19% to 50%. The initial recycling is the easiest: that of glass and paper. It is the harder-to-recycle items that make it more difficult to raise these figures very high.

In some areas where people behave in very green ways, recycling rates may be low because the consumption of items that are more easily recycled is low. More environmentally minded people do not purchase items with much packaging, for instance. Thus, in Brighton & Hove, where people only produce 425 kg of waste each a year, recycling rates have risen by only 1.1% in recent years to 29.5%, whereas, along the coast in Poole, residents now recycle 39.7% of their typical 550 kg of waste. However, in Poole each resident leaves 335 kg a year for landfill or incineration as compared to 304 kg in Brighton & Hove. Thus the greener residents (who also happen to have elected Caroline Lucas, the leader of the Green Party and MP for Brighton Pavilion to Parliament) have the lower recycling rate.

The highest recycling and composting rates per household are found in more rural areas. Often this is because far more people in these areas have gardens, although it would be far better if that material was composted in the gardens it grew in. Map 6.7.2 shows the national pattern of where recycling is most and least common. The lower rates are generally found in mainly urban and poorer areas, with just 15% of waste being recycled in Newman, 20% in Manchester, 25% in Knowsley, 30% in Leeds and 35% in Luton. Compare those rates to 40% in Poole, 45% in York, 50% in Cherwell (Oxfordshire) and 61% in the Cotswolds.

Ultimately what matters most is how much waste you produce of the kind that is not recycled. Map 6.7.3 shows changes in that measure – the reduction in kilograms of residual (non-recycled) waste produced per household in recent years. Here far more of the areas recording large falls and low numbers are within the poorer parts of cities where people tend to consume less in the first place.

Of all the areas where people now produce less than 400 kg of waste each a year, the greatest reductions in recent years, all of over 100 kg a year, have been in: Rochford, Tower Hamlets, Warwick, Kingston upon Thames, Norwich, Ribble Valley, Swale, Richmondshire, Harlow and St Albans. Conversely of all the areas where individual waste estimates per person still exceed 500 kg a year, the ten areas with the lowest rates of improvement in non-recyclable levels are: North Somerset, Milton Keynes, City of London, Peterborough, North Tyneside, Doncaster, Poole, York, Isle of Wight and South Gloucestershire.

Map 6.7.1: 2007/08–2008/09 Change in waste recycled or composted (% point per household), local authorities, England & Wales

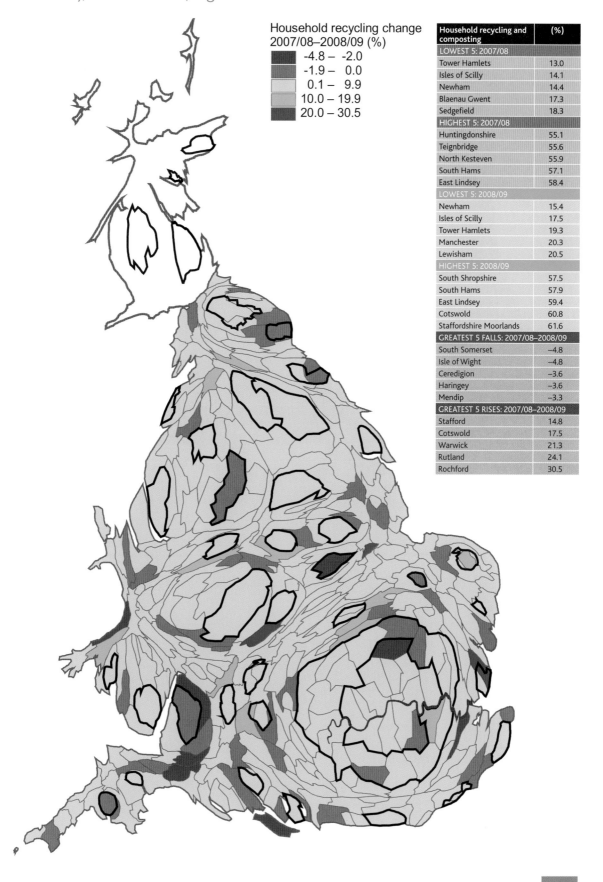

Household recycling change 2007/08–2008/09 (%)

- -4.8 – -2.0
- -1.9 – 0.0
- 0.1 – 9.9
- 10.0 – 19.9
- 20.0 – 30.5

Household recycling and composting	(%)
LOWEST 5: 2007/08	
Tower Hamlets	13.0
Isles of Scilly	14.1
Newham	14.4
Blaenau Gwent	17.3
Sedgefield	18.3
HIGHEST 5: 2007/08	
Huntingdonshire	55.1
Teignbridge	55.6
North Kesteven	55.9
South Hams	57.1
East Lindsey	58.4
LOWEST 5: 2008/09	
Newham	15.4
Isles of Scilly	17.5
Tower Hamlets	19.3
Manchester	20.3
Lewisham	20.5
HIGHEST 5: 2008/09	
South Shropshire	57.5
South Hams	57.9
East Lindsey	59.4
Cotswold	60.8
Staffordshire Moorlands	61.6
GREATEST 5 FALLS: 2007/08–2008/09	
South Somerset	−4.8
Isle of Wight	−4.8
Ceredigion	−3.6
Haringey	−3.6
Mendip	−3.3
GREATEST 5 RISES: 2007/08–2008/09	
Stafford	14.8
Cotswold	17.5
Warwick	21.3
Rutland	24.1
Rochford	30.5

Map 6.7.2: 2008/09 Waste recycled or composted (% per household), local authorities, England & Wales

Map 6.7.3: 2007/08–2008/09 Change in domestic waste collected and not recycled (kg per household), local authorities, England

Household recycling
2008/09 (%)
- 15.4 – 19.9
- 20.0 – 29.9
- 30.0 – 39.9
- 40.0 – 49.9
- 50.0 – 61.6

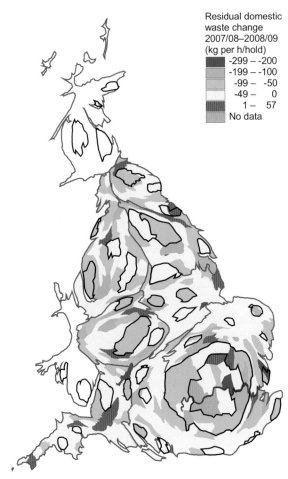

Residual domestic
waste change
2007/08–2008/09
(kg per h/hold)
- -299 – -200
- -199 – -100
- -99 – -50
- -49 – 0
- 1 – 57
- No data

Conclusion

An index of local environmental conditions

We end this atlas by taking just four of the indicators we have mapped in the preceding pages and combining them to create a single index of local environmental conditions. To do this we needed indicators which had been available for the same geographical areas for all of England, Scotland and Wales. They had to be available for the same two pairs of years so that we could see how the index was changing. The most comprehensive sets were available for 2007/08 and 2008/09 – charting the cusp of the crash. Indicators had to be available for every local authority in the country with no missing numbers (otherwise we could not rank our index). These conditions meant that we then had very few choices, as only four sets of data complied with all these requirements. This is data about the general environments of the areas people live in and how they are changing, not so much about individual lives.

Indicator 1 – benzene air pollution

The first indicator we chose was benzene air pollution (see Section 6.3). These emissions come mainly from car exhausts but also from industrial plants, and the lower this measure of how much pollution we have to inhale, the better. In 2007 Falkirk in Scotland, the town adjacent to the Grangemouth oil refinery, recorded the highest recorded emissions with 1.76 tonnes being emitted over every square kilometre of land (t/sq km) in the town. Next highest then was the industrial district of Stockton-on-Tees at 1.11 t/sq km. By 2008 pollution rates in Falkirk had risen to 1.85 t/sq km, but traffic and congestion in central London had produced even more damaging overall rates of 1.88 t/sq km, enough in a year to exceed even the pollution near oil refineries and giant chemical works. In 2008 benzene pollution

rates in Westminster (1.35 t/sq km), Kensington & Chelsea (1.32), Southampton (1.16), Islington (1.15), Lambeth (1.05), Hammersmith & Fulham (1.04), Tower Hamlets (1.02) and Camden (0.95) ranked from third to tenth highest after the City of London and Falkirk, and all exceeded those of Stockton-on-Tees that year, despite the chemical works there.

The lowest recorded rates of benzene pollution were 0.01 t/sq km across Argyll & Bute in 2008, 188 times less than in the City of London. By 2008, people living in the heart of London were breathing in the most chemicals. In the table in the Appendix (page 153) we show these pollution figures, for every local authority in Britain for 2007 and 2008, in units of tens of kilograms per hectare per year to avoid having to include any decimal points.

Indicator 2 – crime rates

The second indicator that was available for these same areas in England, Scotland and Wales, for both years with no missing data, was the number of crimes reported per 100 people per year in the financial years 2007/08 and 2008/09 (see Section 4.5). In the earlier period the highest crime rate was recorded in the City of London at 95 crimes per 100 residents. Clearly most residents of the City are not themselves subject to crime, but it is crimes committed against commuters and tourists travelling through the area that inflate this figure. In the crime tables the City of London was followed that year by Blaenau Gwent (76 crimes recorded per 100 inhabitants) and Wolverhampton (75). Crime rates fell a little in the City in the year 2008/09 but it still held on to first place (91 crimes per 100 residents). This was well above the new second-ranking city for crime, Hull (at 74 crimes per 100 residents), while Wolverhampton retained third place at 72. In general, in most areas, crime rates fell over this period. The lowest recorded rate (3 crimes per 100 residents) was in the Isles of Scilly.

Indicator 3 – electricity consumption

The third indicator that met all the criteria to be included in this index was domestic electricity consumption: how many hundreds of kilowatt hours were being used per household per year in each place; in both 2007 and 2008 (see Section 6.5). Rates were highest in both years in the Shetland and Orkney Islands, in Eilean Siar and in the Scilly Isles, where there was no domestic gas supply. They were next highest in other remote rural areas, where the most homes were which were not connected to supplies of mains gas for heating and cooking. Rates were lowest where people were poorest and could least afford electricity (Blaenau Gwent and South Tyneside in both years). However, rates of consumption generally increased the most between these pairs of years in places where money worries were least: in Weymouth & Portland (+150 kWh per household per year), Kensington & Chelsea (+75), the City of London (+66), Tower Hamlets (+60), New Forest (+41), Westminster (+37) and Poole (+29).

Indicator 4 – malicious calls to fire brigades

The fourth and final indicator we selected was the rate of malicious false alarms being made to the local fire brigade per 10,000 people per year. Here we often had to use data for a larger area than the local authority itself as the statistics were reported for the brigade area as a whole. This was the most comprehensive measure of anti-social behaviour that we could collect for both these years for all three countries of Britain, and was a measure which could be allocated down to all local authorities. In the financial year 2007/08 the malicious callout rate was highest in and around Glasgow at 12.2 calls per 10,000 people per year. The rate there fell rapidly to 9.5 by 2008/09, but still remained the highest in all the three countries. Like crime and electricity consumption, anti-social behaviour was generally in decline. The lowest malicious callout rates were in and around the Cotswolds at one call per 10,000 people per year. No such malicious calls were recorded in the Isles of Scilly.

Creating the index of local environmental conditions

For every local authority area in Britain the table in the following Appendix shows these four measures and the change over time in each of them. It also shows how each area scores at each point in time if the four measures are simply added together to make a score. The four measures contribute to those scores on average in the following proportions: benzene level 18%; reported crime 32%; electricity consumption 46%; malicious false alarms 4%. These proportions, as any would be, are arbitrary. However, they allow us to then rank areas by that score and see how those rankings of local environmental conditions have been changing as a result of changes to local pollution levels, crime rates, electricity use and anti-social behaviour. Individual scores can be affected by particularly unusual local factors, which are unlikely to affect the other parameters. The use of an overall score reduces the effect of that. Ranking then shows how one authority compares with another. The original arbitrary units used in the separate measures have little impact on the changes in ranking over time.

By 2008 the place with the worst local environmental conditions according to our overall score was the City of London (333), followed by Falkirk (281), Westminster (208), Tower Hamlets (208) and Kensington & Chelsea (207). At the other extreme the areas which ranked best out of all 408 local authorities by 2008 were Durham, in North East England (scoring 72), South Lakeland, in Cumbria (72), Purbeck, in Dorset (71), Broadland, in Norfolk (71), and the Ribble Valley, in Lancashire (71). But perhaps what is most interesting is not finding that pollution, crime, consumption and anti-social behaviour are lowest in rural and northern England and highest in areas of old polluting industry and oil refineries and also in the banking heart of London. What is most interesting is how these rankings are changing.

Table 7.1 shows the ten areas of Britain which experienced the greatest overall deterioration in their local environmental conditions score as measured between the two most recent years for which comprehensive data are available (rank 1 has the worst/highest score):

Table 7.1: Local environmental conditions: highest deterioration in scores between 2007/08 and 2008/09

Local environmental conditions score (most deteriorated)							
Rank of change in score	Local Authority	2007 score	2008 score	Change in score	2007 rank	2008 rank	Change in rank
1	City of London	252	333	80	2	1	1
2	Westminster	151	208	57	17	3	14
3	Kensington & Chelsea	154	207	53	16	5	11
4	Tower Hamlets	164	208	44	9	4	5
5	Islington	165	205	41	8	6	2
6	Lambeth	158	198	40	14	7	7
7	Southwark	140	178	38	26	12	14
8	Castle Point	108	141	35	142	41	101
9	Camden	131	165	34	46	19	27
10	Hammersmith & Fulham	151	185	34	18	10	8

Note: A high score means poor local environmental conditions.

Table 7.2: Local environmental conditions: greatest improvement in scores between 2007/08 and 2008/09

Local environmental conditions score (most improved)							
Rank of change score	Local Authority	2007 score	2008 score	Change in score	2007 rank	2008 rank	Change in rank
399	Sedgefield	107	91	−16	147	228	−81
400	North Lincolnshire	172	156	−16	6	25	−19
401	Blaenau Gwent	139	120	−18	31	84	−53
402	Wakefield	135	116	−18	36	94	−58
403	Rossendale	107	87	−20	148	263	−115
404	Stockton-on-Tees	205	183	−21	3	11	−8
405	Barnsley	132	109	−22	42	121	−79
406	Doncaster	128	106	−22	52	134	−82
407	Redcar & Cleveland	179	156	−24	5	24	−19
408	Rotherham	136	105	−31	33	138	−105

Note: A high score means poor local environmental conditions.

Table 7.2 shows the ten areas that saw their scores improve the most between the latest years for which we have data:

Overall environmental conditions still remain worse in a few of the ten most improving local authorities; but the bigger picture shows that when it comes to environmental sustainability and sociability in Britain, these two sets of areas are moving apart.

In much of the north of England, and especially in South Yorkshire, some of the worst government cuts are being planned, but, prior to this period, air pollution was improving, crime falling, domestic consumption of electricity dropping and anti-social behaviour declining. Part of the reason will be further industrial decline in places such as Barnsley,

Doncaster and Rotherham: fewer cars on the roads, fewer people able to go out and get drunk, get into a fight and commit a criminal offence, fewer people being able to heat their homes so well, but also fewer people tolerating the waste when teenagers ring to see if a fire engine will turn up when there is no real fire.

The country as whole needs to consume less, emit less benzene into the air, commit (and suffer) less crime, consume less and be less malicious. Living conditions in the heart of bailed-out London are not to be envied despite all the profligacy there: City lungs are slowly filling up with chemicals, City minds are growing weary constantly thinking about where their wallets are in case of theft and how full they are in preparation for the next crash, City offices and homes burn up power as air conditioners whirr and a thousand and one gadgets are charged.

This index, set out in full in the Appendix, allows places to be ranked by things in life that can matter more than money, and illustrates how they are changing.

Bankruptcy

The best stories are those which have a twist at the end. The twist in this story has been to find environmental conditions worsening fastest in the wealthiest places. This atlas has mapped just the beginning of the socio-economic fall-out of what, for all practical purposes, has been the London-based banks' near bankruptcy of Britain.

The New Labour administration was complicit in allowing those bankers to gamble, not just with their customers' money but with the futures of all the country's citizens. The Coalition government, as Labour's successor, has been even more acquiescent to the call of those who still call themselves 'wealth creators' for cuts that result in rises in poverty concentrated far away from their own homes. However, none of this means that one group is necessarily doing much better at the expense of the rest.

Everyone suffers when greed is allowed to rule, including the greedy. Although it its certainly true that the social and financial impact of the fall-out from our over-dependence on banking has been most concentrated in the poorest parts of the country – and among the poorest social groups in those parts – this does not mean that all is good where most wealth remains.

In those parts of Britain that remain the wealthiest, many people are becoming even richer than they were before. As we write this conclusion, in the spring of 2011, despite GDP falling nationally by half of one percentage point, property values in the most expensive parts of London and the South East continue to rise, huge bonuses are still being paid to bankers, the Prime Minister gives

speeches suggesting that multiculturalism has failed in a pathetic attempt to divert attention away from the thousands of jobs being lost through the cuts, and even those growing increasingly rich (often through the bankruptcy or near bankruptcy of so many others) are growing more fearful –and understandably so.

In January 2011 we discovered that the bankers were again beginning to receive the huge annual bonus payments that so many had taken before the economic crash. In February, it became apparent that the Coalition government had no intention of preventing this further widening of income, and hence wealth, inequalities. In March it was announced that there had been just over a 10% increase in the number of billionaires living in Britain – just as the incomes of many of the poorest were about to be reduced by a similar proportion due to redundancy, cuts in benefits, higher inflation, and minimal wage rises, or the taking by stealth of their meagre pension rights. In April, the *Sunday Times* rich list was unveiled to garner yet more shocked responses to the excesses of the rich. However, all was not well, even among the wealthiest people living in Britain.

The wealthy know that as the gap between rich and poor grows, the future for their own children becomes less and less secure. Increasingly these children know that their parents, and the convoluted way British society is currently arranged and the direction in which it is travelling, *are responsible for* a huge part of the problems that are slowly bankrupting the country in so many ways. Future generations, including those now just becoming adults, may well have very different view, both rich and poor.

Financially, residentially, politically, morally, emotionally and environmentally, we appear to be heading towards certain forms of bankruptcy. This atlas has charted some of the most recent evidence of where we may be going in the wrong direction.

Notes

Introduction

[1] Bauman, Z. (2010) 'Letter 34: Is there an end to depression?', *44 Letters from the Liquid Modern World*, Cambridge: Polity Press, p 139 (originally published in *La Repubblica delle Donne*, 2009).

[2] Dorling, D. and Thomas, B. (2004) *People and places: A census atlas of the UK*, Bristol: The Policy Press.

[3] HM Treasury (2011), *Budget 2011*, http://cdn.hm-treasury.gov.uk/2011budget_complete.pdf

[4] Taylor-Gooby, P. and Stoker, G. (2011) 'The Coalition Programme', *Political Quarterly*, vol 82, no 1, pp 4-27.

[5] Institute for Fiscal Studies (2011) *Living standards during the recession*, www.ifs.org.uk/bns/bn117.pdf

How to use this atlas

[1] Gastner, M.T. and Newman, M.E.J. (2004) 'Diffusion-based method for producing density equalizing maps', *Proceedings of the National Academy of Sciences of the United States of America*, vol 101, pp 7499–504. The code can be found here: www-personal.umich.edu/~mejn/car

[2] http://scapetoad.choros.ch

[3] Bauman, Z. (2010) 'Letter 41: Drawing boundaries', in *44 Letters from the Liquid Modern World*, Cambridge: Polity Press, p 171 (originally published in *La Repubblica delle Donne*, 2009, emphasis as in the original).

Chapter 1

[1] www.creditaction.org.uk/debt-statistics.html

[2] www.statistics.gov.uk/downloads/theme_economy/ukea-10q1.pdf (Table A1, GDP 2009) £1,392,705 million, or around £23,212 for every person in the UK, 11.9% of which is £2,762. In 2008 the average number of people per household in the UK was 2.37 and so national debt per household was £6,546: www.statistics.gov.uk/downloads/theme_compendia/GLF08/GLFoverview2008.pdf

[3] *Households Below Average Income*, p 15, Median income after household costs £17,836 per year. See: http://statistics.dwp.gov.uk/asd/hbai/hbai_2009/pdf_files/full_hbai10.pdf

[4] On national wealth see: www.equalities.gov.uk/national_equality_panel/publications/charts_and_statistical_annex/statistical_annex.aspx

[5] www.aib.gov.uk/About/annualtargets/quarterlyreports/q1stats201011

[6] www.insolvency.gov.uk/bankruptcy/alternativestobankruptcy.htm

[7] See UNICEF's Innocenti Research Centre's Report Card 7: www.unicef-irc.org/publications/pdf/rc7_eng.pdf

[8] This still differs from the EU measure in requiring that children's families are in receipt of these credits or benefits to be poor. Thus a child of a family not qualifying, say because their parents are seeking refugee status, will not be counted as poor despite usually being among the poorest in Britain. It is also possible by the UK definition for a 17-year-old not to be considered a child. This is because: 'A person will also be defined as a child if they are 16 to 19 years old and they are:

- not married nor in a Civil Partnership nor living with a partner; and
- living with parents; and
- in full-time non-advanced education or in unwaged government training

This is the same definition as used within tax credits, Child Benefit and Income Support and Jobseeker's Allowance.'

See Technical information for National Indicator 116: www.hmrc.gov.uk/stats/personal-tax-credits/menu. htm

[9] See *Households Below Average Income* statistics: 2008/9 report, p 15: http://statistics.dwp.gov.uk/asd/hbai/hbai_2009/pdf_files/full_hbai10.pdf

[10] 'In general, the older the age of the pensioners, the greater the likelihood of low income': *Households Below Average Income* (HBAI) 2008/9 (p 141 and Table 6.3, p 152 on living alone and tenure – on the after housing cost basis). http://statistics.dwp.gov.uk/asd/hbai/hbai_2009/pdf_files/full_hbai10.pdf

[11] Ibid, Table 6.5. Note that HBAI statistics now include data on what items poorer pensioners have to live without.

[12] www.hmrc.gov.uk/stats/income_distribution/menu-by-year.htm

[13] See Dorling, D. (2010) *Injustice: Why social inequality persists*, Bristol: The Policy Press, for a summary of all these claims and sources.

[14] See ONS, Introduction of automatic occupation coding in ASHE: www.statistics.gov.uk/cci/article.asp?id=1843

[15] This document can be found at www.communities.gov.uk/documents/localgovernment/pdf/1611330.pdf, And more similar ones here: www.communities.gov.uk/localgovernment/localgovernmentfinance/

[16] *New IFS research challenges Chancellor's 'progressive Budget' claim*, www.ifs.org.uk/publications/5245

Chapter 2

[1] 'Western Europe has most millionaires, study finds', *National Geographic* 'News', 11 July 2003, http://news.nationalgeographic.com/news/2003/07/0711_030711_money.html

[2] Peter Rachman was the 1950s Notting Hill landlord whose name became synonymous with greed and unscrupulousness. On the right-to-sell see Dorling, D. (2011) *Housing and identity: How place makes race*, London: Race Equality Foundation, www.better-housing.org.uk/files/housing/housing-brief17.pdf

[3] The sale was widely misreported at £70 million, before accurate figures became available from HM Land Registry, where records state that on 30 June 2004, 18-19 Kensington Palace Gardens, along with three mews houses at the rear of the property, sold for £57,145,967: http://en.wikipedia.org/wiki/Kensington_Palace_Gardens

[4] http://scotland.shelter.org.uk/housing_issues/preventing_homelessness

Chapter 3

[1] http://en.wikipedia.org/wiki/Rotten-and-pocket-boroughs

Chapter 4

[1] See Dorling, D. (2010) *Injustice: Why social inequality persists*, Bristol: The Policy Press, fig 19.

[2] The names of many of the children who suffered cruelty and were killed are listed in David Batty's 'Timeline: a history of child protection': www.guardian.co.uk/society/2005/may/18/childrensservices2

[3] For details see the relevant government department's reports at: www.dcsf.gov.uk/everychildmatters/safeguardingandsocialcare/integratedchildrenssystem/icstechnicalresources/icsphasingoutchildprotectionregister/registerphaseout/

[4] www.dcsf.gov.uk/rsgateway/DB/SFR/s000873/index.shtml

[5] UNICEF (2007) *Child poverty in perspective: An overview of child well-being in rich countries*, Innocenti Report Card 7, Florence: UNICEF Innocenti Research Centre, www.unicef-irc.org/publications/pdf/rc7_eng.pdf

[6] See ibid, summary table, p 2.

[7] Pickett, K.E. and Wilkinson, R.G. (2007) 'Child wellbeing and income inequality in rich societies: ecological cross sectional study', BMJ, vol 355; doi:10.1136/bmj.39377.580162.55

[8] www.fti.communities.gov.uk/DataDownload. aspx?PH=01/01/1900 (This is DCLG's floor target download page, from which the definition of bullying can be searched for.)

[9] Purcell, B. (2010) 'UK poverty: Northerners likely to be poorer, less healthy, and die earlier, says ONS', *Tribune*, 11 June, p 7 (reporting on figures released in *Regional Trends* by ONS that week).

[10] For example, 'A key lesson from the Dutch, who have a very low teen pregnancy rate, is to make the mechanics of reproduction crystal clear': www. guardian.co.uk/commentisfree/2010/feb/27/teen-pregnancy-netherlands-sex. Anastasia de Waal, who made this suggestion, was talking on behalf of Civitas, one of the think tanks that concentrate on issues of morality in Britain.

[11] http://news.bbc.co.uk/1/hi/education/8531227.stm

[12] Shaw, M., Dorling, D. and Davey-Smith, G. (2002) 'Editorial: Mortality and political climate: how suicide rates have risen during periods of Conservative government, 1901–2000', *Journal of Epidemiology and Community Health*, vol 56, no 10, pp 722-7 (http://sasi.group.shef.ac.uk/publications/2002/shaw_et_al_mortality_political_climate.pdf).

[13] www.communities.gov.uk/publications/corporate/statistics/monitorq12009

[14] www.communities.gov.uk/documents/statistics/pdf/154796.pdf - paragraph 6

[15] http://menmedia.co.uk/news/s/208/208810_10m_a_year_cost_of_999_hoax_calls.html

[16] On what is a crime and what should be seen as criminal, see: Dorling, D., Gordon, D., Hillyard, P., Pantazis, C., Pemberton, S. and Tombs, S. (2008) *Criminal obsessions: Why harm matters more than crime*, 2nd edn, London: Centre for Crime and Justice Studies www.crimeandjustice.org.uk/criminalobsessions2.html

[17] www.iainduncansmith.org/article. aspx?id=7&ref=163

[18] http://en.wikipedia.org/wiki/Regulation_of_Investigatory_Powers_Act_2000

[19] www.bigbrotherwatch.org.uk/TheGrimRIPA.pdf

[20] Wilkinson, R. and Pickett, K. (2009) *The spirit level: Why more equal societies almost always do better*, London: Penguin

[21] www.hmrc.gov.uk/tax-evasion/index.htm.

[22] The number 22,210 is calculated by summing all the figures given for individual areas, which have been rounded down to the nearest 10. When the number is less than 20 no figure is given at all. The total number of estates liable for inheritance tax in Britain, including all those estates which have been excluded due to rounding, is 23,400. See www.hmrc.gov.uk/stats/inheritance_tax/table-12-11.xls and www.hmrc.gov.uk/thelibrary/national-statistics.htm

[23] 'RBS chief Sir Phillip Hampton defends "astonishingly high" bankers' pay', (2010) *The Times*, 30 April. The full article can be found here: http://business.timesonline.co.uk/tol/business/industry-sectois/banking_and_finance_/article7112656.ece

Chapter 5

[1] Mitchell, R. (2005) 'The decline of death – how do we measure and interpret changes in self-reported health across cultures and time?', *International Journal of Epidemiology* vol 34, no 2, pp 306-8; doi:10.1093/ije/dyh361

[2] Burrows, R. and Rhodes, D. (2000) 'The geography of misery: area disadvantage and patterns of neighbourhood dissatisfaction in England', in J. Bradshaw and R. Sainsbury (eds) *Researching Poverty*, Aldershot: Ashgate.

3 www.audit-commission.gov.uk/localgov/audit/nis/Pages/NI050emotionalhealthofchildrenn.aspx

4 We don't include the Isles of Scilly here as their 'results are based on responses from all children and young people in school years 6, 8 and 10 in the local authority'. Also, the City of London did not take part in the survey. It might be expected that the children there might not be so happy, given the general relationship we are finding, but officially: 'This is because with just one primary school to survey, the same school would always be surveyed, as opposed to a sample of the schools in an authority being surveyed. Also as Sir John Cass Primary School has a number of children from other local authorities and as the majority of City children go to school in other boroughs, the result from the one school, were it to take part in TellUs, would not necessarily be a reflection of the work of the local authority, seeing as some of the questions are based around experiences of the children not during the school time.'

5 Dorling, D. (2010) *Injustice: Why social inequality persists*, Bristol: The Policy Press, ch 7.

6 Caan, W. (2009) Editorial, *Journal of Public Mental Health*, vol 8, no 4, pp 2-3.

7 Aggarwal, R. (2010) 'Why we still need free prescriptions in Wales', *Western Mail*, 19 July, www.walesonline.co.uk/news/health-news/2010/07/19/why-we-still-need-free-prescriptions-in-wales-91466-26878783/

8 The data source is the Mental Health Minimum Dataset (MHMDS) 2008–09 annual returns. This work remains the sole and exclusive property of the Health and Social Care Information Centre and may only be reproduced where there is explicit reference to the ownership of the Health and Social Care Information Centre.

9 www.neighbourhood.statistics.gov.uk/dissemination/MetadataDownloadPDF.do?downloadId=25934

10 CEPMHPG (2006) *The depression report: A new deal for depression and anxiety disorders*, London: London School of Economics Centre for Economic Performance's Mental Health Policy Group,

11 James, O. (2007) *Affluenza: How to be successful and stay sane*, London: Vermilion; James, O. (2008) *The selfish capitalist: Origins of* Affluenza, London: Vermilion.

12 Friedli, L. (2009) *Mental health, resilience and inequalities*, Copenhagen: WHO, www.euro.who.int/__data/assets/pdf_file/0012/100821/E92227.pdf

13 Wilkinson, R. and Pickett, K. (2010) *The Spirit Level*, 2nd edn, London: Allen Lane.

Chapter 6

1 Barford, A. et al (2010) 'Re-evaluating self-evaluation. A commentary on Jen, Jones, and Johnston (68:4, 2009)', *Social Science & Medicine*, vol 70, no 4, pp 496-7.

2 King, R. 'Representing: 20's Plenty For Us – The campaign for 20 mph to become the default speed limit for residential roads', www.20splentyforus.org.uk/UsefulReports/Evidence%20to%20Transport%20Committee%20inquiry%20into%20Road%20Safety.pdf

3 'Local and regional CO_2 emissions estimates for 2005–2007', produced by AEA for the Department of Energy and Climate Change (see http://www.decc.gov.uk/en/content/cms/statistics/climate_change/localco2/localco2.aspx).

4 Monbiot, G. (2006) *Heat: How to stop the planet burning*, London: Allen Lane.

5 The Stern Review on the Economics of Climate Change (2006), http://en.wikipedia.org/wiki/Stern_Review

6 Dorling, D. (2010) *Injustice: Why social inequality persists*, Bristol: The Policy Press, Chapter 6, relying for this statistic on: Beck, U. (2000) *World risk society*, 2nd edn, Cambridge: Polity (see page 6 of Beck's book on how the richest fifth of people on the planet consume six times more than their parents did).

7 Scott Cato, M. (2009) *Green economics: An introduction to theory, policy and practice*, London: Earthscan.

Data sources

Maps

Map 1.1.1	www.insolvency.gov.uk/otherinformation/statistics/regionalstats/Total%20Personal%20Insolvencies.xls
	www.insolvency.gov.uk/otherinformation/statistics/regionalstatisticsmenu.htm
Map 1.1.2	www.insolvency.gov.uk/otherinformation/statistics/regionalstats/Total%20Personal%20Insolvencies.xls
	www.insolvency.gov.uk/otherinformation/statistics/regionalstatisticsmenu.htm
Map 1.1.3	www.insolvency.gov.uk/otherinformation/statistics/regionalstats/DROs.xls
	www.insolvency.gov.uk/otherinformation/statistics/regionalstatisticsmenu.htm
Map 1.2.1	www.hmrc.gov.uk/stats/personal-tax-credits/child_poverty.htm
	www.sns.gov.uk
Map 1.2.2	www.hmrc.gov.uk/stats/personal-tax-credits/child_poverty.htm
	www.sns.gov.uk
Map 1.2.3	www.hmrc.gov.uk/stats/personal-tax-credits/child_poverty.htm
	www.sns.gov.uk
Map 1.3.1	www.hmrc.gov.uk/stats/income_distribution/menu-by-year.htm
Map 1.3.2	www.hmrc.gov.uk/stats/income_distribution/menu-by-year.htm
Map 1.3.3	www.hmrc.gov.uk/stats/income_distribution/menu-by-year.htm
Map 1.4.1	www.nomisweb.co.uk
Map 1.4.2	www.nomisweb.co.uk
Map 1.4.3	www.nomisweb.co.uk
Map 1.4.4	www.nomisweb.co.uk
Map 1.5.1	www.nomisweb.co.uk
Map 1.5.2	www.nomisweb.co.uk
Map 1.5.3	www.nomisweb.co.uk
Map 1.6.1	www.communities.gov.uk/documents/localgovernment/xls/1611273.xls
	www.communities.gov.uk/localgovernment/localgovernmentfinance
	www.communities.gov.uk/news/newsroom/1611369
Map 1.6.2	www.nomisweb.co.uk
Map 1.6.3	www.nomisweb.co.uk
Map 1.7.1	www.hmrc.gov.uk/stats/income_distribution/menu-by-year.htm
Map 1.7.2	www.hmrc.gov.uk/stats/income_distribution/menu-by-year.htm
Map 1.7.3	www.hmrc.gov.uk/stats/income_distribution/menu-by-year.htm
Map 1.7.4	www.hmrc.gov.uk/stats/income_distribution/menu-by-year.htm
Map 2.1.1	www.neighbourhood.statistics.gov.uk
	www.sns.gov.uk
Map 2.2.1	www.neighbourhood.statistics.gov.uk
	www.sns.gov.uk
Map 2.3.1	www.justice.gov.uk/publications/docs/mortgage-landlord-possession-local-authority-1999-2009-q1.xls
	www.justice.gov.uk/publications/mortgatelandlordpossession.htm
Map 2.3.2	www.justice.gov.uk/publications/docs/mortgage-landlord-possession-local-authority-1999-2009-q1.xls
	www.justice.gov.uk/publications/mortgatelandlordpossession.htm

Map 2.4.1	www.communities.gov.uk/documents/housing/xls/table-702.xls
	www.communities.gov.uk/housing/housingresearch/housingstatistics/housingstatisticsby/rentslettings/livetables/
	www.scotland.gov.uk/Resource/Doc/1125/0091491.xls
	www.scotland.gov.uk/Topics/Statistics/Browse/Housing-Regeneration/HSfS/HRATables
	http://dissemination.dataunitwales.gov.uk
Map 2.4.2	www.communities.gov.uk/documents/housing/xls/table-702.xls
	www.communities.gov.uk/housing/housingresearch/housingstatistics/housingstatisticsby/rentslettings/livetables/
	www.scotland.gov.uk/Resource/Doc/1125/0091491.xls
	www.scotland.gov.uk/Topics/Statistics/Browse/Housing-Regeneration/HSfS/HRATables
	http://dissemination.dataunitwales.gov.uk
Map 2.5.1	www.justice.gov.uk/publications/docs/mortgage-landlord-possession-local-authority-1999-2009-q1.xls
	www.justice.gov.uk/publications/mortgatelandlordpossession.htm
Map 2.5.2	www.justice.gov.uk/publications/docs/mortgage-landlord-possession-local-authority-1999-2009-q1.xls
	www.justice.gov.uk/publications/mortgatelandlordpossession.htm
Map 2.6.1	www.communities.gov.uk/documents/housing/xls/144458.xls
	www.communities.gov.uk/housing/housingresearch/housingstatistics/housingstatisticsby/rentslettings/livetables
Map 2.6.2	www.communities.gov.uk/documents/housing/xls/144458.xls
	www.communities.gov.uk/housing/housingresearch/housingstatistics/housingstatisticsby/rentslettings/livetables
Map 2.7.1	www.communities.gov.uk/documents/housing/xls/141476.xls
	www.communities.gov.uk/housing/housingresearch/housingstatistics/housingstatisticsby/homelessnessstatistics
	www.communities.gov.uk/documents/housing/xls/144458.xls
	www.communities.gov.uk/housing/housingresearch/housingstatistics/housingstatisticsby/rentslettings/livetables
Map 3.1.1	Local Government Chronicle Elections Centre, University of Plymouth
	http://spreadsheets.google.com/ccc?key=tdLut_gO0qo_C0JevIxnZ2g
Map 3.1.2	Local Government Chronicle Elections Centre, University of Plymouth
Map 3.1.3	http://spreadsheets.google.com/ccc?key=tdLut_gO0qo_C0JevIxnZ2g
Map 3.2.1	Local Government Chronicle Elections Centre, University of Plymouth
	http://spreadsheets.google.com/ccc?key=tdLut_gO0qo_C0JevIxnZ2g
Map 3.2.2	Local Government Chronicle Elections Centre, University of Plymouth
Map 3.2.3	http://spreadsheets.google.com/ccc?key=tdLut_gO0qo_C0JevIxnZ2g
Map 3.3.1	Local Government Chronicle Elections Centre, University of Plymouth
Map 3.4.1	http://spreadsheets.google.com/ccc?key=tTzJxdN1wUiTFjJoPv6903g
Map 3.4.2	http://spreadsheets.google.com/ccc?key=tTzJxdN1wUiTFjJoPv6903g
Map 3.5.1	http://spreadsheets.google.com/ccc?key=tdLut_gO0qo_C0JevIxnZ2g
Map 3.6.1	http://spreadsheets.google.com/ccc?key=tdLut_gO0qo_C0JevIxnZ2g
Map 3.6.2	http://spreadsheets.google.com/ccc?key=tdLut_gO0qo_C0JevIxnZ2g
Map 3.7.1	www.gwydir.demon.co.uk/uklocalgov/makeup.htm
Map 3.7.2	http://spreadsheets.google.com/ccc?key=tdLut_gO0qo_C0JevIxnZ2g
Map 4.1.1	www.dcsf.gov.uk/rsgateway/DB/SFR/s000873/FINALAdditionalTables1to13.xls
	www.dcsf.gov.uk/rsgateway/DB/SFR/s000873/index.shtml
	http://dissemination.dataunitwales.gov.uk/nesstar/temp/EGMS20081211165720568/DOCEN.pdf
	www.scotland.gov.uk/Resource/Doc/286274/0087182.pdf
	www.scotland.gov.uk/Topics/Statistics/Browse/Children/PubChildProtection

Map 4.1.2	www.dcsf.gov.uk/rsgateway/DB/SFR/s000873/FINALAdditionalTables1to13.xls
	www.dcsf.gov.uk/rsgateway/DB/SFR/s000873/index.shtml
	http://dissemination.dataunitwales.gov.uk/nesstar/temp/EGMS20081211165720568/DOCEN.pdf
	www.scotland.gov.uk/Resource/Doc/286274/0087182.pdf
	www.scotland.gov.uk/Topics/Statistics/Browse/Children/PubChildProtection
Map 4.2.1	www.fti.communities.gov.uk/DataDownload.aspx
Map 4.3.1	www.dcsf.gov.uk/everychildmatters/resources-and-practice/IG00200
	www.dcsf.gov.uk/everychildmatters/healthandwellbeing/teenagepregnancy/statistics/statistics/
	www.statswales.wales.gov.uk/TableViewer/tableView.aspx?ReportId=11297#
	www.isdscotland.org/isd/servlet/FileBuffer?namedFile=mat_tp_table3_new_method_06.xls
	www.isdscotland.org/isd/2071.html
Map 4.3.2	www.dcsf.gov.uk/everychildmatters/resources-and-practice/IG00200
	www.dcsf.gov.uk/everychildmatters/healthandwellbeing/teenagepregnancy/statistics/statistics/
	www.statswales.wales.gov.uk/TableViewer/tableView.aspx?ReportId=11297#
	www.isdscotland.org/isd/servlet/FileBuffer?namedFile=mat_tp_table3_new_method_06.xls
	www.isdscotland.org/isd/2071.html
Map 4.4.1	www.communities.gov.uk/documents/statistics/xls/1403046.xls
	www.communities.gov.uk/publications/corporate/statistics/monitorq12009
Map 4.4.2	www.communities.gov.uk/documents/statistics/xls/1403046.xls
	www.communities.gov.uk/publications/corporate/statistics/monitorq12009
Map 4.5.1	http://rds.homeoffice.gov.uk/rds/pdfs09/rec-crime-la-data.xls
	http://rds.homeoffice.gov.uk/rds/soti.html
	www.scotland.gov.uk/Publications/2008/09/29155946/15
	www.scotland.gov.uk/Publications/2008/09/29155946/0
	www.scotland.gov.uk/Resource/Doc/925/0087801.xls
	www.scotland.gov.uk/Publications/2009/09/28155153/0
Map 4.5.2	http://rds.homeoffice.gov.uk/rds/pdfs09/rec-crime-la-data.xls
	http://rds.homeoffice.gov.uk/rds/soti.html
	www.scotland.gov.uk/Publications/2008/09/29155946/15
	www.scotland.gov.uk/Publications/2008/09/29155946/0
	www.scotland.gov.uk/Resource/Doc/925/0087801.xls
	www.scotland.gov.uk/Publications/2009/09/28155153/0
Map 4.5.3	http://rds.homeoffice.gov.uk/rds/pdfs09/rec-crime-la-data.xls
	http://rds.homeoffice.gov.uk/rds/soti.html
	www.scotland.gov.uk/Publications/2008/09/29155946/15
	www.scotland.gov.uk/Publications/2008/09/29155946/0
	www.scotland.gov.uk/Resource/Doc/925/0087801.xls
	www.scotland.gov.uk/Publications/2009/09/28155153/0
Map 4.6.1	www.bigbrotherwatch.org.uk/TheGrimRIPA.pdf
Map 4.6.2	www.bigbrotherwatch.org.uk/TheGrimRIPA.pdf
Map 4.6.3	www.bigbrotherwatch.org.uk/TheGrimRIPA.pdf
Map 4.7.1	www.hmrc.gov.uk/stats/inheritance_tax/table-12-11.xls
	www.hmrc.gov.uk/thelibrary/national-statistics.htm
	ONS for England & Wales mortality data & General Register Office for Scotland for Scotland mortality data
Map 4.7.2	www.hmrc.gov.uk/stats/inheritance_tax/table-12-11.xls
	www.hmrc.gov.uk/thelibrary/national-statistics.htm
Map 5.1.1	www.fti.communities.gov.uk/DataDownload.aspx
Map 5.2.1	www.fti.communities.gov.uk/DataDownload.aspx
Map 5.2.2	www.fti.communities.gov.uk/DataDownload.aspx
Map 5.2.3	www.fti.communities.gov.uk/DataDownload.aspx

Map 5.3.1	www.fti.communities.gov.uk/DataDownload.aspx
Map 5.3.2	www.fti.communities.gov.uk/DataDownload.aspx
Map 5.3.3	www.fti.communities.gov.uk/DataDownload.aspx
Map 5.4.1	https://iview.ic.nhs.uk/pctprescribing/Default.aspx
	http://isdscotland.org/isd/information-and-statistics.jsp?p_service=Content. show&pContentID=3671&p_applic=CCC&
	Health Solutions Wales
Map 5.4.2	Health Solutions Wales
	http://isdscotland.org/isd/information-and-statistics.jsp?p_service=Content. show&pContentID=3671&p_applic=CCC&
Map 5.4.3	https://iview.ic.nhs.uk/pctprescribing/Default.aspx
Map 5.5.1	www.ic.nhs.uk/webfiles/publications/pharmserv9808/General%20Pharmaceutical%20 Services%20in%20England%20and%20Wales%202007_08%20PCT%20LHB%20level%20 Appendix.xls
	www.ic.nhs.uk/webfiles/publications/Primary%20Care/Pharmacies/pharmserv9909/General_ Pharmaceutical_Services_in_England_1999_2000_to_2008_09.xls
	http://isdscotland.org/isd/information-and-statistics.jsp?pContentID=2227&p_applic=CCC&p_ service=Content.show&
	www.statswales.wales.gov.uk/TableViewer/tableView.aspx
Map 5.5.2	www.ic.nhs.uk/webfiles/publications/genphmsvcengwaldecade05/ GeneralPharmaceuticalServices270106_PDF.pdf
	www.ic.nhs.uk/webfiles/publications/gps0506/GeneralPharmaceuticalServicesTables211106_XLS. xls
	www.ic.nhs.uk/webfiles/publications/generalpharmservices200607/General%20 Pharmaceutical%20Services%20in%20England%20and%20Wales%20200607.%20 Community%20Pharmacy%20Appendix.xls
	www.ic.nhs.uk/webfiles/publications/pharmserv9808/General%20Pharmaceutical%20 Services%20in%20England%20and%20Wales%202007_08%20PCT%20LHB%20level%20 Appendix.xls
	www.ic.nhs.uk/webfiles/publications/Primary%20Care/Pharmacies/pharmserv9909/General_ Pharmaceutical_Services_in_England_1999_2000_to_2008_09.xls
	http://isdscotland.org/isd/information-and-statistics.jsp?pContentID=2227&p_applic=CCC&p_ service=Content.show&
	www.statswales.wales.gov.uk/TableViewer/tableView.aspx
Map 5.5.3	www.ic.nhs.uk/webfiles/publications/Primary%20Care/Pharmacies/pharmserv9909/General_ Pharmaceutical_Services_in_England_1999_2000_to_2008_09.xls
	http://isdscotland.org/isd/information-and-statistics.jsp?pContentID=2227&p_applic=CCC&p_ service=Content.show&
	www.statswales.wales.gov.uk/TableViewer/tableView.aspx
Map 5.6.1	www.neighbourhood.statistics.gov.uk
Map 5.7.1	www.fti.communities.gov.uk/DataDownload.aspx
Map 5.7.2	www.fti.communities.gov.uk/DataDownload.aspx
	www.sns.gov.uk
Map 6.2.1	www.dft.gov.uk/pgr/statistics/datatablespublications/accidents/casualtieslatables/ roadcasualtieslocal08
	www.dft.gov.uk/pgr/statistics/datatablespublications/accidents/casualtieslatables/ roadcasualtieslocal08
	www.scotland.gov.uk/Resource/Doc/933/0090597.xls
	www.scotland.gov.uk/Topics/Statistics/Browse/Transport-Travel/RoadAccidentTables/ExtraRCS- Nov09

	Statistical Directorate of the Welsh Assembly
Map 6.2.2	www.dft.gov.uk/excel/173025/221412/221552/228038/625030/datatables2009.xls
	www.dft.gov.uk/pgr/statistics/datatablespublications/vehicles/licensing/vehiclelicensingstatistics2009
Map 6.2.3	www.dft.gov.uk/pgr/statistics/datatablespublications/accidents/casualtieslatables/roadcasualtieslocal08
	www.dft.gov.uk/pgr/statistics/datatablespublications/accidents/casualtieslatables/roadcasualtieslocal08
	www.scotland.gov.uk/Resource/Doc/933/0090597.xls
	www.scotland.gov.uk/Topics/Statistics/Browse/Transport-Travel/RoadAccidentTables/ExtraRCS-Nov09
	http://wales.gov.uk/docs/statistics/2009/091027wts2009ch4ency.xls
	http://wales.gov.uk/topics/statistics/publications/transport2009/?lang=en
Map 6.3.1	www.naei.org.uk/mapping/mapping_2008.php
Map 6.3.2	www.naei.org.uk/mapping/mapping_2007.php
	www.naei.org.uk/mapping/mapping_2008.php
Map 6.3.3	www.naei.org.uk/mapping/mapping_2007.php
	www.naei.org.uk/mapping/mapping_2008.php
Map 6.4.1	www.decc.gov.uk/en/content/cms/statistics/climate_change/gg_emissions/uk_emissions/2007_local/2007_local.aspx
Map 6.5.1	www.decc.gov.uk/en/content/cms/statistics/regional/electricity/electricity.aspx
Map 6.5.2	www.decc.gov.uk/en/content/cms/statistics/regional/electricity/electricity.aspx
Map 6.5.3	www.decc.gov.uk/en/content/cms/statistics/regional/gas/gas.aspx
Map 6.6.1	www.defra.gov.uk/evidence/statistics/environment/wastats/archive/mwb200708a.xls
	www.defra.gov.uk/evidence/statistics/environment/wastats/bulletin08.htm
	www.defra.gov.uk/evidence/statistics/environment/wastats/archive/mwb200809a.xls
	www.defra.gov.uk/evidence/statistics/environment/wastats/bulletin09.htm
Map 6.6.2	www.defra.gov.uk/evidence/statistics/environment/wastats/archive/mwb200809a.xls
	www.defra.gov.uk/evidence/statistics/environment/wastats/bulletin09.htm
Map 6.6.3	www.defra.gov.uk/evidence/statistics/environment/wastats/archive/mwb200809a.xls
	www.defra.gov.uk/evidence/statistics/environment/wastats/bulletin09.htm
Map 6.7.1	www.defra.gov.uk/evidence/statistics/environment/wastats/archive/mwb200708a.xls
	www.defra.gov.uk/evidence/statistics/environment/wastats/bulletin08.htm
	www.defra.gov.uk/evidence/statistics/environment/wastats/archive/mwb200809a.xls
	www.defra.gov.uk/evidence/statistics/environment/wastats/bulletin09.htm
	www.statswales.wales.gov.uk/TableViewer/dimView.aspx
Map 6.7.2	www.defra.gov.uk/evidence/statistics/environment/wastats/archive/mwb200809a.xls
	www.defra.gov.uk/evidence/statistics/environment/wastats/bulletin09.htm
	www.statswales.wales.gov.uk/TableViewer/dimView.aspx
Map 6.7.3	www.defra.gov.uk/evidence/statistics/environment/wastats/archive/mwb200708a.xls
	www.defra.gov.uk/evidence/statistics/environment/wastats/bulletin08.htm
	www.defra.gov.uk/evidence/statistics/environment/wastats/archive/mwb200809a.xls
	www.defra.gov.uk/evidence/statistics/environment/wastats/bulletin09.htm

Figures

Figure 1.0.1	http://stats.oecd.org/Index.aspx?DataSetCode=SNA_TABLE720
Figure 1.0.2	http://epp.eurostat.ec.europa.eu/tgm/table.do?tab=table&init=1&plugin=1&language=en&pcode=tsieb080
Figure 2.1.1	www.neighbourhood.statistics.gov.uk
	www.sns.gov.uk

Figure 2.3.1   www.justice.gov.uk/publications/docs/mortgage-landlord-possession-local-authority-1999-2009-q1.xls

www.justice.gov.uk/publications/mortgatelandlordpossession.htm

Figure 2.4.1   www.communities.gov.uk/documents/housing/xls/table-702.xls www.communities.gov.uk/housing/housingresearch/housingstatistics/housingstatisticsby/rentslettings/livetables

www.scotland.gov.uk/Resource/Doc/1125/0091491.xls

www.scotland.gov.uk/Topics/Statistics/Browse/Housing-Regeneration/HSfS/HRATables

http://dissemination.dataunitwales.gov.uk

Figure 2.5.1   www.justice.gov.uk/publications/docs/mortgage-landlord-possession-local-authority-1999-2009-q1.xls

http://www.justice.gov.uk/publications/mortgatelandlordpossession.htm

Figure 2.7.1   www.communities.gov.uk/documents/housing/xls/141476.xls

www.communities.gov.uk/housing/housingresearch/housingstatistics/housingstatisticsby/homelessnessstatistics

www.communities.gov.uk/documents/housing/xls/144458.xls

www.communities.gov.uk/housing/housingresearch/housingstatistics/housingstatisticsby/rentslettings/livetables

Figure 2.7.2   www.communities.gov.uk/documents/housing/xls/141476.xls

www.communities.gov.uk/housing/housingresearch/housingstatistics/housingstatisticsby/homelessnessstatistics

www.communities.gov.uk/documents/housing/xls/144458.xls

www.communities.gov.uk/housing/housingresearch/housingstatistics/housingstatisticsby/rentslettings/livetables

Figure 2.7.3   www.communities.gov.uk/documents/housing/xls/141476.xls

www.communities.gov.uk/housing/housingresearch/housingstatistics/housingstatisticsby/homelessnessstatistics

www.communities.gov.uk/documents/housing/xls/144458.xls

www.communities.gov.uk/housing/housingresearch/housingstatistics/housingstatisticsby/rentslettings/livetables

Figure 3.2.1   Local Government Chronicle Elections Centre, University of Plymouth

http://spreadsheets.google.com/ccc?key=tdLut_gO0qo_C0JevlxnZ2g

Figure 3.5.1   Local Government Chronicle Elections Centre, University of Plymouth

http://spreadsheets.google.com/ccc?key=tdLut_gO0qo_C0JevlxnZ2g

Figure 4.5.1   Calculated by authors from data from:

http://rds.homeoffice.gov.uk/rds/pdfs09/rec-crime-la-data.xls

http://rds.homeoffice.gov.uk/rds/soti.html

www.scotland.gov.uk/Publications/2008/09/29155946/15

www.scotland.gov.uk/Publications/2008/09/29155946/0

www.scotland.gov.uk/Resource/Doc/925/0087801.xls

www.scotland.gov.uk/Publications/2009/09/28155153/0

Figure 4.7.1   www.hmrc.gov.uk/stats/inheritance_tax/table-12-11.xls

www.hmrc.gov.uk/thelibrary/national-statistics.htm

Figure 5.1.1   www.communities.gov.uk/documents/localgovernment/doc/880053.doc

Figure 5.1.2   www.fti.communities.gov.uk/DataDownload.aspx

www.neighbourhood.statistics.gov.uk

Figure 5.2.1   www.tellussurvey.org.uk (note this website is now defunct)

Figure 5.4.1   http://isdscotland.org/isd/information-and-statistics.jsp?p_service=Content.show&pContentID=3671&p_applic=CCC&

Figure 5.5.1   https://iview.ic.nhs.uk/pctprescribing/Default.aspx

www.ic.nhs.uk/webfiles/publications/genphmsvcengwaldecade05/GeneralPharmaceuticalServices270106_PDF.pdf

http://isdscotland.org/isd/information-and-statistics.jsp?pContentID=2227&p_applic=CCC&p_
service=Content.show&

www.statswales.wales.gov.uk/TableViewer/tableView.aspx

Figure 5.7.1   www.communities.gov.uk/documents/statistics/pdf/164191.pdf

www.communities.gov.uk/publications/corporate/statistics/citizenshipsurveyq4200910

Figure 6.1.1   ONS for England & Wales mortality data & General Register Office for Scotland for Scotland
mortality data

Figure 6.1.2   ONS for England & Wales mortality data & General Register Office for Scotland for Scotland
mortality data

Figure 6.1.3   ONS for England & Wales mortality data & General Register Office for Scotland for Scotland
mortality data

Figure 6.1.4   ONS for England & Wales mortality data & General Register Office for Scotland for Scotland
mortality data

Figure 6.1.5   ONS for England & Wales mortality data & General Register Office for Scotland for Scotland
mortality data

Figure 6.1.6   ONS for England & Wales mortality data & General Register Office for Scotland for Scotland
mortality data

Figure 6.1.7   ONS for England & Wales mortality data & General Register Office for Scotland for Scotland
mortality data

Figure 6.1.8   ONS for England & Wales mortality data & General Register Office for Scotland for Scotland
mortality data

Figure 6.1.9   ONS for England & Wales mortality data & General Register Office for Scotland for Scotland
mortality data

Figure 6.1.10   ONS for England & Wales mortality data & General Register Office for Scotland for Scotland
mortality data

Tables

Table 1.4.1   www.nomisweb.co.uk

Table 1.7.1   www.equalities.gov.uk/docs/200608_Wealth_tables.xls

www.equalities.gov.uk/national_equality_panel/publications/charts_and_statistical_annex/
statistical_annex.aspx

Table 2.6.1   www.statistics.gov.uk/downloads/theme_social/Social-Trends40/10_19.xls

http://www.statistics.gov.uk/downloads/theme_social/Social-Trends40/ST40_2010_FINAL.pdf

Table 2.7.1   www.communities.gov.uk/documents/housing/xls/141476.xls

www.communities.gov.uk/housing/housingresearch/housingstatistics/housingstatisticsby/
homelessnessstatistics

http://dissemination.dataunitwales.gov.uk

www.scotland.gov.uk/Resource/Doc/1033/0085962.xls

www.scotland.gov.uk/Topics/Statistics/Browse/Housing-Regeneration/RefTables

Table 3.6.1   www.sasi.group.shef.ac.uk/injustice/files/Figure13.xls (updated for 2010)

Table 3.7.1   http://www.worldmapper.org/data/nomap/360_worldmapper_data.xls

Table 4.2.1   www.fti.communities.gov.uk/DataDownload.aspx

Table 4.6.1   www.bigbrotherwatch.org.uk/TheGrimRIPA.pdf

Table 4.7.1   www.hmrc.gov.uk/stats/inheritance_tax/table-12-11.xls

www.hmrc.gov.uk/thelibrary/national-statistics.htm

Table 5.1.1   www.fti.communities.gov.uk/DataDownload.aspx

www.neighbourhood.statistics.gov.uk

Table 6.1.1   ONS for England & Wales mortality data & General Register Office for Scotland for Scotland
mortality data

Table 6.4.1   www.decc.gov.uk/en/content/cms/statistics/climate_change/
gg_emissions/uk_emissions/2007_local/2007_local.aspx

Appendix

The columns in the table have the following headings

Region/Country	
Local Authority	
LA code	
Benzene mean emissions 2007 (tens of kg/ha)	A
Benzene mean emissions 2008 (tens of kg/ha)	B
Benzene mean emissions change 2007–08 (tens of kg/ha)	C
Reported crime rate 2007/08 (per 100 residents)	D
Reported crime rate 2008/09 (per 100 residents)	E
Reported crime rate 2007/08–2008/09 (per 100 residents)	F
Average domestic electricity consumption 2007 (100 kWh)	G
Average domestic electricity consumption 2008 (100 kWh)	H
Average domestic electricity consumption 2007–08 (100 kWh)	I
Malicious false alarms rate 2007/08 (per 10,000 population)	J
Malicious false alarms rate 2008/09 (per 10,000 population)	K
Malicious false alarms rate 2007/08–2008/09 (per 10,000 population)	L
2007 score	M
2008 score	N
Change in score	O
2007 rank	P
2008 rank	Q
Change in rank	R

Region/Country	Local Authority	LA Code	A	B	C	D	E	F	G	H	I	J	K	L	M	N	O	P	Q	R
NORTH EAST	Darlington UA	00EH	15	14	-1	49	45	-4	43	41	-1.51	4.0	3.2	-0.8	111	103	-7	121	144	-23
	Hartlepool UA	00EB	20	24	4	65	68	3	38	37	-0.91	3.8	2.9	-0.9	127	132	5	57	51	6
	Middlesbrough UA	00EC	25	35	10	67	71	4	39	37	-1.96	3.8	2.9	-0.9	135	146	11	37	35	2
	Redcar & Cleveland UA	00EE	77	57	-21	58	58	0	40	38	-2.40	3.8	2.9	-0.9	179	156	-24	5	24	-19
	Stockton-on-Tees UA	00EF	111	94	-16	50	48	-2	40	38	-2.13	3.8	2.9	-0.9	205	183	-21	3	11	-8
Durham	Chester-le-Street	20UB	10	10	0	39	34	-5	39	37	-1.65	4.0	3.2	-0.8	92	84	-7	265	286	-21
	Derwentside	20UD	10	10	0	48	38	-10	41	39	-1.43	4.0	3.2	-0.8	103	90	-12	172	232	-60
	Durham	20UE	10	10	0	28	22	-6	39	37	-2.60	4.0	3.2	-0.8	81	72	-9	377	404	-27
	Easington	20UF	10	10	0	50	47	-3	39	36	-2.84	4.0	3.2	-0.8	103	97	-7	166	188	-22
	Sedgefield	20UG	10	10	0	55	42	-13	38	36	-1.71	4.0	3.2	-0.8	107	91	-16	147	228	-81
	Teesdale	20UH	10	10	0	28	22	-6	52	49	-2.70	4.0	3.2	-0.8	94	85	-10	237	281	-44
	Wear Valley	20UJ	10	10	0	59	47	-12	41	39	-1.73	4.0	3.2	-0.8	114	100	-15	108	168	-60
Northumberland	Alnwick	35UB	4	5	1	29	25	-4	54	51	-3.11	2.4	2.0	-0.4	90	83	-7	280	302	-22
	Berwick-upon-Tweed	35UC	4	5	1	23	22	-1	67	64	-2.99	2.4	2.0	-0.4	97	93	-3	212	208	4
	Blyth Valley	35UD	4	5	1	48	42	-6	37	35	-2.02	2.4	2.0	-0.4	92	84	-7	264	285	-21
	Castle Morpeth	35UE	4	5	1	30	22	-8	49	47	-1.90	2.4	2.0	-0.4	86	76	-9	338	375	-37
	Tynedale	35UF	4	5	1	23	21	-2	50	47	-2.80	2.4	2.0	-0.4	79	75	-4	391	389	2
	Wansbeck	35UG	4	5	1	59	50	-9	37	36	-1.51	2.4	2.0	-0.4	103	93	-10	171	214	-43
Tyne & Wear (Met County)	Gateshead	00CH	23	29	6	50	46	-4	39	37	-1.58	6.3	5.5	-0.8	118	117	0	92	91	1
	Newcastle upon Tyne	00CJ	25	34	9	46	42	-4	41	39	-2.22	6.3	5.5	-0.8	118	120	2	91	83	8
	North Tyneside	00CK	26	37	11	46	42	-4	39	37	-1.89	6.3	5.5	-0.8	117	122	4	93	79	14
	South Tyneside	00CL	25	31	6	65	61	-4	35	34	-1.57	6.3	5.5	-0.8	132	131	0	45	54	-9
	Sunderland	00CM	26	31	5	57	50	-7	37	35	-1.65	6.3	5.5	-0.8	126	122	-4	59	76	-17

Region/Country	Local Authority	LA Code	A	B	C	D	E	F	G	H	I	J	K	L	M	N	O	P	Q	R
NORTH WEST	Blackburn with Darwen UA	00EX	13	15	2	48	42	-6	44	42	-1.55	5.6	4.8	-0.8	110	104	-6	125	143	-18
	Blackpool UA	00EY	23	38	14	49	50	1	45	43	-1.68	5.6	4.8	-0.8	123	136	13	75	46	29
	Halton UA	00ET	24	32	7	59	50	-9	43	41	-1.99	2.7	2.2	-0.5	129	125	-4	51	64	-13
	Warrington UA	00EU	17	23	6	40	33	-7	45	42	-3.07	2.7	2.2	-0.5	104	100	-5	159	166	-7
Cheshire																				
	Chester	13UB	16	23	7	31	26	-5	48	45	-2.99	2.7	2.2	-0.5	98	97	-1	200	189	11
	Congleton	13UC	6	12	5	29	22	-7	46	43	-2.90	2.7	2.2	-0.5	84	79	-5	357	346	11
	Crewe & Nantwich	13UD	6	12	5	37	34	-3	49	46	-2.69	2.7	2.2	-0.5	94	94	-1	233	203	30
	Ellesmere Port & Neston	13UE	16	23	7	42	35	-7	43	41	-2.54	2.7	2.2	-0.5	104	101	-3	164	158	6
	Macclesfield	13UG	6	12	5	27	22	-5	54	50	-3.08	2.7	2.2	-0.5	89	87	-4	287	266	21
	Vale Royal	13UH	16	23	7	37	31	-6	46	43	-3.17	2.7	2.2	-0.5	102	99	-3	173	173	0
Cumbria																				
	Allerdale	16UB	3	4	1	28	28	0	49	46	-2.83	2.4	1.9	-0.5	82	80	-2	372	340	32
	Barrow-in-Furness	16UC	11	26	16	34	35	1	40	38	-1.83	2.4	1.9	-0.5	87	101	15	314	154	160
	Carlisle	16UD	3	4	1	31	29	-2	46	43	-2.66	2.4	1.9	-0.5	82	78	-4	374	361	13
	Copeland	16UE	3	3	0	32	32	0	46	43	-2.39	2.4	1.9	-0.5	83	80	-3	360	329	31
	Eden	16UF	2	4	2	13	11	-2	60	56	-3.28	2.4	1.9	-0.5	77	73	-4	399	396	3
	South Lakeland	16UG	2	4	1	13	12	-1	56	54	-2.00	2.4	1.9	-0.5	74	72	-3	407	405	2
Greater Manchester (Met County)																				
	Bolton	00BL	20	31	11	48	44	-4	44	42	-2.03	6.6	3.5	-3.1	119	121	2	87	81	6
	Bury	00BM	20	27	7	39	35	-4	45	42	-2.70	6.6	3.5	-3.1	111	108	-3	122	128	-6
	Manchester	00BN	30	49	19	50	50	0	44	42	-1.87	6.6	3.5	-3.1	130	145	14	48	36	12
	Oldham	00BP	17	23	5	51	47	-4	41	39	-2.18	6.6	3.5	-3.1	115	112	-4	102	110	-8
	Rochdale	00BQ	17	20	3	57	51	-6	42	41	-1.20	6.6	3.5	-3.1	123	115	-7	73	97	-24
	Salford	00BR	23	36	13	49	48	-1	46	44	-2.57	6.6	3.5	-3.1	125	131	6	65	53	12
	Stockport	00BS	24	33	9	36	32	-4	45	43	-2.18	6.6	3.5	-3.1	111	111	0	116	116	0
	Tameside	00BT	24	31	7	48	44	-4	41	40	-1.85	6.6	3.5	-3.1	120	118	-2	82	90	-8
	Trafford	00BU	23	32	9	34	32	-2	46	44	-2.57	6.6	3.5	-3.1	110	111	1	127	114	13
	Wigan	00BW	23	26	3	49	43	-6	43	40	-2.51	6.6	3.5	-3.1	121	113	-9	77	108	-31

Region/Country	Local Authority	LA Code	A	B	C	D	E	F	G	H	I	J	K	L	M	N	O	P	Q	R
NORTH WEST (continued)	Lancashire																			
	Burnley	30UD	12	12	0	47	43	-4	42	40	-2.17	5.6	4.8	-0.8	107	100	-7	146	165	-19
	Chorley	30UE	10	12	2	29	23	-6	45	42	-2.50	5.6	4.8	-0.8	89	82	-7	285	314	-29
	Fylde	30UF	9	11	2	20	17	-3	48	47	-1.46	5.6	4.8	-0.8	83	79	-3	366	347	19
	Hyndburn	30UG	18	18	0	42	35	-7	42	40	-2.55	5.6	4.8	-0.8	108	97	-10	139	185	-46
	Lancaster	30UH	4	6	1	31	27	-4	42	40	-2.51	5.6	4.8	-0.8	83	77	-6	365	366	-1
	Pendle	30UJ	12	10	-2	39	33	-6	41	40	-1.10	5.6	4.8	-0.8	98	88	-10	207	245	-38
	Preston	30UK	11	18	7	40	36	-4	44	42	-2.03	5.6	4.8	-0.8	101	101	0	181	156	25
	Ribble Valley	30UL	4	5	1	16	13	-3	51	48	-2.98	5.6	4.8	-0.8	76	71	-6	401	408	-7
	Rossendale	30UM	13	8	-5	41	29	-12	47	45	-2.12	5.6	4.8	-0.8	107	87	-20	148	263	-115
	South Ribble	30UN	14	19	5	27	21	-6	44	42	-2.52	5.6	4.8	-0.8	91	87	-4	268	260	8
	West Lancashire	30UP	7	11	4	43	34	-9	48	45	-2.99	5.6	4.8	-0.8	104	95	-9	163	195	-32
	Wyre	30UQ	5	8	3	22	19	-3	46	44	-1.52	5.6	4.8	-0.8	78	76	-2	395	380	15
	Merseyside (Met County)																			
	Knowsley	00BX	26	50	25	66	57	-9	42	39	-2.69	6.0	2.9	-3.1	140	149	10	29	32	-3
	Liverpool	00BY	29	46	17	71	63	-8	43	41	-2.73	6.0	2.9	-3.1	149	153	3	19	29	-10
	St. Helens	00BZ	20	25	4	50	43	-7	40	38	-2.64	6.0	2.9	-3.1	116	108	-9	97	125	-28
	Sefton	00CA	22	31	9	51	46	-5	44	42	-2.29	6.0	2.9	-3.1	123	122	-1	71	78	-7
	Wirral	00CB	18	25	7	55	45	-10	44	42	-2.05	6.0	2.9	-3.1	123	115	-8	72	98	-26
YORKSHIRE AND THE HUMBER	East Riding of Yorkshire UA	00FB	15	10	-5	31	28	-3	46	44	-1.85	4.3	3.7	-0.6	96	86	-10	216	273	-57
	Kingston upon Hull, City of UA	00FA	38	47	9	73	74	1	40	39	-1.82	4.3	3.7	-0.6	156	163	8	15	21	-6
	North East Lincolnshire UA	00FC	35	24	-11	59	58	-1	41	39	-1.70	4.3	3.7	-0.6	139	125	-14	30	65	-35
	North Lincolnshire UA	00FD	76	68	-8	49	43	-6	42	41	-1.60	4.3	3.7	-0.6	172	156	-16	6	25	-19
	York UA	00FF	25	15	-10	28	25	-3	42	40	-1.92	2.8	2.5	-0.3	98	82	-15	209	309	-100
	North Yorkshire																			
	Craven	36UB	6	4	-2	19	20	1	52	49	-2.91	2.8	2.5	-0.3	80	75	-4	390	387	3
	Hambleton	36UC	14	11	-3	21	18	-3	53	49	-3.32	2.8	2.5	-0.3	90	81	-10	275	327	-52
	Harrogate	36UD	12	9	-3	21	17	-4	49	46	-2.27	2.8	2.5	-0.3	84	75	-10	353	391	-38
	Richmondshire	36UE	7	7	0	17	15	-2	55	52	-2.60	2.8	2.5	-0.3	81	77	-5	378	370	8

Region/Country	Local Authority	LA Code	A	B	C	D	E	F	G	H	I	J	K	L	M	N	O	P	Q	R
YORKSHIRE AND THE HUMBER (continued)	Ryedale	36UF	8	7	-1	20	18	-2	52	49	-2.54	2.8	2.5	-0.3	82	77	-6	371	372	-1
	Scarborough	36UG	9	7	-2	37	37	0	47	45	-2.03	2.8	2.5	-0.3	96	92	-4	218	220	-2
	Selby	36UH	22	16	-6	31	28	-3	51	48	-2.65	2.8	2.5	-0.3	107	95	-12	145	199	-54
South Yorkshire (Met County)	Barnsley	00CC	38	23	-14	51	46	-5	39	37	-1.78	4.4	3.2	-1.1	132	109	-22	42	121	-79
	Doncaster	00CE	28	15	-14	55	50	-5	41	38	-2.37	4.4	3.2	-1.1	128	106	-22	52	134	-82
	Rotherham	00CF	40	20	-20	53	45	-8	39	37	-1.80	4.4	3.2	-1.1	136	105	-31	33	138	-105
	Sheffield	00CG	23	27	4	43	41	-2	39	37	-2.02	4.4	3.2	-1.1	109	108	-1	130	126	4
West Yorkshire (Met County)	Bradford	00CX	24	22	-3	49	45	-4	45	43	-2.28	6.3	5.3	-1.0	124	115	-10	67	99	-32
	Calderdale	00CY	19	15	-5	49	44	-5	45	43	-2.40	6.3	5.3	-1.0	119	107	-13	84	130	-46
	Kirklees	00CZ	26	20	-6	46	41	-5	43	40	-2.11	6.3	5.3	-1.0	121	107	-14	78	131	-53
	Leeds	00DA	31	26	-5	45	41	-4	44	41	-2.84	6.3	5.3	-1.0	126	114	-13	58	106	-48
	Wakefield	00DB	44	36	-8	44	37	-7	40	38	-2.43	6.3	5.3	-1.0	135	116	-18	36	94	-58
EAST MIDLANDS	Derby UA	00FK	36	49	13	47	45	-2	44	41	-2.49	4.2	3.3	-0.9	131	138	8	47	44	3
	Leicester UA	00FN	36	54	18	60	57	-3	41	39	-2.35	3.9	2.0	-1.9	141	152	11	25	30	-5
	Nottingham UA	00FY	34	51	17	55	52	-3	41	39	-2.36	5.0	4.4	-0.6	135	146	11	35	34	1
	Rutland UA	00FP	5	4	-1	16	14	-2	56	53	-2.67	3.9	2.0	-1.9	81	73	-8	386	400	-14
Derbyshire	Amber Valley	17UB	9	9	0	35	32	-3	46	43	-2.63	4.2	3.3	-0.9	94	87	-7	238	250	-12
	Bolsover	17UC	14	8	-6	42	36	-6	41	38	-2.10	4.2	3.3	-0.9	101	86	-15	182	274	-92
	Chesterfield	17UD	28	28	1	43	38	-5	39	37	-2.23	4.2	3.3	-0.9	115	107	-7	106	133	-27
	Derbyshire Dales	17UF	4	2	-1	20	16	-4	54	51	-3.31	4.2	3.3	-0.9	82	72	-9	369	403	-34
	Erewash	17UG	14	16	2	44	41	-3	43	40	-2.30	4.2	3.3	-0.9	105	101	-4	156	159	-3
	High Peak	17UH	10	7	-3	34	28	-6	45	43	-2.53	4.2	3.3	-0.9	93	81	-12	244	325	-81
	North East Derbyshire	17UJ	12	8	-5	35	29	-6	42	40	-1.98	4.2	3.3	-0.9	93	80	-14	250	337	-87
	South Derbyshire	17UK	9	7	-1	28	22	-6	47	45	-1.75	4.2	3.3	-0.9	88	77	-10	303	365	-62

Region/Country	Local Authority	LA Code	A	B	C	D	E	F	G	H	I	J	K	L	M	N	O	P	Q	R
EAST MIDLANDS	Leicestershire																			
(continued)	Blaby	31UB	11	12	2	27	21	-6	45	43	-2.37	3.9	2.0	-1.9	87	78	-8	316	360	-44
	Charnwood	31UC	10	9	0	30	22	-8	45	43	-2.70	3.9	2.0	-1.9	89	76	-13	286	382	-96
	Harborough	31UD	4	3	-1	23	16	-7	52	51	-0.89	3.9	2.0	-1.9	83	72	-11	362	402	-40
	Hinckley & Bosworth	31UE	7	6	-1	31	24	-7	46	45	-1.85	3.9	2.0	-1.9	88	77	-12	300	371	-71
	Melton	31UG	4	3	-1	29	20	-9	51	49	-2.61	3.9	2.0	-1.9	88	74	-15	296	395	-99
	North West Leicestershire	31UH	10	9	-1	30	24	-6	49	46	-2.28	3.9	2.0	-1.9	93	81	-11	254	321	-67
	Oadby & Wigston	31UJ	22	29	7	31	26	-5	41	39	-2.31	3.9	2.0	-1.9	98	96	-2	203	191	12
	Lincolnshire																			
	Boston	32UB	4	5	1	36	33	-3	51	50	-0.72	3.5	2.5	-1.0	94	91	-4	232	230	2
	East Lindsey	32UC	4	4	0	29	27	-2	52	50	-2.09	3.5	2.5	-1.0	88	83	-5	295	297	-2
	Lincoln	32UD	29	31	3	53	49	-4	41	38	-3.31	3.5	2.5	-1.0	127	121	-5	55	82	-27
	North Kesteven	32UE	4	4	0	24	20	-4	50	48	-1.41	3.5	2.5	-1.0	81	75	-6	379	392	-13
	South Holland	32UF	4	3	0	34	29	-5	54	53	-1.28	3.5	2.5	-1.0	95	87	-7	223	256	-33
	South Kesteven	32UG	4	4	0	30	26	-4	51	49	-1.46	3.5	2.5	-1.0	88	82	-6	293	315	-22
	West Lindsey	32UH	6	5	-1	34	32	-2	51	48	-2.77	3.5	2.5	-1.0	94	88	-7	235	249	-14
	Northamptonshire																			
	Corby	34UB	16	20	4	62	48	-14	44	43	-1.76	3.8	3.5	-0.3	126	114	-12	60	104	-44
	Daventry	34UC	5	5	0	31	22	-9	58	55	-2.80	3.8	3.5	-0.3	97	85	-12	211	278	-67
	East Northamptonshire	34UD	4	4	-1	33	26	-7	51	49	-2.69	3.8	3.5	-0.3	92	82	-11	259	311	-52
	Kettering	34UE	8	8	0	42	34	-8	47	45	-1.97	3.8	3.5	-0.3	101	90	-10	185	234	-49
	Northampton	34UF	26	39	13	48	40	-8	47	44	-2.68	3.8	3.5	-0.3	124	127	2	66	61	5
	South Northamptonshire	34UG	5	4	-1	22	14	-8	57	54	-2.75	3.8	3.5	-0.3	87	75	-12	313	384	-71
	Wellingborough	34UH	10	9	-1	48	40	-8	45	42	-2.13	3.8	3.5	-0.3	106	95	-11	150	196	-46
	Nottinghamshire																			
	Ashfield	37UB	17	16	-1	43	38	-5	41	39	-2.29	5.0	4.4	-0.6	106	98	-9	149	184	-35
	Bassetlaw	37UC	8	7	-1	33	28	-5	46	44	-2.28	5.0	4.4	-0.6	92	83	-9	263	301	-38
	Broxtowe	37UD	16	21	6	31	28	-3	41	39	-2.18	5.0	4.4	-0.6	93	93	0	241	215	26
	Gedling	37UE	10	11	0	33	29	-4	45	43	-2.52	5.0	4.4	-0.6	93	87	-7	246	257	-11
	Mansfield	37UF	21	19	-2	42	37	-5	41	39	-2.09	5.0	4.4	-0.6	109	100	-10	129	169	-40

Region/Country	Local Authority	LA Code	A	B	C	D	E	F	G	H	I	J	K	L	M	N	O	P	Q	R
EAST MIDLANDS	Newark & Sherwood	37UG	6	5	-1	29	23	-6	47	45	-2.47	5.0	4.4	-0.6	87	77	-10	315	367	-52
(continued)	Rushcliffe	37UJ	6	5	-1	21	18	-3	47	45	-1.26	5.0	4.4	-0.6	79	73	-6	394	401	-7
WEST MIDLANDS	Herefordshire, County of UA	00GA	5	9	3	28	22	-6	52	50	-2.77	3.0	3.1	0.1	88	84	-6	291	288	3
	Stoke-on-Trent UA	00GL	34	41	7	57	48	-9	40	38	-2.02	3.3	2.3	-1.0	134	129	-5	39	57	-18
	Telford & Wrekin UA	00GF	14	14	1	46	39	-7	41	40	-1.42	3.1	2.0	-1.1	104	95	-9	158	197	-39
Shropshire	Bridgnorth	39UB	5	9	4	26	21	-5	54	51	-2.65	3.1	2.0	-1.1	88	83	-5	304	298	6
	North Shropshire	39UC	5	9	4	28	27	-1	52	49	-3.01	3.1	2.0	-1.1	88	87	-1	294	253	41
	Oswestry	39UD	5	9	4	33	30	-3	49	46	-3.48	3.1	2.0	-1.1	90	87	-4	273	259	14
	Shrewsbury & Atcham	39UE	5	9	4	29	25	-4	49	46	-2.46	3.1	2.0	-1.1	86	82	-4	340	313	27
	South Shropshire	39UF	5	9	4	22	20	-2	59	58	-0.12	3.1	2.0	-1.1	89	89	1	290	238	52
Staffordshire	Cannock Chase	41UB	17	17	0	49	38	-11	46	44	-2.16	3.3	2.3	-1.0	115	101	-14	104	151	-47
	East Staffordshire	41UC	6	8	1	36	29	-7	48	46	-1.62	3.3	2.3	-1.0	93	86	-9	247	276	-29
	Lichfield	41UD	9	9	-1	33	24	-9	52	49	-3.84	3.3	2.3	-1.0	98	84	-15	208	290	-82
	Newcastle-under-Lyme	41UE	13	14	1	35	31	-4	41	40	-0.93	3.3	2.3	-1.0	93	88	-5	253	248	5
	South Staffordshire	41UF	10	9	-1	33	27	-6	48	46	-2.99	3.3	2.3	-1.0	95	84	-11	228	291	-63
	Stafford	41UG	8	10	2	27	23	-4	48	47	-1.40	3.3	2.3	-1.0	86	82	-4	325	312	13
	Staffordshire Moorlands	41UH	10	11	1	26	19	-7	48	46	-2.06	3.3	2.3	-1.0	87	78	-9	317	358	-41
	Tamworth	41UK	28	32	3	47	37	-10	47	45	-2.28	3.3	2.3	-1.0	125	116	-10	63	95	-32
Warwickshire	North Warwickshire	44UB	8	8	0	38	28	-10	51	48	-2.95	3.7	1.7	-2.0	101	86	-15	184	275	-91
	Nuneaton & Bedworth	44UC	19	24	6	51	41	-10	46	44	-1.45	3.7	1.7	-2.0	119	111	-7	86	117	-31
	Rugby	44UD	6	6	1	39	32	-7	53	51	-2.23	3.7	1.7	-2.0	102	90	-10	177	233	-56
	Stratford-on-Avon	44UE	6	9	3	23	16	-7	60	56	-3.88	3.7	1.7	-2.0	93	83	-10	251	304	-53
	Warwick	44UF	11	13	2	29	22	-7	48	46	-2.55	3.7	1.7	-2.0	92	82	-10	261	308	-47
West Midlands (Met County)	Birmingham	00CN	34	51	17	74	69	-5	44	42	-1.69	8.3	7.1	-1.2	160	169	9	13	17	-4
	Coventry	00CQ	26	42	16	54	49	-5	43	41	-2.44	8.3	7.1	-1.2	132	139	7	43	42	1

Region/Country	Local Authority	LA Code	A	B	C	D	E	F	G	H	I	J	K	L	M	N	O	P	Q	R
WEST MIDLANDS (continued)	Dudley	00CR	32	46	14	55	49	-6	45	42	-2.47	8.3	7.1	-1.2	140	144	4	27	38	-11
	Sandwell	00CS	48	62	14	71	66	-5	42	41	-1.64	8.3	7.1	-1.2	170	176	6	7	13	-6
	Solihull	00CT	18	23	5	42	36	-6	50	48	-2.56	8.3	7.1	-1.2	119	114	-5	89	105	-16
	Walsall	00CU	41	42	1	69	61	-8	45	43	-2.07	8.3	7.1	-1.2	163	153	-10	10	27	-17
	Wolverhampton	00CW	34	50	17	75	72	-3	44	42	-2.03	8.3	7.1	-1.2	162	171	11	12	16	-4
Worcestershire	Bromsgrove	47UB	11	14	3	36	30	-6	52	49	-2.87	3.0	3.1	0.1	102	96	-6	175	190	-15
	Malvern Hills	47UC	7	12	5	25	23	-2	56	53	-3.31	3.0	3.1	0.1	91	91	0	270	231	39
	Redditch	47UD	29	72	43	53	42	-11	45	42	-2.14	3.0	3.1	0.1	130	159	30	49	22	27
	Worcester	47UE	35	50	15	43	36	-7	45	42	-2.26	3.0	3.1	0.1	126	131	6	62	52	10
	Wychavon	47UF	9	14	4	33	24	-9	53	51	-1.97	3.0	3.1	0.1	98	92	-7	201	219	-18
	Wyre Forest	47UG	12	15	4	43	36	-7	46	44	-2.27	3.0	3.1	0.1	104	98	-5	157	179	-22
EAST	Luton UA	00KA	35	53	18	48	46	-2	43	41	-2.03	3.3	2.7	-0.7	129	143	13	50	40	10
	Peterborough UA	00JA	7	10	3	49	44	-5	44	42	-2.15	5.0	2.4	-2.6	105	99	-7	155	176	-21
	Southend-on-Sea UA	00KF	23	38	14	48	45	-3	48	46	-2.56	5.8	5.1	-0.8	125	134	8	64	47	17
	Thurrock UA	00KG	26	29	3	40	38	-2	50	48	-2.59	5.8	5.1	-0.8	122	120	-2	76	85	-9
Bedfordshire	Bedford	09UD	5	6	1	40	36	-4	46	44	-1.99	3.3	2.7	-0.7	95	89	-6	231	239	-8
	Mid Bedfordshire	09UC	6	7	0	25	19	-6	50	48	-2.11	3.3	2.7	-0.7	84	77	-9	355	369	-14
	South Bedfordshire	09UE	6	7	0	34	30	-4	49	47	-2.81	3.3	2.7	-0.7	93	86	-8	252	267	-15
Cambridgeshire	Cambridge	12UB	23	36	13	22	19	-3	43	41	-2.59	5.0	2.4	-2.6	93	98	5	248	182	66
	East Cambridgeshire	12UC	4	4	0	22	19	-3	54	51	-3.23	5.0	2.4	-2.6	85	77	-9	343	368	-25
	Fenland	12UD	4	5	1	38	35	-3	52	49	-2.81	5.0	2.4	-2.6	99	91	-7	194	226	-32
	Huntingdonshire	12UE	4	5	1	28	22	-6	49	47	-2.77	5.0	2.4	-2.6	86	76	-10	326	379	-53
	South Cambridgeshire	12UG	6	5	-1	18	13	-5	57	55	-1.63	5.0	2.4	-2.6	86	75	-10	339	385	-46
Essex	Basildon	22UB	16	25	8	41	36	-5	47	46	-1.77	5.8	5.1	-0.8	110	112	0	124	112	12
	Braintree	22UC	4	5	1	33	28	-5	53	50	-2.88	5.8	5.1	-0.8	95	88	-8	224	246	-22

Region/Country	Local Authority	LA Code	A	B	C	D	E	F	G	H	I	J	K	L	M	N	O	P	Q	R
EAST (continued)	Brentwood	22UD	7	9	2	21	22	1	52	51	-1.83	5.8	5.1	-0.8	86	87	0	327	261	66
	Castle Point	22UE	20	61	42	33	29	-4	49	46	-2.59	5.8	5.1	-0.8	108	141	35	142	41	101
	Chelmsford	22UF	7	9	2	27	23	-4	52	49	-2.64	5.8	5.1	-0.8	92	86	-5	266	268	-2
	Colchester	22UG	6	8	2	30	25	-5	48	46	-2.64	5.8	5.1	-0.8	90	84	-6	278	289	-11
	Epping Forest	22UH	6	7	1	32	28	-4	54	52	-2.02	5.8	5.1	-0.8	97	92	-6	210	221	-11
	Harlow	22UJ	24	38	14	49	43	-6	42	40	-1.84	5.8	5.1	-0.8	121	126	5	79	62	17
	Maldon	22UK	3	4	1	28	22	-6	57	55	-2.51	5.8	5.1	-0.8	94	86	-8	236	272	-36
	Rochford	22UL	5	7	1	23	21	-2	49	47	-2.37	4.1	3.5	-0.7	81	78	-4	383	356	27
	Tendring	22UN	6	6	0	42	39	-3	47	45	-1.97	5.8	5.1	-0.8	100	95	-6	188	201	-13
	Uttlesford	22UQ	4	4	0	20	16	-4	61	59	-2.38	5.8	5.1	-0.8	91	84	-7	269	287	-18
Hertfordshire	Broxbourne	26UB	16	23	7	34	31	-3	51	49	-2.50	1.5	1.6	0.0	103	104	2	169	142	27
	Dacorum	26UC	9	11	2	31	25	-6	49	46	-2.75	1.5	1.6	0.0	90	84	-7	277	295	-18
	East Hertfordshire	26UD	5	6	1	22	17	-5	56	53	-2.56	1.5	1.6	0.0	84	78	-7	354	359	-5
	Hertsmere	26UE	11	16	5	27	26	-1	52	50	-2.18	1.5	1.6	0.0	91	93	2	267	209	58
	North Hertfordshire	26UF	6	7	1	29	25	-4	49	46	-2.31	1.5	1.6	0.0	85	80	-5	344	336	8
	St Albans	26UG	10	14	4	20	18	-2	49	48	-1.24	1.5	1.6	0.0	81	82	1	384	318	66
	Stevenage	26UH	28	45	17	40	39	-1	42	41	-1.02	1.5	1.6	0.0	111	126	15	117	63	54
	Three Rivers	26UJ	12	16	4	23	20	-3	52	49	-2.79	1.5	1.6	0.0	88	87	-2	297	265	32
	Watford	26UK	34	55	21	32	30	-2	48	46	-2.17	1.5	1.6	0.0	116	133	17	100	50	50
	Welwyn Hatfield	26UL	10	14	4	26	24	-2	48	45	-3.40	1.5	1.6	0.0	86	84	-1	337	283	54
Norfolk	Breckland	33UB	3	4	1	32	28	-4	53	50	-3.13	2.0	1.4	-0.6	90	84	-7	271	292	-21
	Broadland	33UC	4	5	1	21	18	-3	49	46	-2.77	2.0	1.4	-0.6	76	71	-5	403	407	-4
	Great Yarmouth	33UD	6	9	3	51	48	-3	50	47	-2.75	2.0	1.4	-0.6	109	105	-3	134	137	-3
	King's Lynn & West Norfolk	33UE	3	4	1	32	29	-3	61	57	-3.51	2.0	1.4	-0.6	98	92	-6	206	222	-16
	North Norfolk	33UF	3	4	1	29	25	-4	60	56	-3.30	2.0	1.4	-0.6	94	87	-7	239	258	-19
	Norwich	33UG	28	44	16	43	41	-2	38	35	-2.43	2.0	1.4	-0.6	111	122	11	120	77	43
	South Norfolk	33UH	4	5	1	23	20	-3	56	53	-2.53	2.0	1.4	-0.6	85	80	-5	347	339	8

Region/Country	Local Authority	LA Code	A	B	C	D	E	F	G	H	I	J	K	L	M	N	O	P	Q	R
EAST	Suffolk																			
(continued)	Babergh	42UB	4	4	1	27	21	-6	56	53	-3.05	1.9	1.0	-0.9	88	79	-9	292	352	-60
	Forest Heath	42UC	4	5	1	25	21	-4	57	52	-5.64	1.9	1.0	-0.9	88	79	-10	298	350	-52
	Ipswich	42UD	30	42	12	45	43	-2	46	43	-2.65	1.9	1.0	-0.9	123	129	6	70	56	14
	Mid Suffolk	42UE	3	4	1	20	18	-2	61	57	-3.61	1.9	1.0	-0.9	86	80	-6	335	331	4
	St. Edmundsbury	42UF	4	5	1	28	23	-5	52	49	-3.14	1.9	1.0	-0.9	86	78	-8	336	362	-26
	Suffolk Coastal	42UG	3	4	1	20	17	-3	57	54	-2.90	1.9	1.0	-0.9	82	76	-6	375	383	-8
	Waveney	42UH	4	5	0	40	37	-3	47	44	-2.84	1.9	1.0	-0.9	93	87	-7	249	255	-6
LONDON	Inner London																			
	Camden	00AG	60	95	35	32	32	0	36	35	-0.74	3.6	3.4	-0.3	131	165	34	46	19	27
	City of London	00AA	104	188	83	95	91	-4	50	51	0.66	3.6	3.4	-0.3	252	333	80	2	1	1
	Hackney	00AM	57	90	33	63	63	0	39	39	-0.35	3.6	3.4	-0.3	163	195	32	11	8	3
	Hammersmith & Fulham	00AN	65	104	39	44	39	-5	38	38	-0.03	3.6	3.4	-0.3	151	185	34	18	10	8
	Haringey	00AP	43	70	27	59	60	1	44	41	-2.37	3.6	3.4	-0.3	149	175	25	20	14	6
	Islington	00AU	73	115	43	51	50	-1	38	37	-0.57	3.6	3.4	-0.3	165	205	41	8	6	2
	Kensington & Chelsea	00AW	79	132	53	28	28	0	43	44	0.75	3.6	3.4	-0.3	154	207	53	16	5	11
	Lambeth	00AY	65	105	40	51	52	1	39	38	-0.91	3.6	3.4	-0.3	158	198	40	14	7	7
	Lewisham	00AZ	45	75	30	49	48	-1	40	39	-1.58	3.6	3.4	-0.3	138	165	27	32	20	12
	Newham	00BB	39	68	28	63	63	0	39	39	0.22	3.6	3.4	-0.3	145	174	28	24	15	9
	Southwark	00BE	52	90	38	44	46	2	40	39	-1.84	3.6	3.4	-0.3	140	178	38	26	12	14
	Tower Hamlets	00BG	56	102	46	61	59	-2	43	44	0.60	3.6	3.4	-0.3	164	208	44	9	4	5
	Wandsworth	00BJ	52	86	35	30	29	-1	42	41	-1.11	3.6	3.4	-0.3	128	159	33	54	23	31
	Westminster	00BK	79	135	56	25	26	1	44	44	0.37	3.6	3.4	-0.3	151	208	57	17	3	14
	Outer London																			
	Barking & Dagenham	00AB	32	46	14	52	53	1	44	42	-2.06	3.6	3.4	-0.3	132	144	13	44	37	7
	Barnet	00AC	26	43	18	31	29	-2	51	49	-2.02	3.6	3.4	-0.3	112	124	14	115	68	47
	Bexley	00AD	28	37	10	34	30	-4	45	44	-1.70	3.6	3.4	-0.3	111	114	4	118	101	17
	Brent	00AE	43	66	23	54	54	0	45	43	-1.63	3.6	3.4	-0.3	146	167	21	22	18	4
	Bromley	00AF	17	25	8	31	26	-5	47	46	-1.63	3.6	3.4	-0.3	99	100	1	195	164	31
	Croydon	00AH	26	40	14	41	41	0	44	43	-0.65	3.6	3.4	-0.3	115	128	13	105	58	47
	Ealing	00AJ	39	63	24	41	39	-2	43	42	-1.33	3.6	3.4	-0.3	127	147	20	56	33	23

Region/Country	Local Authority	LA Code	A	B	C	D	E	F	G	H	I	J	K	L	M	N	O	P	Q	R
LONDON	Enfield	00AK	24	37	13	47	47	0	49	46	-2.45	3.6	3.4	-0.3	123	134	10	69	48	21
(continued)	Greenwich	00AL	30	48	18	49	48	-1	40	39	-0.52	3.6	3.4	-0.3	123	139	16	74	43	31
	Harrow	00AQ	28	45	17	29	27	-2	48	46	-2.25	3.6	3.4	-0.3	108	121	12	136	80	56
	Havering	00AR	17	24	8	35	33	-2	49	46	-2.32	3.6	3.4	-0.3	104	107	3	162	132	30
	Hillingdon	00AS	30	45	15	34	31	-3	46	44	-2.04	3.6	3.4	-0.3	114	124	10	109	70	39
	Hounslow	00AT	30	54	23	33	30	-3	47	46	-1.49	3.6	3.4	-0.3	114	133	18	110	49	61
	Kingston upon Thames	00AX	30	50	19	22	17	-5	45	44	-1.57	3.6	3.4	-0.3	101	114	12	180	102	78
	Merton	00BA	32	53	21	27	24	-3	40	39	-1.53	3.6	3.4	-0.3	103	119	16	167	87	80
	Redbridge	00BC	28	45	17	40	39	-1	44	43	-1.12	3.6	3.4	-0.3	116	131	15	99	55	44
	Richmond upon Thames	00BD	25	42	18	21	16	-5	46	45	-1.25	3.6	3.4	-0.3	96	106	11	220	135	85
	Sutton	00BF	29	49	20	29	26	-3	46	44	-2.02	3.6	3.4	-0.3	108	122	15	143	74	69
	Waltham Forest	00BH	35	54	20	55	55	0	42	40	-1.49	3.6	3.4	-0.3	136	153	18	34	28	6
SOUTH EAST	Bracknell Forest UA	00MA	12	17	5	25	22	-3	49	46	-3.04	4.2	3.0	-1.2	90	88	-2	276	243	33
	Brighton & Hove UA	00ML	21	31	10	41	36	-5	43	41	-1.71	4.1	3.5	-0.7	109	112	3	132	113	19
	Isle of Wight UA	00MW	7	12	4	36	31	-5	47	47	-0.28	4.4	3.6	-0.8	95	94	-2	227	205	22
	Medway UA	00LC	17	17	0	42	38	-4	44	43	-0.89	3.0	2.7	-0.3	106	101	-5	153	161	-8
	Milton Keynes UA	00MG	10	14	4	46	40	-6	47	45	-1.94	2.9	2.6	-0.3	105	101	-4	154	152	2
	Portsmouth UA	00MR	35	47	12	37	35	-2	40	39	-0.26	2.8	2.2	-0.5	115	124	9	107	71	36
	Reading UA	00MC	39	53	14	41	35	-6	50	47	-2.39	4.2	3.0	-1.2	134	138	4	40	45	-5
	Slough UA	00MD	57	65	8	40	37	-3	44	44	0.12	4.2	3.0	-1.2	145	149	4	23	31	-8
	Southampton UA	00MS	93	116	23	40	31	-9	44	44	-0.13	2.8	2.2	-0.5	180	193	13	4	9	-5
	West Berkshire UA	00MB	9	14	5	25	20	-5	61	57	-4.17	4.2	3.0	-1.2	99	94	-5	191	204	-13
	Windsor & Maidenhead UA	00ME	14	16	3	24	19	-5	56	53	-2.72	4.2	3.0	-1.2	98	91	-6	205	229	-24
	Wokingham UA	00MF	15	18	3	20	14	-6	53	50	-3.39	4.2	3.0	-1.2	92	85	-8	256	280	-24
	Buckinghamshire																			
	Aylesbury Vale	11UB	6	6	1	21	17	-4	53	50	-3.10	2.9	2.6	-0.3	83	75	-6	364	386	-22
	Chiltern	11UC	9	9	0	20	16	-4	58	55	-3.29	2.9	2.6	-0.3	90	83	-8	274	305	-31
	South Bucks	11UE	12	16	4	19	14	-5	59	57	-2.25	2.9	2.6	-0.3	93	90	-4	243	236	7
	Wycombe	11UF	10	13	3	29	24	-5	54	52	-1.94	2.9	2.6	-0.3	96	91	-4	221	227	-6

Region/Country	Local Authority	LA Code	A	B	C	D	E	F	G	H	I	J	K	L	M	N	O	P	Q	R
SOUTH EAST																				
(continued)	East Sussex																			
	Eastbourne	21UC	15	21	7	36	34	-2	41	40	-1.04	4.1	3.5	-0.7	96	99	3	214	175	39
	Hastings	21UD	17	25	8	53	56	3	43	43	0.01	4.1	3.5	-0.7	117	127	10	96	59	37
	Lewes	21UF	6	6	0	27	25	-2	48	47	-0.64	4.1	3.5	-0.7	85	81	-3	352	320	32
	Rother	21UG	4	4	0	29	27	-2	53	52	-1.71	4.1	3.5	-0.7	90	86	-4	272	270	2
	Wealden	21UH	4	5	1	19	14	-5	56	54	-2.35	4.1	3.5	-0.7	83	76	-7	361	376	-15
	Hampshire																			
	Basingstoke & Deane	24UB	9	13	5	26	22	-4	49	48	-1.25	2.8	2.2	-0.5	87	85	-1	319	279	40
	East Hampshire	24UC	7	9	2	21	15	-6	54	54	-0.19	2.8	2.2	-0.5	85	80	-5	349	335	14
	Eastleigh	24UD	29	41	12	25	19	-6	45	43	-2.01	2.8	2.2	-0.5	101	105	3	178	141	37
	Fareham	24UE	27	33	6	20	16	-4	45	44	-0.30	2.8	2.2	-0.5	94	96	1	234	194	40
	Gosport	24UF	28	31	4	29	25	-4	45	44	-0.10	2.8	2.2	-0.5	104	103	-1	160	148	12
	Hart	24UG	8	10	2	17	13	-4	52	51	-0.58	2.8	2.2	-0.5	80	76	-3	389	373	16
	Havant	24UH	15	20	5	37	30	-7	44	43	-0.49	2.8	2.2	-0.5	99	96	-3	196	193	3
	New Forest	24UJ	18	16	-2	22	17	-5	47	47	0.41	2.8	2.2	-0.5	89	82	-7	283	310	-27
	Rushmoor	24UL	29	33	3	31	23	-8	43	43	-0.30	2.8	2.2	-0.5	106	101	-6	151	153	-2
	Test Valley	24UN	7	13	5	19	15	-4	53	51	-1.44	2.8	2.2	-0.5	81	81	-1	376	319	57
	Winchester	24UP	7	9	2	17	13	-4	52	52	0.11	2.8	2.2	-0.5	79	76	-2	393	374	19
	Kent																			
	Ashford	29UB	5	6	1	26	24	-2	52	50	-1.75	3.0	2.7	-0.3	86	83	-3	341	306	35
	Canterbury	29UC	7	8	1	24	21	-3	44	43	-1.04	3.0	2.7	-0.3	78	74	-3	396	393	3
	Dartford	29UD	20	21	1	32	31	-1	47	44	-2.23	3.0	2.7	-0.3	102	99	-3	176	172	4
	Dover	29UE	7	6	-1	33	32	-1	43	42	-0.45	3.0	2.7	-0.3	86	83	-3	334	303	31
	Gravesham	29UG	20	16	-4	41	36	-5	44	43	-1.83	3.0	2.7	-0.3	108	97	-11	135	186	-51
	Maidstone	29UH	7	8	1	25	23	-2	50	49	-1.39	3.0	2.7	-0.3	85	82	-3	345	307	38
	Sevenoaks	29UK	7	8	1	21	17	-4	57	54	-2.90	3.0	2.7	-0.3	88	82	-6	309	316	-7
	Shepway	29UL	5	6	1	38	39	1	47	46	-1.45	3.0	2.7	-0.3	93	94	0	242	207	35
	Swale	29UM	8	8	-1	36	34	-2	47	44	-1.16	3.0	2.7	-0.3	94	90	-4	240	235	5
	Thanet	29UN	11	13	2	51	50	-1	44	44	-0.56	3.0	2.7	-0.3	109	109	0	131	120	11
	Tonbridge & Malling	29UP	11	10	0	23	19	-4	50	49	-1.35	3.0	2.7	-0.3	87	80	-6	321	332	-11
	Tunbridge Wells	29UQ	6	7	1	21	17	-4	55	53	-1.84	3.0	2.7	-0.3	85	80	-5	346	338	8

Region/Country	Local Authority	LA Code	A	B	C	D	E	F	G	H	I	J	K	L	M	N	O	P	Q	R
SOUTH EAST	Oxfordshire																			
(continued)	Cherwell	38UB	10	15	4	25	18	-7	51	49	-1.32	2.0	1.3	-0.6	88	84	-5	312	294	18
	Oxford	38UC	29	42	12	26	23	-3	43	42	-1.57	2.0	1.3	-0.6	100	108	7	189	129	60
	South Oxfordshire	38UD	7	8	1	19	15	-4	60	57	-3.02	2.0	1.3	-0.6	88	82	-7	299	317	-18
	Vale of White Horse	38UE	8	10	2	18	16	-2	55	52	-2.52	2.0	1.3	-0.6	83	80	-3	363	343	20
	West Oxfordshire	38UF	7	8	2	17	13	-4	59	56	-2.72	2.0	1.3	-0.6	85	78	-5	350	354	-4
	Surrey																			
	Elmbridge	43UB	14	21	7	18	15	-3	55	53	-1.45	5.4	3.8	-1.6	92	93	1	260	211	49
	Epsom & Ewell	43UC	16	25	9	21	17	-4	50	46	-3.17	5.4	3.8	-1.6	92	92	0	262	218	44
	Guildford	43UD	10	10	0	19	17	-2	52	50	-1.80	5.4	3.8	-1.6	87	81	-5	323	323	0
	Mole Valley	43UE	6	7	0	17	13	-4	56	55	-1.56	5.4	3.8	-1.6	85	79	-7	348	351	-3
	Reigate & Banstead	43UF	11	17	5	21	18	-3	51	49	-1.25	5.4	3.8	-1.6	88	88	-1	307	242	65
	Runnymede	43UG	14	21	7	18	15	-3	50	47	-2.90	5.4	3.8	-1.6	88	87	-1	310	254	56
	Spelthorne	43UH	22	28	6	25	22	-3	48	46	-1.87	5.4	3.8	-1.6	101	100	0	183	163	20
	Surrey Heath	43UJ	12	16	4	19	18	-1	53	52	-1.49	5.4	3.8	-1.6	90	90	0	279	237	42
	Tandridge	43UK	6	6	0	19	16	-3	56	55	-1.86	5.4	3.8	-1.6	87	80	-6	322	330	-8
	Waverley	43UL	7	8	1	17	14	-3	54	54	-0.15	5.4	3.8	-1.6	83	80	-4	359	344	15
	Woking	43UM	15	18	4	24	20	-4	52	51	-1.44	5.4	3.8	-1.6	97	93	-3	213	213	0
	West Sussex																			
	Adur	45UB	13	19	5	34	27	-7	48	45	-2.30	3.3	3.0	-0.3	98	94	-5	202	202	0
	Arun	45UC	9	12	3	31	25	-6	45	44	-0.54	3.3	3.0	-0.3	88	84	-4	301	284	17
	Chichester	45UD	5	8	3	23	19	-4	57	57	0.07	3.3	3.0	-0.3	88	87	-1	305	262	43
	Crawley	45UE	33	47	13	37	33	-4	42	41	-1.26	3.3	3.0	-0.3	116	124	7	101	69	32
	Horsham	45UF	6	7	1	23	18	-5	54	52	-1.52	3.3	3.0	-0.3	86	80	-6	331	334	-3
	Mid Sussex	45UG	7	8	1	19	16	-3	53	51	-1.95	3.3	3.0	-0.3	82	78	-4	368	355	13
	Worthing	45UH	20	31	12	36	30	-6	47	45	-2.08	3.3	3.0	-0.3	106	109	4	152	123	29
SOUTH WEST	Bath & North East Somerset UA	00HA	7	12	5	21	18	-3	48	45	-2.37	5.4	3.5	-1.9	81	79	-2	380	348	32
	Bournemouth UA	00HN	21	34	13	37	33	-4	47	47	0.05	2.6	2.4	-0.2	108	117	9	140	93	47
	Bristol, City of UA	00HB	31	48	17	38	33	-5	42	40	-2.29	5.4	3.5	-1.9	117	125	8	94	67	27
	North Somerset UA	00HC	10	19	9	25	20	-5	45	43	-1.89	5.4	3.5	-1.9	86	86	0	333	271	62

Region/Country	Local Authority	LA Code	A	B	C	D	E	F	G	H	I	J	K	L	M	N	O	P	Q	R
SOUTH WEST (continued)	Plymouth UA	00HG	34	42	8	39	35	-4	42	39	-2.40	2.1	2.0	0.0	117	118	2	95	89	6
	Poole UA	00HP	21	30	9	28	22	-6	46	47	0.29	2.6	2.4	-0.2	98	101	3	204	155	49
	South Gloucestershire UA	00HD	8	14	6	23	18	-5	46	44	-1.92	5.4	3.5	-1.9	83	80	-3	367	341	26
	Swindon UA	00HX	14	18	4	48	35	-13	47	44	-2.89	1.6	1.6	0.0	111	99	-12	119	174	-55
	Torbay UA	00HH	14	21	7	40	35	-5	43	42	-1.05	2.1	2.0	0.0	99	100	1	190	162	28
Cornwall & Isles of Scilly	Caradon	15UB	4	9	5	22	20	-2	58	55	-2.52	1.9	1.7	-0.2	86	86	0	332	269	63
	Carrick	15UC	4	9	5	24	21	-3	57	55	-2.08	1.9	1.7	-0.2	87	87	0	320	264	56
	Kerrier	15UD	4	9	5	25	23	-2	56	54	-2.38	1.9	1.7	-0.2	87	87	0	318	252	66
	North Cornwall	15UE	4	9	5	20	18	-2	64	63	-0.56	1.9	1.7	-0.2	89	92	2	281	224	57
	Penwith	15UF	4	9	5	27	24	-3	55	54	-0.88	1.9	1.7	-0.2	88	89	1	306	240	66
	Restormel	15UG	4	9	5	29	24	-5	58	57	-0.86	1.9	1.7	-0.2	93	91	-1	255	225	30
	Isles of Scilly	15UH	1	8	6	2	3	1	86	84	-1.92	0.0	0.0	0.0	89	95	5	289	198	91
Devon	East Devon	18UB	4	8	4	18	15	-3	50	48	-1.95	2.1	2.0	0.0	74	73	-1	405	398	7
	Exeter	18UC	26	35	9	28	23	-5	40	38	-2.23	2.1	2.0	0.0	96	98	2	215	180	35
	Mid Devon	18UD	3	6	3	22	17	-5	53	51	-2.46	2.1	2.0	0.0	81	76	-4	385	378	7
	North Devon	18UE	2	4	2	22	18	-4	51	49	-2.23	2.1	2.0	0.0	78	73	-4	397	397	0
	South Hams	18UG	3	7	3	19	14	-5	61	58	-2.98	2.1	2.0	0.0	85	81	-5	342	322	20
	Teignbridge	18UH	4	8	4	24	18	-6	49	47	-1.95	2.1	2.0	0.0	79	75	-4	392	390	2
	Torridge	18UK	2	5	3	29	23	-6	53	51	-2.19	2.1	2.0	0.0	86	81	-5	328	324	4
	West Devon	18UL	2	4	2	18	16	-2	55	53	-1.89	2.1	2.0	0.0	77	75	-2	398	388	10
Dorset	Christchurch	19UC	10	15	5	24	18	-6	44	44	0.03	2.6	2.4	-0.2	80	79	-1	387	349	38
	East Dorset	19UD	5	8	3	18	14	-4	49	49	-0.22	2.6	2.4	-0.2	74	73	-1	404	399	5
	North Dorset	19UE	3	6	3	16	13	-3	53	53	0.13	2.6	2.4	-0.2	74	74	0	406	394	12
	Purbeck	19UG	2	4	1	18	15	-3	50	50	-0.22	2.6	2.4	-0.2	73	71	-2	408	406	2
	West Dorset	19UH	3	6	3	14	12	-2	57	56	-0.89	2.6	2.4	-0.2	76	76	0	402	377	25
	Weymouth & Portland	19UJ	10	36	25	29	25	-4	40	42	1.50	2.6	2.4	-0.2	82	105	22	373	139	234

Region/Country	Local Authority	LA Code	A	B	C	D	E	F	G	H	I	J	K	L	M	N	O	P	Q	R
SOUTH WEST (continued)	Gloucestershire																			
	Cheltenham	23UB	21	30	9	39	30	-9	46	44	-2.76	1.0	1.2	0.1	107	105	-3	144	140	4
	Cotswold	23UC	3	5	2	20	15	-5	65	62	-3.34	1.0	1.2	0.1	89	83	-6	284	299	-15
	Forest of Dean	23UD	5	8	3	34	26	-8	55	52	-2.42	1.0	1.2	0.1	95	87	-7	230	251	-21
	Gloucester	23UE	25	39	15	43	36	-7	46	43	-3.07	1.0	1.2	0.1	115	120	5	103	86	17
	Stroud	23UF	5	7	2	30	22	-8	53	51	-2.93	1.0	1.2	0.1	89	81	-9	282	326	-44
	Tewkesbury	23UG	6	8	1	29	22	-7	50	47	-2.81	1.0	1.2	0.1	86	78	-9	330	353	-23
	Somerset																			
	Mendip	40UB	4	7	4	26	21	-5	49	48	-1.51	2.1	2.0	0.0	81	78	-3	382	364	18
	Sedgemoor	40UC	5	11	6	30	26	-4	52	49	-2.76	2.1	2.0	0.0	89	88	-1	288	241	47
	South Somerset	40UD	5	10	5	21	16	-5	54	53	-1.75	2.1	2.0	0.0	82	81	-2	370	328	42
	Taunton Deane	40UE	5	11	6	25	21	-4	48	46	-2.20	2.1	2.0	0.0	80	80	0	388	345	43
	West Somerset	40UF	2	3	2	20	19	-1	59	56	-3.21	2.1	2.0	0.0	83	80	-2	358	333	25
	Wiltshire																			
	Kennet	46UB	4	8	4	21	18	-3	72	69	-2.45	1.6	1.6	0.0	98	97	-1	199	187	12
	North Wiltshire	46UC	4	8	4	27	22	-5	56	53	-2.76	1.6	1.6	0.0	88	84	-4	302	282	20
	Salisbury	46UD	4	8	4	20	17	-3	51	51	-0.03	1.6	1.6	0.0	77	78	1	400	363	37
	West Wiltshire	46UF	4	8	4	31	24	-7	51	50	-1.12	1.6	1.6	0.0	88	84	-4	311	293	18
WALES	Isle of Anglesey	00NA	7	11	4	40	43	3	61	53	-7.18	2.3	2.5	0.2	110	110	0	128	119	9
	Gwynedd	00NC	4	6	2	28	28	0	61	56	-5.22	2.3	2.5	0.2	95	92	-3	225	217	8
	Conwy	00NE	5	7	2	38	35	-3	47	43	-3.69	2.3	2.5	0.2	92	88	-4	258	247	11
	Denbighshire	00NG	6	9	2	38	34	-4	47	42	-4.61	2.3	2.5	0.2	93	88	-6	245	244	1
	Flintshire	00NJ	23	24	1	36	33	-3	46	43	-3.62	2.3	2.5	0.2	108	102	-5	138	149	-11
	Wrexham	00NL	12	14	2	39	35	-4	46	42	-3.91	2.3	2.5	0.2	99	93	-6	192	210	-18
	Powys	00NN	3	4	1	26	20	-6	50	46	-3.85	5.4	5.3	-0.1	85	76	-9	351	381	-30
	Ceredigion	00NQ	4	6	2	18	17	-1	54	51	-2.33	5.4	5.3	-0.1	81	80	-1	381	342	39
	Pembrokeshire	00NS	13	15	2	31	32	1	49	48	-0.67	5.4	5.3	-0.1	98	101	2	197	160	37
	Carmarthenshire	00NU	6	9	3	31	29	-2	42	40	-1.58	5.4	5.3	-0.1	84	83	-1	356	296	60
	Swansea	00NX	15	15	0	39	34	-5	40	39	-0.86	5.4	5.3	-0.1	99	93	-6	193	212	-19
	Neath Port Talbot	00NZ	27	21	-6	44	36	-8	37	37	0.16	5.4	5.3	-0.1	114	100	-14	111	167	-56

Region/Country	Local Authority	LA Code	A	B	C	D	E	F	G	H	I	J	K	L	M	N	O	P	Q	R
WALES (continued)	Bridgend	00PB	23	21	-1	47	37	-10	40	38	-2.08	6.3	5.3	-1.0	116	101	-14	98	157	-59
	The Vale of Glamorgan	00PD	14	17	3	39	35	-4	42	41	-1.28	6.3	5.3	-1.0	102	99	-3	174	177	-3
	Cardiff	00PT	33	42	8	39	39	0	41	41	-0.77	6.3	5.3	-1.0	120	127	6	83	60	23
	Rhondda, Cynon, Taf	00PF	21	16	-5	48	40	-8	37	36	-0.89	6.3	5.3	-1.0	113	98	-15	112	183	-71
	Merthyr Tydfil	00PH	14	15	0	68	59	-9	38	37	-1.02	6.3	5.3	-1.0	126	116	-11	61	96	-35
	Caerphilly	00PK	20	18	-2	55	47	-8	37	36	-1.19	6.3	5.3	-1.0	118	106	-12	90	136	-46
	Blaenau Gwent	00PL	22	16	-5	76	65	-11	35	34	-0.76	6.3	5.3	-1.0	139	120	-18	31	84	-53
	Torfaen	00PM	19	26	7	50	41	-9	37	36	-0.72	6.3	5.3	-1.0	112	109	-4	113	124	-11
	Monmouthshire	00PP	7	8	1	28	20	-8	47	45	-1.87	6.3	5.3	-1.0	88	78	-10	308	357	-49
	Newport	00PR	33	32	-1	56	49	-7	39	39	-0.83	6.3	5.3	-1.0	135	125	-10	38	66	-28
SCOTLAND	Aberdeen City	00QA	27	27	0	20	22	2	49	47	-1.72	4.4	3.2	-1.2	100	100	-1	187	170	17
	Aberdeenshire	00QB	3	5	2	14	13	-1	65	62	-3.13	4.4	3.2	-1.2	86	83	-3	324	300	24
	Angus	00QC	3	4	2	33	33	0	60	57	-2.94	6.7	7.7	1.0	103	102	0	168	150	18
	Argyll & Bute	00QD	1	1	0	30	29	-1	76	75	-1.57	12.2	9.5	-2.7	119	114	-5	85	103	-18
	Clackmannanshire	00QF	5	11	5	49	50	1	46	44	-1.78	10.7	9.6	-1.2	110	114	3	123	100	23
	Dumfries & Galloway	00QH	2	2	0	33	33	0	58	56	-1.90	1.9	0.8	-1.1	95	92	-3	229	223	6
	Dundee City	00QJ	31	29	-2	54	54	0	56	53	-2.96	6.7	7.7	1.0	148	144	-4	21	39	-18
	East Ayrshire	00QK	3	7	5	53	56	3	42	40	-1.45	12.2	9.5	-2.7	110	113	4	126	107	19
	East Dunbartonshire	00QL	7	13	6	28	29	1	49	47	-2.11	12.2	9.5	-2.7	96	98	2	217	178	39
	East Lothian	00QM	6	7	1	28	31	3	50	49	-1.80	11.1	9.1	-2.0	96	96	0	222	192	30
	East Renfrewshire	00QN	6	8	2	25	25	0	52	50	-1.99	12.2	9.5	-2.7	95	92	-3	226	216	10
	Edinburgh, City of	00QP	17	24	7	30	31	1	46	44	-2.17	11.1	9.1	-2.0	104	108	4	161	127	34
	Eilean Siar	00RJ	2	3	1	33	30	-3	83	78	-4.85	2.9	1.5	-1.4	121	112	-8	80	109	-29
	Falkirk	00QQ	176	185	9	42	40	-2	49	46	-2.07	10.7	9.6	-1.2	277	281	4	1	2	-1
	Fife	00QR	8	12	3	45	44	-1	46	43	-2.20	4.2	3.7	-0.5	103	103	-1	170	146	24
	Glasgow City	00QS	26	39	13	57	63	6	44	43	-1.69	12.2	9.5	-2.7	140	154	15	28	26	2
	Highland	00QT	1	2	1	26	26	0	78	74	-4.02	2.9	1.5	-1.4	108	103	-4	141	145	-4
	Inverclyde	00QU	9	11	2	56	49	-7	51	49	-1.25	12.2	9.5	-2.7	128	119	-9	53	88	-35
	Midlothian	00QW	6	16	10	32	36	4	43	42	-1.43	11.1	9.1	-2.0	92	103	11	257	147	110
	Moray	00QX	2	4	2	24	25	1	56	53	-2.65	4.4	3.2	-1.2	86	85	-1	329	277	52

Region/Country	Local Authority	LA Code	A	B	C	D	E	F	G	H	I	J	K	L	M	N	O	P	Q	R
SCOTLAND (continued)	North Ayrshire	00QY	3	5	2	61	63	2	48	46	-2.12	12.2	9.5	-2.7	124	123	-1	68	73	-5
	North Lanarkshire	00QZ	11	16	5	51	54	3	45	43	-2.01	12.2	9.5	-2.7	119	122	3	88	75	13
	Orkney Islands	00RA	2	3	1	9	15	6	95	93	-2.56	2.9	1.5	-1.4	109	112	3	133	111	22
	Perth & Kinross	00RB	2	3	1	21	22	1	66	62	-4.01	6.7	7.7	1.0	96	95	-1	219	200	19
	Renfrewshire	00RC	7	12	5	43	46	3	46	44	-2.24	12.2	9.5	-2.7	108	111	3	137	115	22
	Scottish Borders	00QE	2	2	0	27	27	0	58	56	-2.56	11.1	9.1	-2.0	98	94	-5	198	206	-8
	Shetland Islands	00RD	2	2	0	14	14	0	113	106	-7.65	2.9	1.5	-1.4	132	123	-9	41	72	-31
	South Ayrshire	00RE	3	4	1	38	40	2	47	46	-1.58	12.2	9.5	-2.7	101	99	-1	186	171	15
	South Lanarkshire	00RF	5	7	1	43	44	1	52	50	-1.79	12.2	9.5	-2.7	112	110	-2	114	118	-4
	Stirling	00RG	2	3	1	31	31	0	57	54	-2.86	10.7	9.6	-1.2	101	98	-3	179	181	-2
	West Dunbartonshire	00QG	7	11	4	57	54	-3	44	42	-1.73	12.2	9.5	-2.7	120	117	-3	81	92	-11
	West Lothian	00RH	8	14	6	40	43	3	44	43	-1.73	11.1	9.1	-2.0	103	109	5	165	122	43